WATCHING
MOVIES

Rick Lyman

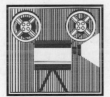

WATCHING MOVIES

The Biggest Names in Cinema Talk
about the Films That Matter Most

Times Books · Henry Holt and Company, New York

Times Books
Henry Holt and Company, LLC
Publishers since 1866
115 West 18th Street
New York, New York 10011

Library of Congress Cataloging-in-Publication Data

Lyman, Rick.
   Watching movies : the biggest names in cinema talk about the films that matter most /
Rick Lyman.—1st ed.
      p.   cm.
   Includes index.
   ISBN: 0-8050-7098-2
   1. Motion pictures—United States. 2. Motion picture actors and actresses—United
States—Interviews. 3. Motion picture producers and directors—United States—Interviews.
I. Title.
PN1993.5.U6 L96 2003
791.43'75'0973—dc21   2002032495

Henry Holt books are available for special promotions and premiums.
For details contact: Director, Special Markets.

First Edition 2003

Designed by Fritz Metsch

Printed in the United States of America
1   3   5   7   9   10   8   6   4   2

To Barb,

even though she keeps telling

me to turn it down

CONTENTS

Introduction: The Way It Worked   xi

1. Quentin Tarantino on *The Golden Stallion*   1
2. Janusz Kaminski on *Vanishing Point*   11
3. Ron Howard on *The Graduate*   21
4. Curtis Hanson on *In a Lonely Place*   33
5. Kevin Costner on *Cool Hand Luke*   43
6. Steven Soderbergh on *All the President's Men*   55
7. Ang Lee on *Love Eternal*   67
8. Wolfgang Petersen on *High Noon*   79
9. Harvey Weinstein on *Exodus*   91
10. Michael Bay on *West Side Story*   103
11. Julianne Moore on *Rosemary's Baby*   115
12. Kevin Smith on *A Man for All Seasons*   127
13. Woody Allen on *Shane*   139

Contents

14. Denzel Washington on *Ordinary People*   153

15. John Travolta on *Yankee Doodle Dandy*   165

16. Brian Grazer on *Blazing Saddles*   177

17. Wes Anderson on *Small Change*   189

18. Sissy Spacek on *To Kill a Mockingbird*   201

19. Nicole Kidman on *The Shining*   213

20. Barry Sonnenfeld on *Dr. Strangelove*   225

21. Barry Levinson on *On the Waterfront*   237

Acknowledgments   249

Index   251

INTRODUCTION:
THE WAY IT WORKED

———————

Once the thing got started—which took forever, by the way—the question I was most often asked was: Which one was the most fun?

I'd always try to answer it, and even came up with a few little anecdotes that hadn't made it into the finished pieces. But the truth is that the most memorable, "fun" moments were ones that had nothing to do with the job at hand, the watching of the movie. I remember sharing a humongous platter of sushi with John Travolta and listening to him describe dinner parties at his hilltop house, including one he had for Marlon Brando that attracted, if my memory's right, just about every A-list leading man in Hollywood. He had a group picture to prove it. And the best part of spending an afternoon with Quentin Tarantino at his Mediterranean spread in the Hollywood Hills was not watching the Roy Rogers movie he'd chosen to project on his living room wall with a 16-millimeter projector. It was staying afterward and talking, talking, talking about all sorts of movies, including his own, one topic spilling into the next in his febrile brain. The movie lasted only forty minutes, but it was five hours before I got out of his house. Or how about standing in a corridor on the Warner Bros. lot with Steven Soderbergh as the projectionist rewound the print of *All the President's Men* and talking about his eagerness to begin filming *Ocean's 11* in Las Vegas while dryly taking a few digs at the *New York Times,* with which he'd had a couple of gripes over the years?

To me, those things were fun. But I don't think that's what people were really asking about, any more than when they asked: Who was the nicest? Who was the meanest? Who did you like? Who didn't you like?

What they really wanted to know was: Did you get inside? That's what all the entertainment television shows and the slick magazine covers promise. Exclusive! Inside! Did I get past the stone-faced handlers and the celebrity facades? Did I catch a true glimpse of the Hollywood paradise that everyone imagines, where the boldface names live in hedonistic splendor?

And the answer to that is really kind of disappointing for people. I can see it in their faces. Yes, I saw some nice houses and got to spend some pleasant time with famous people, far away from the niggling of publicists and the straitjacket schedules of location shooting and press junkets. But mostly, it was work. Fun work, but work. No one started snorting cocaine or dove into a hot tub full of *Baywatch* beauties. And the fact is, everyone was nice. Everyone. After all, are you going to invite the *New York Times* over and then be mean? When you're dealing with people at this level, both actors and directors, people who have risen to the top of a hotly competitive, deeply uncertain business, you are dealing for the most part with extremely smart people. How then to tell a real emotion when it comes from someone so adept at manufacturing fake ones? In that, I think, it was the conceit of the series that saved the day. In the end, they couldn't help themselves. When they began talking about some scene or performance in a movie that truly touched them, they opened up, bit by bit. I think I got about as far "inside" as you can get, at least through the uncertain filter of an interview.

That's the secret, hidden between the lines of all of these pieces: Although it seems they're talking about some old movie, what they're really talking about is themselves.

They can't help it. Get anyone down to the level of talking about something that really matters to them—not in a money way or even an ego way, but in a deep, powerful, emotional way—and they're as naked as you're ever likely to see them.

People also often asked: Was the series your idea?

I liked that question, because I had an answer for it: Yes and no.

While I was still in the process of packing up to move to California to take over the movie beat for the *New York Times,* I took a trip back to the newsroom to confer with my editors about what kinds of stories I ought to try to do. One of the editors I talked to was Myra Forsberg, who runs the Weekend section. She said she was looking for ways to get more movie copy into the section, especially for those weekends when there was no big review that could run on the cover. "Why don't you do a series like that one where you walked around neighborhoods with people?" she asked. "Except with movies."

A few years earlier, I'd done a series of pieces that also ran in the Weekend section in which I spent a few hours walking around sections of New York with a celebrity who had some connection to it. We had Martin Scorsese rambling around Little Italy, Tony Randall on the Upper West Side, Billy Crystal at Yankee Stadium. The idea was to show a part of the city already familiar to readers through the eyes of someone who interested them. It was fun, and most of the people really did open up. But the series didn't last long, just six or seven installments. I got transferred to Houston, to be the paper's bureau chief there, and my concerns shifted to floods, droughts, and the weird world of Texas politics.

But suddenly, there I was, back on the culture staff, this time in Hollywood, and once again trying to figure out how to feed the Weekend section. What kind of series would duplicate that earlier one—but be about movies?

I came up with an answer in the time-tested way of many who came before me in American newsrooms. I stole it.

A few years earlier, the paper's chief art critic, Michael Kimmelman, had done an extraordinary series in which he walked around museums with famous, accomplished artists—seeing the art through the artists' eyes and, in the process, revealing more about their creative lives than any straight-ahead interview could ever accomplish. Simple. I'd do that! I'd get some famous Hollywood figure to sit down and watch a movie that had some deep resonance to them, perhaps something they saw as a teenager that convinced them to become an actor, or something that they've returned to time and again over the years, uncertain really why they can't shake it out of their head. Surely, I figured, they'd trip all over themselves to take part, just the sort of thing they're always carping that journalists are never interested in, preferring instead the snide wisecrack in an assassination-by-interview.

Fat chance. In fact, it was more than a year after I arrived in Los Angeles before the first piece ran. I cannot tell you how many people turned me down. Dozens. Men and women, old and young, bald and furry. They all said no. (Actually, it was hard to tell if they actually said no or were never even told about it, since you're always dealing with assistants or publicists or some other human barrier at the very beginning.) Important publicists looked at me as if I was asking their clients to strangle a kitten. The idea fit into no category with which they were familiar. "I don't get it," more than one said. My favorite was one of the minions of publicists, managers, and studio handlers for Julia Roberts who said, after a truly puzzled pause: "Why would she want to spend two hours talking about somebody else's movie?" How to begin to answer?

Finally, I was saved by Quentin Tarantino, who eagerly agreed to be the first guinea pig almost the instant the idea was put to him by his publicist, Bumble Ward (who had her own motive, to remind readers that Tarantino was alive and active after a four-year directing hiatus). Quickly thereafter Ron Howard agreed, and then Curtis Hanson, and the dam was broken.

After there had been three or four installments and people could see what the series was all about, I had them beating down the doors. Really. Major directors were calling up their publicists and saying, get me in that. It was journalist heaven. Brilliant and accomplished people, some of them downright legends, who wouldn't have given me five minutes on the phone without a couple of weeks of negotiations with their handlers, were suddenly inviting me up to the house, spending hours and hours. And asking *me* questions. Who was the nicest? Which one was the most fun? Who did you like? Who was the meanest?

By simply following the path of least resistance, taking the cream of the names who agreed to take part, I was able to get most of the top directors of the moment, and a pretty good smattering of the top actors. But the problem was, it was turning into a parade of White Guys. I found that I needed to work harder and push more persistently to make sure that more non-white and non-male faces took part. Even at the series' height, when I found I could get almost anyone to take part, there were still those who didn't feel comfortable doing it, and actors were always harder to corral than directors. I was turned down by a couple of the top women directors, and there aren't a whole lot of those, Hollywood being what it is. I never did get an answer from Sidney Poitier, after practically stalking him for months. But I got lucky, too. Denzel Washington agreed to do it around the time *Training Day* was opening, the film that would win him an Oscar a few months later. And when I was able to bring more actresses into the series, I got really good ones who picked wonderful movies, resulting in what, in my opinion, were some of the best installments in the series (I mean, Sissy Spacek on *To Kill a Mockingbird,* what's better than that?).

The idea was simple: Pick the best, most accomplished people we could find and match them with the right movie. My rule of thumb was to go only with people who didn't need to be introduced. If we had to have a paragraph explaining to readers who this person was, he or she wasn't right for the series. This left out the hot new up-and-comers and the one- or two-hit wonders whose ultimate fate was still in the balance. And then, once the people agreed to take part, we tried to come up with a movie that really, truly meant something to them—as opposed to something picked by their publicist to massage their client's image in one direction or another. The only rule was that they could not pick a movie someone else had already picked. We didn't want half of Hollywood's A-list all talking about *Citizen Kane* or *The Godfather.* In the end, this never became a problem. Never once did someone pick a movie that someone else had already claimed.

The most interesting thing, of course, was who picked what. There were a lot of surprises. Woody Allen goes with *Shane*? Harvey Weinstein picks *Exodus*? Michael Bay wants *West Side Story*?

And then there was the list of the movies that were chosen.

For one thing, look at what's missing. No one picked *Citizen Kane,* as it turned out, or any Orson Welles film. Hitchcock is missing, too. And so, strangely, is Billy Wilder. And who is there? Fred Zinnemann is represented twice, with *High Noon* and *A Man for All Seasons.* Stanley Kubrick, too, for *Dr. Strangelove* and *The Shining.* Robert Redford makes an appearance as a director—*Ordinary People*—and an actor—*All the President's Men.* Paul Newman is a recurring face. Since most of the people who took part in the series were between forty and sixty, and had come of age in the 1950s and 1960s, most of the films came from that era, from cherished moments in some long-vanished neighborhood cinema where little so-and-so was sitting dreaming in the dark about the movies they'd make someday.

I tried to keep myself out of the installments in the series, as much as I could. I hate interviews where you hear more about the interviewer than the subject. I guess I saved it all for this introduction.

And so, the one final question that almost everyone asked, including many of those interviewed: If it were me being interviewed, what movie would I choose?

A hard one, but fun to toy around with. That was always part of the attraction for doing the series. The process was fun. These are smart, talented people who probably could have made a nice life for themselves in a variety of professions, but something drove them to the movies. This is an attempt to put a name to that something. And me? When I think back on the movies that really meant a lot to me when I was a child, and later on, I come up with a strange assortment that I'm sure my publicist, if I had one, would not like me to share with others. *Abbott and Costello Meet Frankenstein*? I loved it—*loved it*—and awaited its occasional appearances on television like other people wait for the annual broadcast of *The Wizard of Oz.* And I was, and remain, a complete nut for James Bond. I can't explain it, especially now that I'm no longer a teenager. But I make no apologies. It's just the way it is. Beyond that, yes, *Citizen Kane.* And *Psycho,* that perfect little gem. *Lawrence of Arabia,* definitely. And *Ride the High Country* and *Rio Bravo,* my favorite westerns. Maybe *Five Graves to Cairo,* my favorite war movie (unless you count *Schindler's List* as a war movie, which I guess it is). And something from De Sica, probably *Umberto D.* And Kurosawa, let's say *Ikiru*—no, *Yojimbo.*

But if you get right down to it, and I had to pick the movie that reaches in deepest and that I watch again and again, always with delight, I guess I'd have to go with *Double Indemnity.* May the late Mr. Wilder rest in well-earned peace and find good conversation, wherever he is.

Or, wait a minute—what about *His Girl Friday?*

I'll get back to you.

WATCHING
MOVIES

Quentin Tarantino on
The Golden Stallion

When Quentin Tarantino agreed—almost instantly—to be the first subject of the fledgling series, relief was mixed with a high degree of anticipation and curiosity. Tarantino, who had not made a movie since *Jackie Brown* (1997), had been almost the living embodiment of the American independent film scene in the 1990s, a period of explosive growth and creative ferment. But the former video clerk turned auteur, famous for a febrile mind packed with all manner of film trash and arcana, had proven to be much less productive as a director than many of the B-grade filmmakers he most admired. Instead, he had spent much of his time in recent years trying to establish an acting career. But he had been hard at work writing, he insisted, and in fact did return to directing in the summer of 2002 with *Kill Bill*. Most of the people who would take part in the series were also, at the same time, trying to promote one of their films, hitting theaters around the time the installment was to appear. Tarantino had no movie to promote. He seemed to have no agenda at all, other than the film geek's desire to talk about movies. But it turned out he did have an agenda, which only became clear during the watching of the film he chose, an obscure, 40-minute

Roy Rogers movie that seemed to have little in common with the world of *Pulp Fiction* and *Reservoir Dogs*.

■

The six-by-eight-foot flickering rectangle of light turns the white wall to amber above Quentin Tarantino's fireplace. Not far away, back through a Spanish archway, a 16-millimeter projector rattles with a persistent click that never quite disappears beneath the bleating of the sound track, like static on a shortwave radio.

"I love this scene," Mr. Tarantino says. "It's a really tough scene, a tough, tough scene. But it's not the kind of scene you expect, all right. The emotion is right out there. But if you buy it, and I totally buy it, then it can make you cry."

This is the guy who made ear-severing a dance routine, turned sadomasochistic basement torture into comic relief, and created the scene where Uma Thurman takes a six-inch hypodermic in the chest. So when the director of *Reservoir Dogs* and *Pulp Fiction,* the celebrity prototype for an entire generation of Sundance-bred, film-geek auteurs, tells you that you are about to see a scene that is tough, you listen to him, don't you?

Roy Rogers is standing off to one side, elegant and stoic, with that thin, shiny mouth and those exotic eyes. Dale Evans is a few steps behind him, plump and fretting. A few steps away, the sheriff's men have Trigger, Rogers's famous stallion, held tightly on a rope. Trigger bobs his head up and down, shifts from foot to foot, his preternaturally floppy mane slapping across his forehead. It doesn't look good for the good guys. Rogers and Trigger have been found standing next to the body of a villain whose head has been bashed. We know the horse is innocent, but circumstantial evidence points to Trigger.

"In this case, Roy, circumstantial evidence is enough," the sheriff sadly intones.

Yes, Trigger is about to get one between the eyes, right now. There is no court of appeals for killer horses. The screen is suddenly filled with the face of Rogers. Somehow, fear, regret, and calculation all begin to wash out of his eyes, even though his face doesn't move a muscle. He drops his head, a decision made. "Wait, Sheriff," Rogers says, and then confesses to the killing. "Roy, don't you know what you're doing?" Dale whimpers. He knows. He's saving his best friend from a bullet, even if it means several years on a chain gang for him.

Mr. Tarantino leans forward and rests his elbows on his lanky legs, his face riveted to the flickering image on his living room wall where *The Golden Stallion* is playing. He says the film is one of the three or four masterpieces of a now all-but-forgotten journeyman director named William Witney.

Mr. Witney, eighty-five, an Oklahoma native now living in quiet retirement in rural California, is the sweetest fruit of what Mr. Tarantino says has been a year and a half of gorging on film history and B-grade filmmakers. Mr. Tarantino says he had a suspicion that there were "forgotten masters" out there, workaday moviemakers who had carefully chosen their assignments and then transformed them into art, but who had been overlooked in the post-auteur critical landscape.

"People think that the only good westerns made in the forties and fifties were by John Ford or maybe Howard Hawks," Mr. Tarantino says. "Film guys might add, oh, Anthony Mann and Budd Boetticher and Andre De Toth. But I just had this suspicion that because they didn't make A-list movies or didn't work with A-list stars, a lot of really great masters were getting lost in the shuffle."

So while he was working on the two screenplays that he intends to begin shooting, one after the other, after the first of the year, Mr. Tarantino says he also indulged his film-scholar fantasies and dived into the world of the forgotten genre flicks.

"I've found directors of some of these movies who I'm really into, but William Witney is ahead of them all, the one whose movies I can show to anyone and they are just blown away," Mr. Tarantino says. "He makes you accept everything on his terms, and his terms are that Roy and Trigger are best friends. Trigger is not just his best horse; he's his best friend. You know, in some movies, a cowboy might go to jail to save his best friend from being shot down dead. Well, Trigger is Roy's best friend. It's the easiest leap to have him do that here, yet it's so powerful and so unexpected. What's great is that you buy it, you absolutely buy it, and I don't know that I really would buy it from anybody else but Roy and Trigger."

The idea behind this series is to sit down—with accomplished filmmakers or actors or screenwriters or cinematographers, people who have contributed something to the history of film—and simply watch a movie, not one of their own films, but someone else's, a film that has some special resonance for them. The goal is to get some sort of understanding of how film artists absorb the movies they love, and how those movies have informed their own work. Instead of just another profile about the last project or the most recent award or the next big deal, this is to be about the work.

That's the idea. And so Mr. Tarantino, champion of everything from B-grade 1950s genres to '70s black exploitation to life as a bitter and ironic cocktail, was asked what he wanted to watch and he said, *The Golden Stallion,* a 1949 minifeature from the days of the Saturday morning cowboy serials, neither bitter nor ironic. Tough? Quentin Tarantino thinks so. You think you know better?

"The thing about William Witney is that he was really a director of genre movies," Mr. Tarantino says. "He started making serials in the late nineteen-thirties, and he made some of the best of them, from the Dick Tracy ones to Spy Smasher to Jungle Girl. And when they stopped making serials, he moved over to Saturday morning cowboy pictures and did pretty much everything Roy Rogers shot between the late forties and the early fifties"—when Rogers stopped making movies and shifted to television.

As the lanky Mr. Tarantino grows more effusive about his subject, he also becomes more mobile, pivoting on his hips as he chatters, then leaping up to pace the room, peppering his long, fast sentences with earnest expletives like "all right" and "cool." The faster he talks, the faster he walks. The more intricate his sentences, the more baroque his gestures.

"When they stopped making Saturday morning cowboy pictures in the fifties, when Republic Pictures closed down, he moved over and made juvenile delinquent films, and they are some of the best of those movies ever made," Mr. Tarantino says. "And when they stopped making those, he moved over and did some rock 'n' roll movies in the sixties. He flirted with the A-list a couple of times, but mostly he was a guy who moved from one B-list genre to another, all right, for something like forty years. And all the while he is churning out TV shows. He did a ton of *Bonanza* and episodes for almost every western of the period. And do you know what his last movie was? A black exploitation flick in the seventies. He ended with *Darktown Strutters* in 1975, about a female black motorcycle gang. I think it's so cool that he began as the king of the cowboy serials and he ended with a black exploitation film. That's a career, man."

A spokesman for McFarland and Company, which published Mr. Witney's 1995 memoirs about his years as a serial director—*In a Door, Into a Fight, Out a Door, Into a Chase*—said that Mr. Witney had suffered a stroke a few years ago and was not able to be interviewed, but that he had been informed about Mr. Tarantino's interest in his work.

The rap on Mr. Tarantino, thirty-seven, is that he doesn't make as many movies as he should; years and years come between his films. It's been three years since his most recent, *Jackie Brown,* and that one was a long time coming. This is all just about to change, he promises. One of his new projects is a tasty little noirish thriller starring Uma Thurman. "My fans are gonna love this one," he says. "They've been waiting a long time, and I think they're really going to happy with it." The other is a big, epic World War II adventure; he is just now trimming and polishing the screenplay.

Yet what does this very deliberate filmmaker, who spent a lot of his time in the last decade trying to generate an acting career, find to love about a true Hollywood salaryman like William Witney, who was making five movies a year when *The Golden Stallion* came out?

The flickering image shifts: Rogers is off in prison now. There was no last-minute reprieve. He had to do his time, and hard time it was. Not only that, but he also had to watch as Trigger became the property of the bad guys. And yet he never became bitter. Mr. Tarantino finds it odd that this is so moving to him.

"Normally, I would be drawn to movies where a good-guy Roy Rogers character becomes corrupted through life," Mr. Tarantino says, transfixed on the screen again. "In one of my movies, this guy would probably have come out of prison wanting to kill somebody. And he would kill somebody—while riding Trigger.

"Nowadays, Roy Rogers seems almost too good, but you buy it from him somehow. I find myself being moved by his common decency. Life's events and other people's actions have no effect on him and his heart. He didn't save Trigger to become a bitter man; he did it because it was what he had to do. His code is his code. The whole world can change, and it doesn't change his code."

Mr. Tarantino first came across Mr. Witney's work when he watched an old print of *The Bonnie Parker Story* (1958), a kind of juvenile delinquent movie set in the Depression, with Dorothy Provine playing the infamous gangster. "I was blown away," he says. "It was like, whoa, who made this? I have to see everything he ever did." And so began the hunt for the half-forgotten works of Mr. Witney. One after another, he found them, watched them, and, with one or two exceptions, found them absolutely riveting, the work of a real lost master, just what he had been looking for.

He has whittled Mr. Witney's oeuvre—more than one hundred films from 1937 to 1975—into what he considers to be his four greatest masterpieces. The earliest is *The Golden Stallion*. Then comes *Stranger at My Door* (1956), another western, this time with Macdonald Carey playing a frontier preacher whose homestead is invaded by a robber on the lam. ("I showed this to a group of friends, all film people, and it just blew them away," Mr. Tarantino says. "We talked about it for hours afterward.") Then *The Bonnie Parker Story* and, in 1959, *Paratroop Command,* a realistic World War II adventure about a platoon pariah who has to prove himself.

"I was showing *Paratroop Command* to Peter Bogdanovich one day, and there comes this moment in the film where he goes, like, hey, wait a minute, what the heck is happening?" Mr. Tarantino says. "These guys, who you've been getting to know throughout the movie, suddenly start dying. And I don't mean a big, glamorous cinema death. They're just dropping like flies, unceremoniously. It's so realistic. You know that it was a movie made by a guy who had been there. William Witney was in the Marines in World War II for something like five years."

The projector is still clicking away, and the wall above the fireplace is filled with motion. Trigger is running through a broad valley, the sun backlighting his mane and a team of wild horses following behind. Dale Evans, in voice-over, is reading a letter she is writing to Rogers, back on the chain gang. "I find this so poetic, so beautiful," Mr. Tarantino says. "The letter is beautifully written, her delivery is great, and these images of the wild horses are just stunning. Wait, I want to run it back."

He jumps up and runs back to the projector and rewinds to catch the last few minutes again.

Appreciating William Witney begins with understanding what he did with Roy Rogers, Mr. Tarantino says. "Roy's movies at this time had turned into these sort of western musicals, like frontier jamborees, where he's singing and walking around in outfits with fringes," Mr. Tarantino says. "After their first few movies together, Witney had gotten Roy out of his fringe-and-sparkle attire and was dressing him in normal attire, blue jeans and stuff. They stopped being these crazy musicals. He turned them into rough, tough violent adventures. Audiences loved it. Nobody had ever seen Roy fight like that, so it was kind of cool to everyone that he was such a good fistfighter. And a fistfight in a William Witney movie is a fistfight. They're tough. People get bloody noses."

Mr. Tarantino says he admires Mr. Witney for his rough and believable action scenes, but also for his taste, as shown in his choice of assignments over the years. He compares him to Howard Hawks, a director who spanned genres but managed to bring something of himself to each of them. "It shows you how important taste is," he says.

And there is something unpretentious about the way Mr. Witney worked that appeals to the young director.

"He's a visual stylist, but he's a visual stylist in the way that a lot of those guys were back then," Mr. Tarantino says. "It's always about moving the camera like 'Hey Mom, look, I'm directing.' He was clever about camera movement. One of the things I got from looking at his films is that the camera movements are so elegant. You have to have made movies for thirty years to be able to move the camera so unpretentiously. His camera movements, when they happen, are so cool. They're either completely artful, in a cool, don't-call-attention-to-yourself kind of way, or they're visually about how to tell the story. These guys were storytellers. They knew how to move the camera to convey information so they didn't have to shoot another dialogue scene to explain something."

And something else has jumped out at Mr. Tarantino.

"Look at the way he uses Trigger in this film," he says. "William Witney is the greatest director when it comes to working with animals. In his films, if there's an animal, it's another character in the movie. If a homesteader has a dog, it's not just yapping in the background. You get to know this dog; you might even follow it on its own little adventure in the middle of the movie. And *Golden Stallion* is his masterpiece when it comes to working with animals, perhaps because he's working with Trigger, the greatest animal actor who ever was."

In the long run, Mr. Tarantino says, he hopes Mr. Witney has influenced him in subtle ways, perhaps helping him build his instinct for when to move the camera and how. He did, while still in the first flush of admiration for Mr. Witney's work, write two animal scenes into his World War II epic, though he says that the script has grown too long and byzantine and must be trimmed back and that both of the animal scenes, sadly, will probably have to go. In one, a refugee girl hiding in a barn is attacked by rats and saved by a dog; in the other, a soldier separated from his platoon finds and befriends a runaway horse. Never to be filmed, he says with a shrug: "That's the way it goes."

Has this year in the film-scholar trenches been worth it? These are, after all, years in which Mr. Tarantino could have been making a lot of money and a lot of films.

"This is a very noble pursuit," he says. "I've turned quite a few friends on to William Witney, so he lives through us, at least."

It's easy, he knows, to "get hung up on somebody when you do something like this," and perhaps exaggerate a filmmaker's gifts or importance. But he has thought about it and really believes that Mr. Witney is the genuine article. So has it been worth it? Yes.

"You know, in this business right now, there are a whole lot of people making movies to pay for their incredibly extravagant lifestyle," he says. "There's just a whole lot of that going on. I'm not judging, but that's not why I came here, to make movies to pay for my pool. I never want to have to do that, and I don't have to do that. But you know, if you come at this as though it's a religion, as opposed to a job, then sometimes you have to keep close to God a little. That's what this last year was. It was my way of renewing myself."

HIGHLIGHTS OF QUENTIN TARANTINO'S CAREER AND INFORMATION ON *THE GOLDEN STALLION*

∎

What They Watched

The Golden Stallion. Directed by William Witney; written by Sloan Nibley. With Roy Rogers, Dale Evans, Estelita Rodriguez, Pat Brady, and Douglas Evans. 1949.

Quentin Tarantino's Films

Jackie Brown. Written and directed by Quentin Tarantino. 1997.

From Dusk Till Dawn. Written by and starring Quentin Tarantino; directed by Robert Rodriguez. 1996.

Natural Born Killers. Written by David Veloz, Richard Rutowski, and Oliver Stone; story by Quentin Tarantino; directed by Oliver Stone. 1994.

Pulp Fiction. Written, directed by, and starring Quentin Tarantino. 1994.

True Romance. Written by Quentin Tarantino; directed by Tony Scott. 1993.

Reservoir Dogs. Written, directed by, and starring Quentin Tarantino. 1992.

Books on Quentin Tarantino

Tarantino A to Zed: The Films of Quentin Tarantino, by Alan Barnes and Marcus Hearn. Brasseys, 2000.

King Pulp: The Wild World of Quentin Tarantino, by Paul A. Woods. Publishers Group, 1998.

Quentin Tarantino: Shooting from the Hip, by Wensley Clarkson. Overlook Press, 1996.

Quentin Tarantino: The Cinema of Cool, by Jeff Dawson. Applause Theater Books Publications, 1995.

Quentin Tarantino: The Man and His Movies, by Jami Bernard. Harper Perennial, 1995.

2

Janusz Kaminski on
Vanishing Point

One of the things I hoped to do with the series, though was never able to bring to full fruition, was to include install-ments that extended beyond the realm of directors and actors. Months of negotiations with DeDe Allen, the legendary film editor of *Bonnie and Clyde* and several other classic films, kept get-ting sidetracked by her trips out of town and some health problems. A couple of top film composers kept nudging up to the idea and then pulling back. Then Janusz Kaminski, one of the most accomplished cinematographers of the past decade, agreed to do it, partly because he was also keen to promote his directorial debut, a low-budget hor-ror film called *Lost Souls*. As with many installments in the series, his participation provided unexpected bonuses. In retrospect, it acts almost as a companion piece to Wolfgang Petersen's viewing of *High Noon*, both examples of how Hollywood films looked to those grow-ing up in very different societies abroad, and how the allure of spe-cific movie moments drew them to the United States.

■

Janusz Kaminski can close his eyes and conjure up the picture of a teenager sitting in the hushed hours after midnight in the living room of a small apartment in Wroclaw, Poland. A television set is on, bathing both the room and the boy in a flickering glow. The young man, of course, is himself. He must have been about sixteen at the time, he thinks, though he's not really sure. Certainly it is sometime in the late 1970s, when the Communist world was approaching twilight, not that anyone knew it.

On the flickering television screen, to the crunch of gravel and the twang of country rock, is Richard C. Sarafian's *Vanishing Point.* Barry Newman plays Kowalski, a drugged-out, alienated, authority-hating hot-rodder who has made a pointless bet that he can deliver a car halfway across the country in just a few days. When the redneck cops close in, he purposely plows the car into a pair of bulldozers rather than surrender.

"Perhaps in the minds of the Communist government, the reason it was allowed to be shown was that it was seen as a decadent American movie," Mr. Kaminski said. "Under the circumstances, it was viewed as negative and a criticism of America. But the people who were responsible for putting on the television programs in the system at that time were not the dumbest. I think they were able to slip this movie through because it appeared to be criticizing capitalism. But it really wasn't, and I think they knew that."

Mr. Kaminski lives in Southern California now, one of the most respected cinematographers in Hollywood, a two-time Oscar winner—for *Saving Private Ryan* in 1998 and *Schindler's List* in 1993. He'd recently directed his first film, a religion-based thriller called *Lost Souls,* with Winona Ryder and Ben Chaplin, and was in the midst of shooting three films in rapid succession (*A.I., Minority Report,* and *Catch Me If You Can*) for his most frequent collaborator, director Steven Spielberg.

It is a long way from that late night in Wroclaw, but when Mr. Kaminski, forty-one, was asked to think back over his life and choose one of the movies that has meant the most to him, that has had the most profound influence on his intellectual and creative life, he settled on this 1971 drive-in cult flick.

Even now, when he looks back on his life, he still feels Barry Newman's Benzedrine jitters throbbing through his veins.

"I am so curious to see this movie again," Mr. Kaminski said. "You know, I have not seen it in more than twenty years, not at all. But I have this great recollection of thinking as I was watching it, 'Wow, this is what America is all about; this is what freedom of expression is all about.' Here is an individual who is willing to sacrifice, even to sacrifice his own life, for the sake of his idea of freedom and independence."

Mr. Kaminski was sitting in the front row of the otherwise deserted 100-seat screening room that New Line Cinema (which will be distributing *Lost Souls*) maintains on the first floor of a Beverly Hills office building on a trendy stretch of Robertson Boulevard. It was a weekend afternoon, and he was dressed casually, a black polo shirt over green corduroy pants. Though he has lived in the United States for two decades (having left not long after he first saw *Vanishing Point,* to attend college in Chicago and begin a career in cinematography), a trace of the Polish accent still clings to his tongue, but lightly.

The print of *Vanishing Point* that was being shown was not the best; actually, it was a fading videotape projected onto the screen. Much of John A. Alonzo's evocative cinematography of the American West was rendered bland. But the movie was always a bit rough, even when it was brand-new, disdaining the kind of slickness that constitutes so much film craft today. Besides, the images in the New Line screening room couldn't possibly be worse than those that must have appeared on a small television set in Poland in the late '70s.

As the film started, Mr. Kaminski leaned forward as if trying to get as close as possible to the screen, studying the dusty roadscapes through small, rectangular glasses that rigidly clutched the bridge of his nose. In his memory, he puts *Vanishing Point* in a class of other films that he saw around the same time on late-night television: Dennis Hopper's *Easy Rider* (1969), Robert Altman's *Three Women* (1977), Jerry Schatzberg's *Panic in Needle Park* (1971).

"These were movies that influenced me and, I think, millions of other young people all across Eastern Europe," he said. They all were slipped in under the guise of exposing American decadence and drug abuse, but they spoke to the young Mr. Kaminski and others in another, more romantic language.

"This is the way we learned about the world, we Eastern Europeans—from the movies," Mr. Kaminski said. "The majority of the kids like me growing up in Poland under Communism, we thought that America is, you know, the place to be. For me, I saw America not as this country of plenty, this country of wealth, where everyone has a car and everyone has a house, but as a country of freedom, where the individual is free, the ideology is free. That is why I so much wanted to come here."

Yet there was a certain amount of looseness in the system in those days, Mr. Kaminski remembered. "Poland was kind of a paradox among Eastern European countries then because it allowed for a certain form of freedom of expression," he said. Unlike the region's other Communist countries, Poland allowed some farmers to own their own land, for people to set up small businesses in the cities, and for stealth apparatchiks—like those programming the late-night movies in Wroclaw—to sneak in a little American freedom, as long as it was presented in the cloak of American decadence.

To watch *Vanishing Point* now with Mr. Kaminski is like recalling two vanished worlds: that of Poland in the late '70s, caught in the ferment just before Solidarity was born, and that of the United States of nearly a decade earlier, the Vietnam War still raging, the '60s youth culture fraying at the edges.

Even in its heyday, *Vanishing Point* was not much more than a cult favorite, raw and perplexing. At its heart, it is a nihilistic, psychological mystery. What is this Kowalski all about? (Are we meant, for instance, to remember Stanley Kowalski from *A Streetcar Named Desire,* or is the name just a coincidence?)

Why is he a pill-popping renegade? What induces him to make a meaningless suicidal bet with his drug dealer to drive his car to San Francisco in an impossibly short time? Why, when the police try to slow him down, does he only drive faster and more recklessly? And why, in the end, when they finally have him trapped in a small dusty crossroads in rural California, does he choose to kill himself—death by bulldozer—rather than knuckle under? After all, no one has been killed. He's only facing a traffic ticket.

Kowalski is the frontier loner, the rugged individualist, as refracted through the hipster ethos of the early '70s, the antihero as stubborn, self-destructive casualty of the '60s. It's *Thunder Road* in bell-bottoms and love beads.

"The idea was completely surreal for us, that a person could be hired to take a car across the United States and to be paid for it," Mr. Kaminski said. "So completely unreal because to us, of course, we would all want to do it. Such freedom. What a vacation."

Another point struck Mr. Kaminski as he watched the weather-worn faces peer from behind dust-flecked storefronts on the main street of a run-down rural town. "This is not a glamorous depiction of America, but it feels very real," he said. Many of the movies that linger in the memory from that period—*Bonnie and Clyde, The Last Picture Show,* even Mr. Spielberg's *Sugarland Express*—were set in this same sort of landscape of rural clapboard seediness, he said, the sort of America that you do not see now in the movies, which tend toward fantasy worlds and sentimental landscapes.

"I think this face of America is still out there," he said. "I think if we get on the freeway and go just an hour outside of Los Angeles, you will see it. But we have stopped looking at it. Filmmakers have stopped looking at it."

Mr. Kaminski was rapt as he watched the film. "It is obviously very much a picture of its time," he said, and not just because of its attitudes. The camera work, for instance, feels old-fashioned with its zooms and quick shifts in focus and the musical montages pasted over greeting-card sunsets. "But I don't know, it is still working for me somehow," Mr. Kaminski said. "The action scenes are very good. This car chase is fantastic. I do not think it feels dated at all." Kowalski is screeching around hairpin curves just ahead of a line of police cars, gravel flying, dust swirling everywhere.

In at least one way, though, *Vanishing Point* today feels like a movie very much ahead of its time. A blind radio disc jockey called Super Soul, played by Cleavon Little, hears about Kowalski's cross-country run and turns the story into a full-blown media event, tracing his progress, helping him outwit the local police, and inflating his essentially pointless adventure into a romantic antiestablishment gesture. At times, one can almost imagine it as grand opera, with Placido Domingo, perhaps, singing the role of Kowalski. It is impossible to watch it today, Mr. Kaminski said, without seeing in it the pre-tremors of O. J. Simpson and JonBenet Ramsey and Elián Gonzalez and every other hyped-up tabloid media frenzy of the last quarter of the twentieth century.

But the film's ending was, and remains, the crux of its appeal: the explosive and defiant embrace of death before submission. "I am just attracted to those kinds of movies," Mr. Kaminski said. "Movies that end tragically, but not really. Because, you see, Kowalski got what he wanted. He was willing to fight for his freedom and to die before losing it."

It is the *Thelma and Louise* ending, but without ambiguity.

"I was a teenager, you know, and you are so much more idealistic when you are younger," Mr. Kaminski said. "For me, the idea of committing suicide on-screen had no relevance to real life; it was just a romantic idea. And I do see myself as a romantic person. You know, the love affair is always tragic, the antihero is always tragic. So that is how I viewed myself at that point, when I was growing up, and some of that view has not gone away, even being here after twenty years."

He is also struck, as a filmmaker in solid standing, a figure of importance in Hollywood, by how difficult it would be to try to make *Vanishing Point* today. In his own work, he has been to the meetings with studio executives, talked to other filmmakers, met with investors, heard the long, sad wail of the marketing department.

"You couldn't have a movie like this today, no way," Mr. Kaminski said. "They would not let you. They would say: 'Why does he have to die? The audience will not go for it.' You know, movies are so much safer now, because there is too much at risk, too much money involved, too many of the wrong people making the decisions, somebody who is an accountant at a studio. The audience will not go for it, they say. I think the audience will go for it. I think the audience is ready for anything, anything that moves or entertains them. Look at *American Beauty*. It was narrated by a dead man, but audiences loved it because it was a good, good movie."

There is one scene in *Vanishing Point* he remembers quite vividly. Kowalski is running short of pills that he needs to stay awake and keep ahead of the police when he meets up with a chopper-riding *Easy Rider* type who agrees to share some of his stash. The young man takes Kowalski home to his ramshackle trailer on the edge of the Nevada desert, and there, riding around on a motorcycle in the sandy scrubland, is a beautiful young flower child with long blond hair. She is blissful and buck naked. (Later she offers herself to Kowalski. Innocently. Hey, it's just for fun. But he's too much of a gentleman.)

As the scene appears, a slow, bittersweet smile spread across Mr. Kaminski's face. American freedom, distilled to its essence—at least as far as a teenager in Communist Poland was concerned.

"This movie still works for me, just like it did when I was younger," Mr. Kaminski said. "I understand now, being a more mature person and older and a filmmaker, that there are problems with the movie and a certain infantile way of thinking. But at the same time, after seeing it again, I think it is a really, really good movie."

And as he looks at those two people —himself today and himself as a young man back in Poland—he can feel the threads that connect them and even, he thinks, how his emotional response to movies like *Vanishing Point* have made a man of the youth.

"Of course, I can see that we are the same person," he said. "But it is a person who has evolved from being a teenager who lived in a Communist country in a very protected environment to a man who is in his forties who lives in a different country, in a different system, but who still has many of the same values. Now I am in America, but I am still idealistic; I am still romantic; money still does not dominate my world. I am the same person, but I am still searching. I am not content yet."

Since making *Saving Private Ryan*, Mr. Kaminski has been working on his directorial debut and also taking the first steps toward a side career shooting television commercials. He enjoys it, he said, and it gives him more freedom. He does not have to shoot two movies every year, as many cinematographers do, but can pick the one that most appeals to him and work only with the directors he most admires, like Mr. Spielberg and Cameron Crowe (for whom he shot the 1996 *Jerry Maguire*). And then, every two or three years, he hopes to direct a movie of his own, just to keep moving forward, kicking up the gravel.

Definitely, he said, he identifies with Kowalski, even today. "I have a very clear sense of independence," he said. "I make sure that I am not connected with any single studio or any single company. I am purposely structuring my life and my career so that I can make the choice with each movie about what I will do and who I will work with. Having this freedom allows me to be brave, allows me not to settle for the more safe resolution in terms of my work. And that is a great comfort, not being afraid."

Not that he intends to go barreling into bulldozers on a dusty highway. "But I definitely still see the romance of it," Mr. Kaminski said. "I see it from an intellectual point of view. I would not go there myself. I am adult enough to understand. But still, it is tremendous, this idea of freedom, of dying for freedom. There is a reason that I maintain myself as independent and a reason that I always try to take chances. It is like Kowalski. Yes, I may fail. But what if I fail, but I win because I tried?"

HIGHLIGHTS OF JANUSZ KAMINSKI'S CAREER AND INFORMATION ON *VANISHING POINT*

■

What They Watched

Vanishing Point. Directed by Richard C. Sarafian; cinematography by John A. Alonzo. With Barry Newman, Cleavon Little, Dean Jagger, and Victoria Medlin. 1971.

Janusz Kaminski's Films

Catch Me If You Can. Directed by Steven Spielberg; cinematography by Janusz Kaminski. 2002.

Minority Report. Directed by Steven Spielberg; cinematography by Janusz Kaminski. 2002.

A.I. Directed by Steven Spielberg; cinematography by Janusz Kaminski. 2001.

Lost Souls. Directed by Janusz Kaminski. With Winona Ryder, Ben Chaplin, and John Hurt. 2000.

Saving Private Ryan. Directed by Steven Spielberg; cinematography by Janusz Kaminski. 1998.

Amistad. Directed by Steven Spielberg; cinematography by Janusz Kaminski. 1997.

The Lost World: Jurassic Park. Directed by Steven Spielberg; cinematography by Janusz Kaminski. 1997.

Jerry Maguire. Written and directed by Cameron Crowe; cinematography by Janusz Kaminski. 1996.

How to Make an American Quilt. Directed by Jocelyn Moorhouse; cinematography by Janusz Kaminski. 1995.

Schindler's List. Directed by Steven Spielberg; cinematography by Janusz Kaminski. 1993.

3

Ron Howard on
The Graduate

lthough it was before *How the Grinch Stole Christmas*
earned a quarter-billion dollars in North American theaters
alone, Ron Howard had already long since grown past his
image as an aw shucks, Norman Rockwell–esque everykid in such
acting roles as the *American Graffiti* class president, Opie Taylor on
The Andy Griffith Show, and Richie Cunningham on *Happy Days.*
Imagine Entertainment, the production company he cofounded with
his producing partner, Brian Grazer, had become a linchpin of one of
the major studios, Universal, and a dependable provider of mass
market entertainments from low comedy to high-minded drama.
Indeed, Howard rested alongside Steven Spielberg and George Lucas
as exemplars of state-of-the-art, mainstream moviemaking, with all
that implied. This interview took place just as Howard was beginning to work on *A Beautiful Mind,* the movie that would win him an
overdue directing Oscar in 2002. Indeed, during the six-mile drive
back to the Greenwich, Connecticut, train station after the screening, he was bubbling with enthusiasm about some of the preliminary
work he'd done on the project with star Russell Crowe, and delighted

that he had just recently been able to sign Jennifer Connelly to play the film's key supporting role (she also got an Oscar for her work).

■

Hello, darkness, my old friend. I've come to talk with you again."

Beneath the halo of the ceiling-mounted video projector in his basement screening room, Ron Howard sprawled across an upholstered seat in the front row and absentmindedly stroked his chin as the rippling glare of the movie played over his upturned face. "When I first saw *The Graduate,* this whole montage sequence, it was magic to me," Mr. Howard said. "I couldn't figure out how they did it."

Dustin Hoffman, his face a cold mask of obliviousness, inert behind a pair of wraparound sunglasses, pulls himself out of a swimming pool. He is Benjamin Braddock, fresh out of college and trapped in a passionless affair with Mrs. Robinson, the wife of his father's business partner. On the sound track Simon and Garfunkel sing "The Sound of Silence." Benjamin moves through the Southern California glare of the pool deck under the worried gaze of his parents, barbecuing nearby. He pulls on a white shirt, slowly, ritualistically, adjusting the collar, fastening the buttons, one by one.

Without a word or a glance to his parents, he passes into the darkness of the house. "In the naked light I saw, ten thousand people, maybe more. . . ." Though there has been no apparent cut, he is no longer in his parents' house, but in a room at a nearby hotel. Anne Bancroft, as Mrs. Robinson, leans over him, wearing nothing but bra and slip, and begins to unbutton the white shirt, one button at a time.

Benjamin barely acknowledges her presence, leaning back against the bed's black headboard. Suddenly, again without an apparent cut, he stands up, and he is back at home, closing the door on his bewildered parents. "People talking without speaking, people hearing without listening. . . ." Back and forth he moves between his aimless life at home and his joyless affair at the hotel, and each time the cuts are invisible, driven by the music.

"You see, it's the black background, that's how they did it," Mr. Howard said. "I was reading an interview a while back with Sam O'Steen, who was Mike Nichols's editor on *The Graduate,* and he described how it was done."

In the dark room at his parents' house, when Benjamin leans back, it is onto a black pillow. The camera moves in so it sees just Benjamin's face surrounded by black, and then Mrs. Robinson begins to move across the frame, and the camera pulls back, and Benjamin is leaning on the black headboard of the bed.

"It's obvious when you see it," Mr. Howard said. "Very simple, very clever. I mean, really, when you think about it, who has black pillows?"

Wander back now to the Summer of Love, psychedelic 1967. LBJ's in the White House, and Lucy's in the sky with diamonds. Dust off your love beads. Switch on the black light. Don't you want somebody to love?

While teenagers all over America were hoping that their parents didn't notice the luxuriant crops of hair sprouting from their self-consciously alienated heads, thirteen-year-old Ronny Howard was in his next-to-last season on *The Andy Griffith Show*. The youth revolution was largely a rumor in Mayberry, but even Opie knew that something was in the air.

"I was a movie fan in those days, but I wasn't thinking about directing," Mr. Howard said. "When people asked me back then what I wanted to be when I grew up, I said a basketball player, and I meant it. But I loved going to the movies. When I think back on those days, there are a cluster of films that I kind of mix together in my mind: *Bonnie and Clyde, Cool Hand Luke, In the Heat of the Night*. But *The Graduate* had the biggest impact on me."

A decade earlier, his father, the veteran character actor Rance Howard, had moved the family from Oklahoma to Hollywood, where they pursued their parallel careers. Ronny Howard, as he was billed at the time, became one of the most ubiquitous child actors of the early '60s, appearing in films like *The Courtship of Eddie's Father* and *The Music Man* and spending eight years as Opie, perhaps the most realistic and fully rounded child character in early sitcoms.

By 1967, though, Ronny was moving into his teens and nudging his way toward becoming Ron. One night his father took him to see *The Graduate* at a theater in Westwood.

"This is the movie that made me realize what it meant to direct a movie, what was really involved," Mr. Howard said. "It's the one I went back to, again and again. I just kept revisiting it. At first, not analyzing, just enjoying it. But then, as I saw it more and more often, analyzing it."

And what did he learn? Several lessons that have deepened over more than two dozen viewings, he estimates. It has to do with point of view, with telling a story through the eyes of one of your characters: Benjamin or Mrs. Robinson.

And it had to do with tone, the way audiences will accept a blend of drama and slapstick if the characters are true and the sight gags are used judiciously. But it also has to do with how to make movies, the nuts and bolts stuff, like this "Sound of Silence" montage, the puzzles that the movie presented to a young actor who was just beginning to realize that he wanted to be a director.

Before *The Graduate,* Mr. Howard said, he was just another face in the audience, having a good time. But something about this Mike Nichols comedy coming at just the right moment in a young actor's life made him want to deconstruct it and to understand it.

"This is the movie that I went to school on," Mr. Howard said.

He is as cheerful and unassuming as you might expect from the characters he has played, but far more thoughtful, even ruminative. Now forty-six, husband and father of four, his eldest already in college, he makes his home in the rolling countryside outside Greenwich, commuting to wherever his latest film needs to be shot.

As often as not, he chooses to make his movies in the East, handy to home. Some, like Jim Carrey in *Dr. Seuss's How the Grinch Stole Christmas*—which was to come out shortly after we watched *The Graduate*—are products of the Hollywood soundstages and necessitate spending chunks of time in Southern California. (His follow-up film, *A Beautiful Mind,* which won Mr. Howard his first directing Oscar and also won best picture, was shot in the East.)

With his partner, Brian Grazer, he runs Imagine Entertainment, a production company that is a mainstay of Universal Pictures, responsible for hits like Eddie Murphy's two *Nutty Professor* films as well as his own movies, like *EdTV, Apollo 13,* and *Ransom.* Ron Howard has so successfully made the transition from sitcom star to filmmaker and Hollywood power broker that it is hard to remember that there was a time when it was difficult to picture young Opie and Richie Cunningham of the *Happy Days* television series as a respected director.

It all started, Mr. Howard said, when his father was directing a play he had written himself in Los Angeles in the mid-'60s, *Look Down on the Hudson*. Young Ronny was allowed to hang around backstage, watching his father direct, and to chat with the actors and the technical workers.

"When I look back on it now, it seems kind of amazing, but they really treated me like a colleague, not like a little kid," Mr. Howard said. "When they had rehearsals or meetings, they'd listen to my ideas just as much as they listened to anyone else's, and they'd explain to me what was going on and why. That's the first time I really had a full idea of what a director's job was."

But not until *The Graduate* did he begin to apply this, in his mind, to the craft of making movies.

"I think I went to see it three or four times during its first run in theaters," Mr. Howard said. "The first time, I went with my father, but then I went back three or four more times. I don't know if you remember, but back then movies used to play in theaters for a lot longer than they do now, and *The Graduate* was in theaters for what seemed like forever."

After that, whenever the movie reappeared in theaters, perhaps as part of a double bill in a repertory cinema or as a midnight show near a college campus, he would try to go see it.

"When we were shooting *American Graffiti* up in San Rafael in 1972, I became good friends with Charlie Martin Smith and discovered that *The Graduate* was his favorite movie, too," Mr. Howard said. "Except he was even more into it than I was. He was the kind of guy who could quote you whole scenes of dialogue off the top of his head."

In that early George Lucas film, Mr. Howard played Steve, the graduating high school jock, and Mr. Smith was his nerdy friend, Terry the Toad.

"The whole movie took place in one long night, if you remember, so that meant that we all had to be up all night every night during the shoot, which lasted something like six weeks," Mr. Howard said. "Charlie and I would spend a lot of time talking about movies, especially *The Graduate*. And then for one stretch *The Graduate* was actually playing on a double bill at a local drive-in, so we went to see it two or three times. We just ate it up."

Even immediately after its release, *The Graduate* was recognized as a groundbreaking film, and one that had a particular hold on the imaginations of the generation of young people who, like Mr. Howard, came of age in the late '60s and early '70s. "It's absolutely true," Mr. Howard said. "I really related to the movie, to the way that it portrayed the world."

Looking at it now, after three decades, it's a little difficult to tell why this strangely anachronistic sex comedy became a generational touchstone for the flower power–Woodstock crowd, because the movie doesn't seem to be taking place in that world at all.

Dustin Hoffman's Benjamin is a clean-cut college kid who seems to wear a tie just about everywhere he goes, even on dates. There's not a shaggy head in sight, and the only faint whiff of a mention of the social turmoil of the period is a comment from a landlord (played with hilarious venom by Norman Fell) that he hopes Benjamin isn't one of those "outside agitators" that he's been reading about.

Vietnam, civil rights, marijuana, free love—all of the hippie-tinged themes associated with the era—are completely absent from *The Graduate*. It's more like the last movie of the '50s than the great clarion of the '60s, full of upper-middle-class people in golf clothes drinking Scotch and centering on the same kind of sex farce that might have been used in a Frank Sinatra comedy or something with Doris Day and Rock Hudson.

"I clearly remember seeing the movie again in the early seventies, when I was in college, and thinking that the young people in the movie sure didn't look anything like the kids I was going to school with," Mr. Howard said.

Yet somehow, more than any of the movies that tried to address the turbulent social upheavals of the '60s more directly, *The Graduate* is the movie that many who actually lived through that time, including Mr. Howard, feel most closely captured the mind-set of the era.

"It has something to do with the view of the world of adult hypocrisy," Mr. Howard said. "It's about the generation that had been through the Great Depression and the Second World War and who had come out on top—people who were living very comfortably, had everything they wanted—and yet there was something phony and hollow about their world. They didn't notice it, but their children did.

"I don't think there is a single character in *The Graduate* that is not a phony, to one degree or another, except Benjamin and Elaine, and only in the scenes when they are alone together." Elaine is Mrs. Robinson's daughter, whom Benjamin has come to love.

The movie has followed Mr. Howard throughout his professional life. It was the first videocassette he bought, and he estimates that he has watched it more than a dozen times since then.

"When I was asked to pick a movie to watch that had had an impact on me, it was the first one that came to mind," he said. "I kind of wondered whether I should pick something more obscure, to seem more impressive. But I decided, no, if the idea was to watch a movie that had really influenced me, then this had to be it."

As he watched the opening credits, he munched on a cookie—an assistant had left a plate outside the basement screening room—and he began to talk animatedly as the first image appeared on the screen.

"Look at this first shot," he said, brushing a crumb off his sleeve. "The camera is right on Dustin."

The actor's impassive face fills the frame, and only as the camera slowly pulls back do we see that he is sitting on an airplane, returning home from college.

"From the very first, the story is told from Benjamin's viewpoint. We keep returning to this image, again and again, to reinforce that the story is from his perspective. We feel the story through Benjamin—his feelings are the ones we are also feeling. That's the first thing this movie taught me, how to tell a story through a character's point of view."

Only two or three times during the movie does Mr. Nichols provide shots from another character's point of view. "And then, it's from Mrs. Robinson's perspective, and it's always done at a point in the story where the result is that it turns up the heat a little more on Benjamin," Mr. Howard said. "And the movie very quickly returns to Benjamin's perspective each time."

Mr. Howard said he had shown the film to his son a few days earlier, just to refresh his memory about it and to see how his son would react.

"He loved it," Mr. Howard said. "I think he was right with the story the whole time. I know there are some things in the movie that are outdated, some camera shots or musical montages that were in style in the late sixties. But I really think that you could release this movie again today, and it would still do well."

Mr. Howard is particularly delighted in pointing out the moments of virtual sitcom slapstick and sight gags found throughout the movie.

"The tone of this movie was so revolutionary at the time, and in a lot of ways it still is," he said. "In some ways it's a traditional kind of sex comedy, but it's not shot like a screwball comedy. It's shot like a drama. Look at all these dark rooms and tense moments." Yet the comedy keeps reasserting itself.

In one scene, Benjamin, desperate to inject some humanity into his relationship, asks Mrs. Robinson whether they could talk about something for a change before making love. She resists, then taunts him, sadly. The whole scene is played in a dark room, nothing but the dim outline of a window in the background, until Mrs. Robinson turns on the bedside lamp and we see that Benjamin is hunched over on the bed on all fours, burying his head in the sheets and looking a little goofy. "It's a sight gag," Mr. Howard said.

Then there's the scene in which Benjamin baffles his parents by announcing that he intends to marry Elaine and then confessing that she knows nothing about it and doesn't even like him. "This whole idea seems pretty half-baked," his father says. "No, it's not, it's completely baked," Benjamin responds and walks out of the room. Stunned silence. A beat. And then the toaster pops up, startling the parents. "Another sight gag," Mr. Howard said.

Sometimes the gags stray into the absurd, and what impresses Mr. Howard particularly is how Mr. Nichols was able to maintain the realistic flavor of the story while injecting brief flashes of an almost vaudeville kind of comedy. In particular he referred to the scene in which Benjamin and Elaine decide they don't want to end their first date, and she suggests that they go for a drink at the same hotel where Benjamin has been carrying on the affair with Elaine's mother. Benjamin's sports car suddenly veers off the road and up on the curb.

"I love the way they shot this, where you're not in the car with them but watching it from a spot down the street," Mr. Howard said. "It's just a classic bit of slapstick, a screwball comedy moment. Even in the context of the movie, it's a little too silly, but you go with it. That's what's great.

"The whole movie is a kind of high-wire act as far as the tone is concerned. That's what I learned, that you can earn a few passes from the audience, in a comedy especially. But if you cash in one of your chips, you better get a laugh."

Mr. Howard watched the film with intense concentration. He was particularly interested in the new things he was noticing in these later viewings.

"It occurred to me when I was watching it with my son that there's just a hint, toward the end, that there's a little bit of Mrs. Robinson in her daughter," Mr. Howard said. Mrs. Robinson had rather coldly manipulated the college graduate, taking a spider's delight in the way she could bend him to her will.

"Let's face it, the guy was way outclassed from the very beginning," Mr. Howard said. "He didn't stand a chance."

But in the movie's final section, when Benjamin follows Elaine to college and tries to persuade her to marry him, Mr. Howard saw hints in the way Elaine keeps Benjamin dangling that she may, just may, be another Mrs. Robinson in the making.

"That never would have occurred to me back then," he said. "All I could see was Katharine Ross playing Elaine, and she was so beautiful."

But the moments that seem to bring Mr. Howard the most delight are technical ones, where he gets small flashes of insight into how the movie was made. There is the "Sound of Silence" montage and later the sequence in which Benjamin drives to the Robinson house to pick up Elaine for their second date, against Mrs. Robinson's wishes.

It is raining as Benjamin pulls to a stop at an intersection not far from the house. We see a woman running through the cloudburst, the door opens, and it is Mrs. Robinson, drenched, warning Benjamin to stay away from Elaine. The entire scene is played inside the car, either seen through the front windshield or with a camera inside.

"This is such a smart way to shoot this scene," Mr. Howard said. "I wouldn't have known this then, but now, after making so many movies of my own, I can see it. First, it's a very effective way to make it more claustrophobic, which is the way Benjamin feels. Again, it keeps the movie on his point of view. But it's also by far the cheapest way to shoot this. All you need is one rainbird."

A rainbird is a contraption that simulates a storm. It hangs over the set like a grid of pipes, sprouting droplets that fall onto the set like real rain. But each rainbird can cover only so much space on the set.

To have a cloudburst that covers an entire street, you need several rainbirds.

"For this, since the whole scene is in the car, they only need one rainbird positioned over the top of the car," Mr. Howard said.

But when Mrs. Robinson threatens Benjamin, he jumps out of the car and begins running down the street.

Mr. Howard sat forward. "Let's see how they shot this," he said. Was he wrong? Did they actually have several rainbirds?

Benjamin, now drenched, his arms flapping at his side, is running down the sidewalk, the rain pelting him. But then, as he reaches the Robinsons' house, he turns and dashes across the lawn toward the front door.

Mr. Howard slapped his knee and a huge grin spread across his face. He might as well have won the lottery. There are, very clearly, no raindrops falling on Benjamin as he crosses the Robinson lawn. Mr. Howard broke into happy laughter.

"Look," he said. "Look! He ran out of the rainbird!"

HIGHLIGHTS OF RON HOWARD'S FILM CAREER AND INFORMATION ON *THE GRADUATE*

■

What They Watched

The Graduate. Directed by Mike Nichols; screenplay by Calder Willingham and Buck Henry; cinematography by Robert Surtees. With Anne Bancroft, Dustin Hoffman, Katharine Ross, William Daniels, and Murray Hamilton. 1967.

Ron Howard's Films

AS A DIRECTOR

A Beautiful Mind. With Russell Crowe, Jennifer Connelly, and Paul Bettany. 2001.

Dr. Seuss's How the Grinch Stole Christmas. With Jim Carrey, Molly Shannon, Christine Baranski, Taylor Momsen, Jeffrey Tambor, Bill Irwin, and Clint Howard. 2000.

EdTV. With Woody Harrelson, Jenna Elfman, Rob Reiner, and Elizabeth Hurley. 1999.

Ransom. With Mel Gibson, Rene Russo, Gary Sinise, Delroy Lindo, and Lili Taylor. 1996.

Apollo 13. With Tom Hanks, Bill Paxton, Kevin Bacon, Gary Sinise, Ed Harris, and Kathleen Quinlan. 1995.

The Paper. With Michael Keaton, Glenn Close, Robert Duvall, Randy Quaid, and Jason Alexander. 1994.

Far and Away. With Tom Cruise, Nicole Kidman, Robert Prosky, and Thomas Gibson. 1992.

Backdraft. With Kurt Russell, William Baldwin, Scott Glenn, Robert De Niro, Rebecca De Mornay, and Donald Sutherland. 1991.

Parenthood. With Steve Martin, Mary Steenburgen, Rick Moranis, Dianne Wiest, Jason Robards, Martha Plimpton, and Keanu Reeves. 1989.

Cocoon. With Don Ameche, Hume Cronyn, Brian Dennehy, Jack Gilford, Steve Guttenberg, Tahnee Welch, Wilford Brimley, Courteney Cox, Maureen Stapleton, and Gwen Verdon. 1985.

Splash. With Tom Hanks, Daryl Hannah, and John Candy. 1984.

Night Shift. With Michael Keaton, Shelley Long, and Kevin Costner. 1982.

AS AN ACTOR

More American Graffiti. Directed by Bill L. Norton. With Cindy Williams, Paul LeMat, Candy Clark, Mackenzie Phillips, Charles Martin Smith, and Scott Glenn. 1979.

The Shootist. Directed by Don Siegel. With John Wayne, James Stewart, and Lauren Bacall. 1976.

American Graffiti. Directed by George Lucas. With Cindy Williams, Richard Dreyfuss, Paul LeMat, Candy Clark, Harrison Ford, Charles Martin Smith, Suzanne Somers, and Wolfman Jack. 1973.

The Courtship of Eddie's Father. Directed by Vincente Minnelli. With Glenn Ford, Shirley Jones, and Stella Stevens. 1963.

The Music Man. Directed by Morton Da Costa. With Robert Preston, Shirley Jones, Hermione Gingold, Paul Ford, and Buddy Hackett. 1962.

4

Curtis Hanson on
In a Lonely Place

Wiry, intense, and ingratiating, Curtis Hanson was happy and eager to keep talking about the film he chose, *In a Lonely Place,* for more than an hour after the screening ended. Already celebrated for his work on *L.A. Confidential,* Hanson was at the time planning for the reissue of his follow-up film, *Wonder Boys,* which many felt had been unjustly overlooked in its release earlier that year and stood a solid chance in the upcoming Oscar race, given a push from Paramount Pictures, its studio. In the end, Paramount came through but the film failed again to connect with audiences on its second go-round. Hanson had been widely praised for his complex, rocket-fast script for *L.A. Confidential,* which successfully boiled down the sprawling James Ellroy book on which it was based. But it was clear from listening to him talk about both *In a Lonely Place* and his own films that his greatest pleasure came from the mysterious process of working with actors.

∎

Curtis Hanson said he wanted to make two points to the actors Russell Crowe and Guy Pearce before they started filming *L.A. Confidential*

33

back in 1996. He wanted them to understand how people really looked and moved and talked back in the early 1950s in Southern California, where the story was set. But just as important, he wanted them to see the kind of naked, emotion-driven acting that he thought the complex, hard-boiled story required.

So he sat them down and showed them Nicholas Ray's *In a Lonely Place*.

Mr. Hanson, fifty-five, sat in the middle of a row in the otherwise vacant James Bridges Theater on the University of California campus at Los Angeles. It was late on a weekday afternoon, and there were a few hours before the auditorium was needed. Mr. Hanson had arranged to borrow a vintage print of Ray's 1950 drama, starring Humphrey Bogart and Gloria Grahame, from the Columbia Pictures archives. A veteran screenwriter and director who had recently released *Wonder Boys,* starring Michael Douglas, and was shortly to begin work on *8 Mile* with Eminem, Mr. Hanson was the chairman of the University of California Film and Television Archives, which explained his pull at the Bridges Theater, the archives' chief venue.

"When I first saw *In a Lonely Place* as a teenager, it frightened me and yet attracted me with an almost hypnotic power," Mr. Hanson said. "Later, I came to understand why. Occasionally, very rarely, a movie feels so heartfelt, so emotional, so revealing that it seems as though both the actor and the director are standing naked before the audience. When that kind of marriage happens between actor and director, it's breathtaking."

By 1950 Humphrey Bogart was in that phase in his career when he seemed to wear bow ties in most of his movies, still exuding the confident masculinity that epitomized his best work in the '30s and '40s, but beginning to edge toward the scowling and the jowly— poised about midway between Sam Spade and Captain Queeg. In the film, he plays Dixon Steele, a talented and bitter screenwriter with a hair-trigger temper, who was mysteriously damaged by his experiences in World War II. Throughout the film, he is either exploding in rage or struggling to suppress it. And yet he appears to be, at heart, an honorable and decent guy.

"To me, what is so incredible about his performance here is that, at the time, he was a major movie star and he could have done just about anything he wanted to do, especially on a movie with a budget as small as this one's," Mr. Hanson said. "Yet this is what he chose, and it's such a naked performance. It is so ugly at times, truly and physically ugly. It's what I love most about actors, their willingness to expose themselves. They won't do it all the time. They won't do it unless there are circumstances where there is trust. But that kind of collaboration between actor and director is, to me, the most important thing to aspire to."

The film is not one of Ray's better-known efforts, certainly not at the level of *Rebel Without a Cause* or *King of Kings,* and even many Bogart enthusiasts have never seen it. But like Ray's quirky 1954 western, *Johnny Guitar,* the film has a strong cult following among a certain breed of film enthusiasts, those who savor ambiguous and emotionally dense stories. Mr. Hanson said he had chosen to watch this film both because of its strong actor-director connection and because of its profound impact on him when he first stumbled across it.

"I think I was about fourteen when I first saw it on television, and it really affected me deeply," Mr. Hanson said. "What was so scary was the raw emotion of Bogart's character, but at the same time I identified with him; I was drawn to him. There was also something about the adult world that was pictured in the film. It feels like a world which is threatening in its darkness and ugliness, and yet there is great tenderness, too."

In later viewings, after he had come into the movie business, he was drawn to some of the Hollywood elements in the story, the notion of a troubled but basically honorable artist trapped in a corrupt world. "He is an honest man in a community of hypocrisy and nepotism," Mr. Hanson said. "He is also an artist in a business that rewards shallowness and commercialism." But those Hollywood elements meant nothing to him when he first saw the film. Back then, he was simply caught by that adrenaline jolt of pure emotion in Bogart's performance.

"It is about a character who is uncontrolled in his honesty and directness, which is not a good thing," Mr. Hanson said. "He's trying to express himself, to be an honorable creative artist, while all of those around him are encouraging him not to. And every now and then, he explodes. I showed this picture to Russell and Guy because I wanted them to see the reality of that period and to see that emotion. This movie, and I'm not saying it's the greatest movie ever made but it represents many things that I think are worth aspiring to, such as having character and emotion be the driving force, rather than the plot."

Mr. Hanson said he put *In a Lonely Place* in a category with a very small number of actor-director collaborations; he mentions James Stewart and Alfred Hitchcock in *Vertigo,* John Wayne and John Ford in *The Searchers,* and Gena Rowlands and John Cassavetes in *A Woman Under the Influence.* In these films, there is obviously so much trust between the director and the actor that the resulting performance exhibits a searing kind of emotional truth.

"These are movies where you feel that the director is right there with the actor, exposing himself along with the performer," Mr. Hanson said. "So many times, actors are out there by themselves, and they get burned, whereas in this picture, Bogart is supported by the movie. Even though you are repulsed and frightened by him, you care about him and you are drawn to him and you reflect on those aspects of yourself that he is portraying."

He finds a particular parallel in *Vertigo* and the way Hitchcock handled Stewart.

"Stewart is so obsessive and repugnant and, at times, cruel and driven, and yet you care about him," Mr. Hanson said. "It's the same with Bogart here. So often actors, you know, they want to be liked. We all want to be liked. And so you often have a situation where actors want to be liked and the studios want to make pictures that are positive, because they are safer. But when you look back at the movies and the books and the plays that really have the power to make you think and that stay with you and disturb you, they are not, quote, 'likable.'"

Mr. Hanson quietly stared up at the screen for a few moments.

Bogart stands off to the side, watching a couple of Hollywood hacks belittle a washed-up actor at a restaurant bar, and he begins to seethe. The scowl deepens. He gets that glint of moisture on his lower lip that, as anyone who has seen a Bogart movie knows, means he is about to erupt. His eyes focus more sharply. And then, with a frightening animal lunge, he lurches forward and flattens one of the men.

"Such a brave performance," Mr. Hanson said, staring raptly up at the screen, one slender arm cocked behind the back of his chair, the other hand cradling his salt-and-pepper beard. "In my capacity as chairman of this archive, I am always asked why film preservation is important. This movie answers the question more eloquently than I ever could. What a tragedy it would be for a film like this to be lost. Through Bogart's performance and through the other characters, we get such a window into the time the movie was made."

At the beginning of the film, Bogart's character cynically takes home a restaurant hatcheck girl who has read the potboiler novel he is being asked to adapt for the screen. Everyone at the restaurant assumes he has improper intentions, even the girl, but in reality all he wants is for her to tell him the story so he doesn't have to read the book himself.

"Notice how Ray shoots this sequence," Mr. Hanson said.

When they reach Bogart's home, in one of those Mission-style garden apartment complexes that seem to exemplify Los Angeles in that period, the woman flirts, accepts a drink, and then excitedly begins to recount the book's ridiculously melodramatic plot. Ray shot the scene so that the actress, Martha Stewart, was telling the story directly into the camera.

"What Ray does here is, he subtly forces us to see the story through the eyes of Bogart's character," Mr. Hanson said. "In this case, literally through his eyes. The way this film is shot, the audience is led to identify with this character who otherwise they might be repulsed by."

Ostensibly, the movie is a mystery. We know Steele is a volatile character. We see him get into several fights. But is he also a murderer?

The hatcheck girl is killed later that evening, and suspicion falls on Steele. But he is saved by a pretty young actress played by Grahame, who lives across the courtyard and tells the police she saw him at the time the murder was being committed.

Like Bogart's Steele, Grahame's character is trapped in her own lonely place: a would-be actress who, it is implied, has had career-enhancing romantic relationships with rich men. "She has been around, too, and this is her chance to become a better kind of person," Mr. Hanson said.

She and Steele are attracted to each other, but simmering beneath the surface, at all times, is the threat of Steele's volcanic temper. And then she begins to suspect that perhaps she was wrong, perhaps he actually did kill that girl. Yet she remains drawn to him. "The very thing that attracts her to him is the thing that scares her about him," Mr. Hanson said.

Mr. Hanson kept apologizing for talking while the movie was running. "I'm not sure how much to talk; I don't want us to miss anything," he said. Frequently, he would stop himself in midsentence and hold up his finger, directing attention back to the screen, indicating that what he thought was an important moment was about to take place.

He was particularly interested in a scene at the house of a couple who are Steele's friends (the man is also a detective who is investigating the murder) in which Steele demonstrates how he thinks the murder of the hatcheck girl was committed. And as he acts out the murder, with the detective's wife seated at his side, pretending they are riding together in a car, he becomes more wrapped up in the performance and begins to squeeze the neck of the detective's wife a little too ferociously. From the look on her face, you see the growing realization that perhaps Steele is guilty.

But really, Mr. Hanson said, it is that Steele is merely caught up in his staging of the scene.

"Here he is, a very talented screenwriter, and it's like he's sitting in the director's chair for a change," Mr. Hanson said. "At least he's getting to show that he's a better director than most of the hacks that he's been forced to work with."

Another scene captures Mr. Hanson's attention. The day after the murder, Steele stops at a florist's shop.

"This is fascinating," Mr. Hanson said. "It's humorous and yet it's serious, at the same time, and about a third of the scene goes by before you can figure out what's going on." In fact, Steele has stopped to buy flowers to be sent, anonymously, to the woman's funeral. This comes right after his first interrogation at police headquarters, where he had reacted with an eerie lack of emotion to the news of her death. "Ray makes the point that, despite that, Steele is basically decent and sentimental," Mr. Hanson said. "This is very precise filmmaking."

Further examples of precision can be found in another aspect of Ray's filmmaking that Mr. Hanson admires: the choice of settings.

"It's so interesting, the very vivid sense of place that you get from this film," Mr. Hanson said. "Really, there are very few locations in the film. Yet when you think back on this movie, there is such a powerful sense of Los Angeles at that time because he is so accurate in the specificity of his sets. There is the courtyard apartment that represents a certain kind of romantic Hollywood architecture; there is the industry restaurant, the car, a scene at the beach. It's a more accurate portrayal of this city than many pictures that were shot on location at the time. His sense of locale and place, not just in this picture but in all of his best pictures, is really very strong."

Probably Ray's most frequently seen movie, *Rebel Without a Cause*, is another prime example.

"Think about that movie, which is really a very good companion piece to this film," Mr. Hanson said. "Those kids in that movie, James Dean and Natalie Wood and Sal Mineo, are also outsiders, just like Steele, and they are trying to find their way in an environment where they don't fit in. In terms of sense of place, in *Rebel* you've got the flatlands, where the school and the police station are, and then you've got the mansion up on the hill and the climax at the Griffith Park Observatory and the scene on the cliff where the kids are playing chicken. Just like this movie, there are not many locations, but they are perfectly chosen, and they are indelibly etched in your mind once you've seen them."

Mr. Hanson said he also took lessons on how to adapt a book to the screen from *In a Lonely Place*. He had liked the movie so much as a teenager, he said, that he tracked down a copy of the original novel by Dorothy B. Hughes. He was surprised to learn that while the characters in the book and the movie had some kernels of similarity, the two stories were entirely different. In the book, Steele is very definitely a serial killer. And there are no Hollywood elements at all.

Ray adds to the story the subplot about Steele's being asked to adapt a book to the screen, mirroring and satirizing his and his screenwriters' adaptation of Hughes's book.

"It's very interesting, but even within the movie they keep talking about how Steele should just follow the book," Mr. Hanson said. "Just follow the book, people keep saying to him, when in reality the problem is that so many adaptations of novels end up being nothing more than CliffsNotes versions of the book. That's because you cannot replicate a book on-screen, even if it is a good book. That is a lesson that every filmmaker must learn. You have to be true to the character and the emotion, rather than to the letter of the book."

It's something that Mr. Hanson said he took away from *In a Lonely Place* and tried to put into practice in *L.A. Confidential* and other films.

"I don't know how this film was developed, but I do know that somehow Nicholas Ray and Humphrey Bogart found themselves consumed by it," Mr. Hanson said. "Ray found himself in this character. I know it because I can feel it. It's the same way that he found something of himself in those kids in *Rebel*, and to me it demonstrates actor-director collaboration at its most fruitful."

The film had ended, but Mr. Hanson kept talking in the half-lighted auditorium, as if seeing the film again had stirred up a flood of memories and impressions that he eagerly wanted to get out. Finally, someone in the back of the room gently cleared his throat. The room was needed. People were waiting outside. So Mr. Hanson walked into the late afternoon sunshine, strolling happily down the leafy walkways of the campus and settling on a cool, shaded bench to talk some more.

He said he had tried, in his own films, to establish the kind of trust with his actors that Bogart and Ray enjoyed. The best actors are always attracted to that kind of work, he said. The problem is that many are either timid or are surrounded by people who caution them to play it safe.

That was one reason he was so happy with his work with Mr. Douglas in *Wonder Boys*, based on the novel by Michael Chabon. The film was released in February and greeted warmly by many critics but did not perform well at the box office. In a remarkable move, Paramount rereleased it in November to give it a second chance. Once again, it did not perform particularly well at the box office, but it did turn up on the National Board of Review's list of the top ten films of the year and is considered a candidate for Oscar nominations this February.

"Actors want to go there," Mr. Hanson said. "Michael wanted to go there. Just like back then, when Bogart made this movie, established actors can make the movies they want to make. They just have to do it. Michael literally made *Wonder Boys* happen."

Too many movies coming out of Hollywood today are driven simply by the plot or by the special effects. "And it's gotten worse in this regard," Mr. Hanson said. "They are about a plot, and everything in them serves the plot, and that means it tends to serve the leading man who is moving along the line of the plot."

That is why seeing a movie like *In a Lonely Place* is such a tonic, he said. Here is a daring film in which a major actor had the courage and the trust to go beyond the ordinary and the expected.

"What is different about this movie, and really striking about it, is that it is really about character and emotion," Mr. Hanson said. "It's not about who killed the girl, not really. It's about how that situation creates the emotion that acts on Bogart's character."

If you look at what Mr. Hanson considers the best movies of the last few years— he mentioned *American Beauty, Three Kings, Election, Boogie Nights*—they were all films that avoided the normal studio development process, which he said had the effect of grinding away the rough edges that make a film like *In a Lonely Place* so distinctive.

"That is one of the sad things about the state of the business these days," Mr. Hanson said. "It's an interesting puzzle because, back in the days of the studio system, there was a rigid production code where the good guy had to win and so forth. There was true censorship, and yet the artists back then found a way to rebel against the system and against the censorship and do dark pictures and ambiguous pictures.

"And yet today, when in effect you don't have a meaningful production code at all, you have a much more pernicious situation, which is a kind of censorship that the artist collaborates in. It's the censorship of trying to achieve success, the censorship of the focus group and the test screening. And it's much, much more pernicious."

HIGHLIGHTS OF CURTIS HANSON'S CAREER AND INFORMATION ON *IN A LONELY PLACE*

■

What They Watched

In a Lonely Place. Directed by Nicholas Ray; screenplay by Edmund H. North and Andrew Solt; cinematography by Burnett Guffey. With Humphrey Bogart and Gloria Grahame. 1950.

Curtis Hanson's Films

AS A DIRECTOR

8 Mile. With Eminem, Kim Basinger, and Brittany Murphy. 2002.

Wonder Boys. With Michael Douglas, Tobey Maguire, Robert Downey Jr., and Frances McDormand. 2000.

The River Wild. With Meryl Streep, Kevin Bacon, Joseph Mazzello, and David Strathairn. 1994.

The Hand That Rocks the Cradle. With Rebecca De Mornay, Annabella Sciorra, Matt McCoy, and Ernie Hudson. 1992.

Losin' It. With Tom Cruise, Jackie Earle Haley, and John Stockwell. 1983.

AS A SCREENWRITER

Never Cry Wolf. Directed by Carroll Ballard. With Charles Martin Smith and Brian Dennehy. 1983.

White Dog. Directed by Samuel Fuller. With Kristy McNichol and Paul Winfield. 1982.

The Silent Partner. Directed by Daryl Duke. With Elliott Gould, Christopher Plummer, Susannah York, and John Candy. 1979.

AS DIRECTOR AND WRITER

L.A. Confidential. With Russell Crowe, Guy Pearce, Kevin Spacey, James Cromwell, Danny DeVito, and Kim Basinger. 1997.

The Bedroom Window. With Steve Guttenberg, Isabelle Huppert, and Elizabeth McGovern. 1987.

5

Kevin Costner on
Cool Hand Luke

Kevin Costner has taken his share of hits. Once praised as the Gary Cooper of the 1990s, the stalwart Everyman who embodied everything noble about the American hero, he had gone from winning Oscars for producing and directing the sprawling *Dances With Wolves* to becoming almost a punch line in the shorthand of many Hollywood journalists. Such big-budget follow-ups as *Waterworld* and *The Postman* had earned him a reputation for narcissism and creative myopia. But it remains somehow difficult to reconcile this image of him with his delicate work in such films as *Bull Durham*, *Field of Dreams*, and *Tin Cup*. This interview came about as Costner was preparing for the release of *Thirteen Days*, a tense drama about the Cuban missile crisis that would draw for him the usual mix of cheers and jeers, the latter mostly for his thick Boston accent. Watching *Cool Hand Luke* with Costner in his basement screening room in the Hollywood Hills, his two Oscars gleaming in a display case, revealed that despite his critics he has a sharp critical mind that has clearly done a lot of productive thinking about what it means to be a movie star and what it takes to remain one.

■

Kevin Costner fidgeted on the plush sofa in the back row of the basement screening room in his Hollywood Hills compound. A slight grimace crossed his face. It's true, Mr. Costner said, he did feel a little uncomfortable. "I don't usually tolerate people talking through movies," he said. "My kids don't talk. They know."

Talking during movies is a common annoyance, as anyone who has felt the fierce wave of shushes roll across a theater at the beginning of a movie can confirm. To many filmmakers it is a particular irritation, and Mr. Costner is one of them. But it can't be helped. It's the nature of the event. Mr. Costner has been asked to choose, from his favorite films, one that has some particular strength or resonance to him and to talk about the impact it has had on him and his fresh impressions of it as he sat through another viewing.

On the screen, *Cool Hand Luke* begins to roll. Directed by Stuart Rosenberg, a journeyman director of the 1960s and '70s who worked with some of the most popular actors of that period, this 1967 film stars Paul Newman as Luke, a cynical rabble-rouser whose deep reservoir of cool makes him a magnet to fellow prisoners on a southern chain gang but whose self-destructive, antiauthoritarian streak makes him a target for the guards. *Cool Hand Luke* comes from a particularly fertile moment in the history of American film, when movies like *Bonnie and Clyde* and *The Graduate* were transforming the landscape, and a whole generation of television-trained actors, led by Mr. Newman, were working at the peak of their skills.

"The planets really lined up for this movie," Mr. Costner said. "And that's when movies are miracles. The director, the writer, the actors—everybody was playing at the top of their game, and that's when you get magic."

Paul Newman is staggering along a gloomy sidewalk in a dark, quiet southern town, methodically unscrewing the heads from a line of parking meters. They fall to the pavement with a clunk. He stoops, wobbling, clearly drunk, and gently places each back on the curb before moving down the line.

"See, he's not an anarchist; he puts the meter back on the curb, right?" Mr. Costner said, smiling happily at the screen. "Paul has great physical movements. You watch. They're vulgar movements, you know. He doesn't look fluid. When he was drunk there, it's a sloppy drunk. It's a laid-down drunk. He doesn't make it pretty or smooth. He makes it real."

Mr. Newman squats on the sidewalk, tired, eager for another pull from the bottle he carries with him. We hear a car pull up offscreen, see the reflection of police lights. Mr. Newman looks up, squints into the lights, and then smiles.

Mr. Costner stirred as he watched. "That's an electric smile," he said. "Look at it. That's the highest order of movie star that there is. That smile, when you give it up, that's a movie star. Newman, McQueen, those guys—they just took their time before they gave it up, but when they did, well, just look at it."

He was particularly interested in watching how Mr. Newman played the role, how the actor chose his moments within his scenes, magnifying his natural magnetism with the subtle choices he made in individual scenes. Once Mr. Costner pointed it out, it was difficult not to notice how Mr. Newman rarely interacted with the other actors in his scenes, often not even looking at them as he talked.

"See, he doesn't look at anybody," Mr. Costner said. On the screen, Mr. Newman is sitting in the dirt along a dusty roadside. The other men on the chain gang clustered around him, a rogues' gallery of actors who went on to have significant careers but were still relatively unknown performers when the movie was released in 1967. They included Wayne Rogers, Dennis Hopper, J. D. Cannon, Ralph Waite, Harry Dean Stanton, and George Kennedy, who won an Oscar for his supporting performance. In the scene, Mr. Newman had recently escaped from the gang, where he was serving a two-year term for his parking meter binge, and lived for several months in the outside world. Now the men wanted him to regale them with how wonderful it was. In fact, it wasn't. But Mr. Newman, his back to the men, smiles to himself and tells the story.

"See, he doesn't look at anybody," Mr. Costner said. "It's like he's saying: 'You want to hear the story? Here's the story.' " He studied the scene with rapt attention.

"If anybody wants to be a leading man, this is how you do it," Mr. Costner said. "It's just the way you have to deliver these lines. It's just really good film instincts."

Mr. Newman is setting himself apart from the group. He always has his own thing going on in his head, and you have to watch him to see what it is.

"Somebody who didn't have the instincts of a leading man would be including the whole group while he told the story, and a director who didn't understand what this role is about might be giving him bad direction, saying: 'Hey, talk to the other guys. They want to hear from you.' But an actor like Paul Newman, who knows, would just say to that director: 'Hey, they can hear me, they can hear me. I don't need to be looking at them. It's better if I'm not.'"

The same sort of thing happens in a half-dozen major scenes in the film. The convicts are jabbering among themselves while Mr. Newman sits aloof, off to the side, listening and perhaps chiming in when something occurs to him, but rarely even looking over at the men. Usually, the other actors are playing to his profile, or even the back of his head.

"He doesn't look at the other actors, but the other actors check in with him," Mr. Costner said. "You watch. I mean, he does, occasionally, but mostly he's enjoying being by himself, in his own head. He's got his own thing going on, but they're checking in with him. They all want to know what he thinks, what he's doing. But he's never checking in to see what they're doing."

As a result, Mr. Costner said, you cannot take your eyes off Mr. Newman. You're checking in with him, too. He gives the other actors nothing, but sometimes nothing can be a really cool hand.

Mr. Costner leaned back in the darkened screening room. Dressed in blue jeans and a gray T-shirt, he rested his feet on a long, benchlike ottoman that stretches the length of the twelve-foot sofa that is the last of three rows in his screening room. "Built it myself," he said of the ottoman. "I like to rest my feet up when I'm watching a movie." His two Oscars, for producing and directing *Dances With Wolves* (1990), shimmer gently in a glass display case set into the right-hand wall.

Mr. Costner, who turned forty-six on Thursday, said that he could not recall when he first saw *Cool Hand Luke,* but that he thought he had seen it ten to twenty times. It is a movie he revisits regularly, he said, and one that he has shown to his children.

"When somebody says to you, 'Pick a favorite movie,' it's hard to narrow them down, especially if you love movies," he said. "So why *Cool Hand Luke*? I think it's a beautiful movie. It's the antihero at its best. It's like *The Searchers*. A lot of kids now don't understand how a western can be a good movie. It's because there are so many bad westerns—you know, so many westerns that are too obvious, too much the black hat–white hat routine. A good movie is very hard to make. In fact, it's almost impossible to make a good movie because there are so many things fighting against it."

Although probably best known as a Hollywood leading man—something he has been at least since *The Untouchables* in 1987—Mr. Costner is also a director whose fights to secure his vision for some of his films (even those he was not directing) have sometimes spilled into public. And since both of the films he directed—the Oscar-winning *Dances With Wolves* and the critically panned *The Postman* (1997)—were longer than average, he has been pegged by some as vain and self-indulgent. This is just a flat-out misunderstanding, he said.

"There's maybe an opinion that I like to be in long movies or that I like the vanity of long movies," he said. "But it's simply a function of style and what it is that you love as a filmmaker. I don't love being a movie star. I love movies. And I've always loved the longer narrative.

"It's not vanity, the vanity of falling in love with yourself. I just love subplots. You know how some people say, and you hear this all the time, that they hated the first hundred pages of a book, but once it got going, they really liked it? Well, I love the first hundred pages. And that's what I've always loved about epic movies or the movies that choose not to force themselves on the audience. They just untangle for you."

Certainly, he said, *Cool Hand Luke* could not be described as an epic. But there is something about the way it unfolds, the slow buildups, the careful and subtle character moments, and the handful of masterly scenes that are allowed to go on longer than the audience might expect, that appeals to Mr. Costner.

"It's a movie that takes its time," he said. "And it has several scenes in it—I'll point them out as we go along—that would, in the way movies are made today, almost certainly have been cut out. The common language among studio executives today is, oh, look, we understand what's happening, you've made the point, don't make it again, let's move on. But I don't think movies can exist without fat. I think movies are actually propped up that way. It's not a negative. It's a positive.

"Certainly you have to be judicious about what stays and what goes. You have to be careful not to fall in love with the individual brush strokes so much that you lose sight of the entire canvas. But if you feel a moment has relevance, you must keep it. You have to keep it, and you have to fight for it. A movie is almost like a patient that can't speak for itself. You have to speak for it."

Take the opening sequence of *Cool Hand Luke,* Mr. Costner said. The parking meters are decapitated, first one, then another, slowly, in real time, the squeak of the metal filling the sound track, the clunk onto the ground, a pause, a few footsteps, then the next meter. "If you made this movie today, that would be done as a montage," he said. And so much would be lost: the sense of real life, time passing, the effort involved, and Luke's awkward, stumbling rebelliousness.

"Great movies are ones that don't rush through their most important moments," he said. "I mean, where are you going when you go to the movies? Are you in a big hurry? If you're in the hands of a careful filmmaker, you should be able to see what it is that sparked him, that made him want to make the movie. But no, nowadays it's hurry up, keep it moving, let's get out of Dodge before the audience gets bored.

"I say, no. No, no, no. Sometimes you've got to just let them hang, to make a point. Isn't that right? I mean, where are they going? They're there to see a movie."

He cracked open a bottle of mineral water and took a couple of slow pulls. From out of the gloom, a tiny kitten insinuated itself onto his lap, and he stroked it once or twice and then gently lifted it onto the floor.

He had been working all day on a thriller called *Dragonfly,* in which he played a doctor whose dead wife tries to talk to him. Another of his films, *Thirteen Days,* about the Cuban missile crisis, was in theaters at the moment, while another drama, *3,000 Miles to Graceland,* was due out later in the year.

It had already been a long day, and he had an early call in the morning to be back on the *Dragonfly* set. But he seemed unhurried as he watched *Cool Hand Luke* unfold.

Mr. Costner may have been a leading man for a decade and a half, but he also remembers the days when he played tiny, supporting roles, sometimes little more than wallpaper in the background, even having his role cut out of the 1983 film *The Big Chill*. And he said one of the pleasures he has in seeing *Cool Hand Luke* again and again is watching the supporting cast members find their little moments, sometimes just moving across the frame in the background, especially now that some of those faces have become more familiar.

"Just keep an eye on Dennis Hopper in this movie," he said. Mr. Hopper appears in a handful of scenes, always part of a group of prisoners, often just peering from the back of the shot. He utters not a word, but he still makes a vivid impression. "Every time he's on-screen, he's trying to invent something," Mr. Costner said. "He's a brilliant actor. Just watch for him, search him out in the background. He's always doing something. This is a guy who is working, working, working, and that's why he's had such a long and successful career."

In one crowd scene, Mr. Hopper can be spotted carrying what looks like a basket and placing it in a kind of locker. After he closes it, he kisses the locker door, for no apparent reason. The camera is not even really focusing on him; he's just one of the prisoners moving through the shot. In another scene, Mr. Newman is working his shovel at the side of the road, talking to another prisoner, when Mr. Hopper glides into the frame, bends down, and picks up an empty soda bottle, which he raises to his eye like a telescope.

"There you go, you see what I'm saying?" Mr. Costner said. "Every time you see him, he's working hard."

The way the prison warden (Strother Martin) and the guards are portrayed also drew Mr. Costner's admiration. They are not cardboard villains, and they are not portrayed as stupid. Pains are taken to give them some humanity and to underscore why they might feel a special sense of vengeance in Luke's case.

"That was a very inspired choice, Strother Martin, for this role," Mr. Costner said. "I know it's easy to see in hindsight, but somebody made a really smart decision there. A lot of directors would have gone with a standard sort of tough guy. But here, he's almost effeminate in his meanness, and it makes you feel how really mean he can be."

Each guard, in turn, is given his own small moment to register a bit of subtlety, perhaps a moment of gentleness or a sudden flash of intelligence in his eyes. The guards' small routines are shown, with tiny details that reveal how careful and canny they are with the prisoners. When one guard, who acts as the movie's silent angel of death, hiding behind mirror shades, wants to use his rifle to shoot some game, he must first pull the bolt from his waistband and slide it into the rifle. A small moment, and wordless.

"Did you notice how the guy put the bolt in the gun to fire?" Mr. Costner asked. "This is a guy who is not going to let his gun be taken away and turned on him. It's just a nice bit, a small thing. But it lets you know how smart these guys are.

"You know, it's a promise I made to myself when I went into movies, and I think I drove Brian De Palma crazy on *The Untouchables* because I was always stopping to load my gun or checking to see how many bullets I had left. I always hated how guns in the movies just kept on firing forever. You know what I mean? And the thing is, there's drama in having only six bullets. There's an opportunity for drama, as opposed to just killing somebody else."

Twice during the movie, Mr. Costner stopped talking altogether and held up his hand as if asking for silence. The first time came when Luke is summoned out of the barracks to meet with his dying mother (Jo Van Fleet), who is lying on a mattress in the back of a pickup truck.

"This is one of my favorite scenes because, again, they let it play," Mr. Costner said.

The mother and son have an almost flirtatious exchange. Mr. Newman spends much of the shot with his face cloaked in a shadow, and some of his best lines are played on his mother's face. When his young nephew gets out of the truck and asks about the chains on his ankles, Mr. Newman says, "You know, these chains aren't medals," and instead of watching Mr. Newman deliver the line, the camera cuts to Ms. Van Fleet's face as she registers the pain.

"Let me tell you, this scene would be cut by nine out of ten movie studios today," Mr. Costner said. "If they were looking to trim the movie—and they're always looking to trim the movie—this scene would have gone in an eye blink."

The second time Mr. Costner gestured for silence was during what has become the movie's most famous scene, largely on the strength of its unforgettable dialogue.

Luke has escaped and has been recaptured, and in the shot he is returned to the chain gang. A car stops on a rise overlooking the ditch where the men are working. Mr. Martin emerges from the car first, and then Mr. Newman. Now, though, Mr. Newman has a new set of chains on his ankles as a punishment for having tried to escape.

"You gonna get used to wearin' those chains after a while, Luke, but you're never gonna get used to listenin' to them clinkin'," Mr. Martin says. "They're gonna remind you of what I've been sayin': they're for your own good."

Luke smirks in response. He says, "I wish you'd stop bein' so good to me, Cap'n."

Mr. Martin, suddenly enraged, lashes out at Mr. Newman, who falls to the ground and rolls into the ditch. Regaining control of his emotions, Mr. Martin tries to explain his outburst to the convicts below. "What we've got here," he says, "is a failure to communicate."

Mr. Costner smiled and gently slapped his knee with one hand as the scene ended.

"What I like about that scene is, well, all of it," he said. "It's just so good. It's really great dialogue. And I like it that when Strother hit him, he hit him in the neck. It looked so sloppy, almost funny. I mean, somebody made that choice. The obvious thing would be to hit him in the face or the stomach, but he just kind of lashes out and hits him on the side of the neck. Kind of clumsy, you know? But it feels more true, because that's the way violence really is. It's sloppy. It's not a perfect fist to the chin."

So many of the moments that catch Mr. Costner's eye are acting moments for Mr. Newman—maybe a physical thing or a small movement of the eyes. Once, when the chain gang breaks for a meal, a shirtless and dirt-streaked Mr. Newman plops down on his back, closing his eyes and stuffing a spoonful of food into his mouth. He lets go and just lets the spoon sit there, sticking out of his mouth like a totem, bobbing back and forth as he chews. "That's a true Paul Newman bit right there," Mr. Costner said.

He also pointed out the different ways that Mr. Waite's and Mr. Newman's characters reacted to being locked in the camp's punishment box, a kind of solitary-confinement outhouse. Mr. Waite blubbers and slinks into a corner as the door shuts on him. Mr. Newman just stands there, emotionless, maybe even a little cocky. "You can tell from the way Paul plays it that Luke is a guy who doesn't feel bad about the idea of being alone," Mr. Costner said.

When the movie ended, the lights slowly came up and Mr. Costner rose and stretched out his back. He was due on the set in less than eight hours.

"I'm glad we watched that," he said, smiling. He walked slowly up the stairs, past a line of posters for movies that he admires, including *Cool Hand Luke,* and out into the warm evening, dark foliage overhanging the courtyard and the lights of the city rolling on to infinity below. As he walked, he tried to explain why he watches *Cool Hand Luke* so often, and why he enjoyed having his children see it, particularly his son, Joe.

"I guess it's because the movie says there's a way that men should behave," Mr. Costner said. "It's about being your own person, about how men will desert you when, somehow, you don't live up to their expectations. And it's just something about the whole figure of the antihero. You know, Luke dies, but everybody still wants to be Luke. You want to be an individual. Right? Sometimes the outcome isn't great, but at least you leave a mark."

HIGHLIGHTS OF KEVIN COSTNER'S CAREER AND INFORMATION ON *COOL HAND LUKE*

■

What They Watched

Cool Hand Luke. Directed by Stuart Rosenberg; screenplay by Donn Pearce and Frank Pierson; cinematography by Conrad L. Hall; music by Lalo Schifrin. With Paul Newman, George Kennedy, Strother Martin, Jo Van Fleet, Dennis Hopper, and J. D. Cannon. 1967.

Kevin Costner's Films

AS A DIRECTOR

The Postman. With Kevin Costner, Will Patton, Olivia Williams, and Laurenz Tate. 1997.

Dances With Wolves. With Kevin Costner, Mary McDonnell, Graham Greene, and Rodney Grant. 1990.

AS AN ACTOR

Dragonfly. Directed by Tom Shadyac. With Joe Morton and Kathy Bates. 2002.

3,000 Miles to Graceland. Directed by Demian Lichtenstein. With Kurt Russell and Christian Slater. 2001.

Thirteen Days. Directed by Roger Donaldson. With Bruce Greenwood and Steven Culp. 2000.

Message in a Bottle. Directed by Luis Mandoki. With Robin Wright Penn, Paul Newman, and John Savage. 1999.

Tin Cup. Directed by Ron Shelton. With Don Johnson, Cheech Marin, and Rene Russo. 1996.

Waterworld. Directed by Kevin Reynolds. With Dennis Hopper and Jeanne Tripplehorn. 1995.

Wyatt Earp. Directed by Lawrence Kasdan. With Dennis Quaid and Gene Hackman. 1994.

A Perfect World. Directed by Clint Eastwood. With Clint Eastwood, Laura Dern, and T. J. Lowther. 1993.

The Bodyguard. Directed by Mick Jackson. With Whitney Houston and Gary Kemp. 1992.

Robin Hood: Prince of Thieves. Directed by Kevin Reynolds. With Mary Elizabeth Mastrantonio and Morgan Freeman. 1991.

JFK. Directed by Oliver Stone. With Sissy Spacek, Joe Pesci, Tommy Lee Jones, and Gary Oldman. 1991.

Field of Dreams. Directed by Phil Alden Robinson. With Amy Madigan, James Earl Jones, Burt Lancaster, and Ray Liotta. 1989.

Bull Durham. Directed by Ron Shelton. With Susan Sarandon and Tim Robbins. 1988.

No Way Out. Directed by Roger Donaldson. With Gene Hackman and Sean Young. 1987.

The Untouchables. Directed by Brian De Palma. With Sean Connery, Robert De Niro, and Charles Martin Smith. 1987.

Silverado. Directed by Lawrence Kasdan. With Kevin Kline and Scott Glenn. 1985.

Fandango. Directed by Kevin Reynolds. With Judd Nelson and Sam Robards. 1985.

6

Steven Soderbergh on
All the President's Men

Oscar season was in full swing as this installment approached, and I approached the three directors who seemed to have the best shot at winning, Steven Soderbergh (*Traffic*), Ang Lee (*Crouching Tiger, Hidden Dragon*), and Ridley Scott (*Gladiator*), in hopes that one would come through. Astonishingly, all three accepted almost immediately. And we'd have done all three of them had Scott's mother not died unexpectedly, drawing him back to England (the movie he'd chosen to watch, incidentally, was *2001: A Space Odyssey,* which would have meant *three* Stanley Kubrick films in the series). Soderbergh, who went on to win the Oscar, was taciturn during much of the screening. All of these sessions are tape-recorded and usually produced anywhere from 6,000 to 10,000 words of transcript. Soderbergh's was only 4,000 words. His humor was dry, sometimes pointed, and he spoke up only when he had something cogent to say. Part of what I tried to do during these screenings was to toss out ideas and half-ideas, hoping to get the subject talking, and this often resulted in subjects trying to give me what I wanted even if they didn't particularly agree with the point I'd made, leading to rhetorical cul-de-sacs that never made it into the final piece. With

Soderbergh, if I said something that he didn't find pertinent or interesting, he'd give me a brief grunt or simply ignore it. The result was no cul-de-sacs. Almost everything he wanted to say about *All the President's Men* made it into the final piece.

■

This is one of the great openings of all time," Steven Soderbergh said.

He was leaning forward, elbows on knees, in the front row of a small upstairs theater on the Universal Studios lot. The bright image on the screen was entirely white, radiant, and stubbornly monochromatic. The seconds crept by, bleached light spilling over the thirty-eight-year-old director's expressionless, upturned face. "We should have timed it," he said. "I think it lasts forty-five seconds."

A gigantic typewriter key streaks into the frame and smacks onto the glowing white rectangle, now revealed as a blank sheet of paper. "Yeah," Mr. Soderbergh exclaimed quietly, like a football fan celebrating a solid tackle.

Mr. Soderbergh was thirteen, a fresh arrival in Baton Rouge, Louisiana, where his father was a college professor and administrator. He had been grounded that autumn weekend in 1976—he can't remember why—forbidden to attend a party that he'd been looking forward to, a newcomer hoping to make friends among the strangers. But somehow he managed to talk his father into letting his sister drive him all the way across town to the theater where, in a sparse audience, he watched Alan J. Pakula's *All the President's Men* for the first time. "I was really looking forward to the movie," Mr. Soderbergh said. "I was a huge Dustin Hoffman fan."

It was a period in his life, he said, when he was really coming alive to film. He would go back and see his favorites again and again. He saw *All the President's Men* about ten times. "It is without question one of my favorite American films of all time," Mr. Soderbergh said. "And it's one that I looked to quite a lot while I was making my last two movies, *Erin Brockovich* and *Traffic,* because in both cases we were trying to make films about serious issues that were also very entertaining.

"*All the President's Men* is one of the better examples of a movie that managed to have a sociopolitical quotient and still be incredibly entertaining. It's my sense that you can balance those things, and that the audience will sit still for it, even today's audience, if they feel there is some real connection between the political content of the film and their lives."

Mr. Soderbergh remembered spending the entire week before the opening of *All the President's Men* in Baton Rouge reading the book by the *Washington Post*'s Bob Woodward and Carl Bernstein, all about how that pair of unheralded metro reporters had doggedly transformed a peculiar late-night break-in at the Watergate office complex into one of the greatest newspaper subjects of all time, bringing down a presidential administration in the process.

"I guess what impressed me most about *All the President's Men*, and what still impresses me, is that there is really no reason why this movie should work," Mr. Soderbergh said. "It's a story that everyone knew. I mean, the movie was released in 1976 and President Nixon had just resigned in 1974. And the movie climaxes with the protagonists' making a huge mistake. And yet it works so completely. I never tire of watching it."

But the movie had been even more prominent in his thoughts lately, as he made *Traffic* and *Erin Brockovich*. Just days before, both had received an Oscar nomination for best picture, and Mr. Soderbergh was nominated twice as best director (he won, for *Traffic*). This was the first time that in one year the same director had two films up for best picture and has been nominated for directing both of them.

"I took my cue from *All the President's Men* in finding oblique ways to handle important issues while still making a film that is satisfying on a pure entertainment level," he said. "You don't want to destroy the pillars that these genres are built on.

"I mean, *Erin Brockovich* is a pure David-and-Goliath story, a kind of *Rocky* film. Our hope was to make a good movie with that. And *Traffic* is more, to our way of thinking, in the vein of *Z* and *Battle of Algiers* and *The French Connection*, all very entertaining films with a sense of realism and of urgency."

All the President's Men settles in for its brief prologue, television images of a packed joint session of Congress awaiting the arrival of President Richard M. Nixon ("Look at all those old white guys," Mr.

Soderbergh said), which blends into late-night shots of the Watergate complex and the dark figures of the burglars making their way into the national headquarters of the Democratic Party.

The opening credits begin to roll. "I tried to duplicate this type-face for *Traffic*," Mr. Soderbergh said.

He was referring to the narrow sans serif type that Pakula used for the title credits in *All the President's Men*. Mr. Soderbergh said he searched but could not duplicate the typeface exactly, so he settled on one that was close.

"You notice, I did steal the placement," he said. The credits for both films appear not in the center of the frame, but in the bottom left-hand corner. "I just liked the feel of it, the simplicity," he said, and it was also, in the back of his mind, a kind of insider's homage to Pakula. That director, who died at seventy in 1998, is also acclaimed for films like *Sophie's Choice* and *Klute*.

The scenes of the break-in that open the film are dark and fore-boding, but it is not immediately clear what creates a strange mixture of intensity and detachment. Nothing is really happening but dark figures moving through dark rooms.

But then there is a particularly arresting image: The camera is out-side, looking in through the window of a hotel across the street from the Watergate. The hotel curtains are half-drawn. A man is stand-ing in the room, talking into a walkie-talkie. There is the sound of crackling and breathless exchanges of terse dialogue, but virtually no movement.

"Wow, look at that," Mr. Soderbergh said. "Gordon Willis was one of the few cinematographers mixing color temperatures like this back then. Look at the greens and the oranges."

It was so obvious, once Mr. Soderbergh pointed it out. The dark exterior of the hotel is a cold mixture of shadows and icy colors, frozen blues and arctic greens, while in the portion of the frame that shows the inside of the hotel room, from a light source apparently hidden behind the half-closed curtain, warmer amber hues take over, like a campfire on a tundra. And Mr. Soderbergh also noted how the director kept the camera utterly still.

We remain hanging in the air, looking into the hotel room from outside, like a Peeping Tom. We are so far away that we cannot read the expression on the actor's face and must, instead, focus on the crackling from the walkie-talkie.

"A lot of filmmakers would have gone with the obvious thing here," Mr. Soderbergh said. "We'd have a close-up here of the guy talking, or the camera would move inside the room. But it is so much creepier like this."

It is an example, he said, of how a filmmaker in command of his craft—like Pakula—can inject emotion, in this case eerie tension, simply by playing against audience expectations. A small point, Mr. Soderbergh said, but telling.

Later in the film he makes the same point about one of his favorite scenes, Mr. Hoffman's nervous, late-night interview with an even more nervous Republican bookkeeper, played by Jane Alexander.

"Look how they shot this," Mr. Soderbergh said. "Throughout the whole scene the camera remains the same distance away from both of them. It never goes in for a close-up. It never changes its distance at all."

The camera ping-pongs between Mr. Hoffman (as Bernstein), sitting on a sofa, and Ms. Alexander, sitting on a chair opposite him. "By not going into a close-up and then releasing, by maintaining the same distance, it keeps the intensity building in the scene," Mr. Soderbergh said. "Normally, you'd go in and out. And shooting a scene that way can be effective, too.

"But there is a different kind of energy that comes from maintaining the same shots. You just get a sense that these filmmakers are so secure, that they have complete confidence in their material and their performers."

Only at the end of the scene does the camera pull back, to a shot of the actors facing each other across the small room. Ms. Alexander leans back in her chair and her head disappears behind a table lamp, as if she is hiding. It is a little signal that the scene is over, Mr. Soderbergh said, the setup for the transition.

"This film is just so secure in its belief that you will be interested in the characters and the situations," he said. "There is no attempt to whistle up some dramatic high points. It is confident, but quietly so. Which is so rare now, you know.

"I think you'd have a tough time making a movie with these

attributes right now. I think if you went in and previewed this movie, you know, the way it is, ninety-five percent of the cards you'd get back from the audience would come back saying, 'Oh, it's too slow, it's too talky.' Although the mitigating factor, I guess, is that the movie had in it two of the biggest movie stars of the time. So maybe if you did that today, you could get away with it. I don't know."

In Mr. Soderbergh's mind, the fertile period in filmmaking that some call the American New Wave began in 1967 with films like *Bonnie and Clyde* and *The Graduate* and ended in 1976, when *All the President's Men* came out. Most people trace the demise of that burst of creativity to the releases of Steven Spielberg's *Jaws* in 1975 and of George Lucas's *Star Wars* in 1977, blockbusters that alerted studios to the lucrative potential of gigantic, audience-pleasing adventures. But Mr. Soderbergh said the era ended for him with the Academy Awards ceremonies for movies released in 1976.

"Look at the five best-picture nominees from that year," he said. "You had *All the President's Men, Bound for Glory, Network, Rocky,* and *Taxi Driver.* Now, I don't know about you, but one of those movies really stands out to me—*Rocky*—and it's the one that won. I happen to like that movie, but it does feel very different from the others to me."

Those others, he said, were more typical of the fertile filmmaking era that was ending, while *Rocky* was the harbinger of the future, the feel-good epidemic that has infected American film for almost a quarter-century.

"Those other four films all have a little more on their minds than *Rocky* does, and I guess that's what I was responding to," Mr. Soderbergh said. "Because I was seeing a lot of movies at that time, a lot of foreign films, and I was drawn to stuff that had layers. Maybe I did also have a sense that that great era was coming to a close."

Mr. Soderbergh raises up in his seat, like a prairie dog sniffing something in the wind, during the first scene in the *Washington Post*'s newsroom, painstakingly reconstructed on a soundstage in Burbank. "There was a book that came out back then on the making of the movie, and I snapped it up," he said. "Mostly it's just a picture book, but there are some really interesting things in it. This newsroom was re-created down to the tiniest detail. They even flew in actual garbage from the *Post*'s newsroom in D.C. for the garbage cans on the set."

Perhaps that was a little excessive? Mr. Soderbergh smiled and shrugged. "I don't know," he said. "I think I can feel it."

What grabbed his attention was the first use in the film of a dioptric lens with a split focus, a toy that was relatively new when the movie was made and that Pakula used to spectacular effect in the film. Essentially, the lens works like bifocal eyeglasses; there is an invisible line down the middle, sometimes vertical and sometimes horizontal, and the focal length is different on each side.

The trick in using it, Mr. Soderbergh said, is figuring out how to hide the line in the shot so that the two focal lengths are not noticed and the image takes on a subliminally deeper and more three-dimensional feel. Sometimes Pakula uses one of the white, tubular pillars in the newsroom to disguise a vertical line, or the edge of a desk for a horizontal line.

If used properly, one image can be very close to the camera on the left side of the lens while the image on the right is relatively far away, and both are in perfect focus.

In *All the President's Men,* Pakula uses the dioptric lens most frequently in the newsroom scenes. Sometimes he has Robert Redford (as Woodward) or Mr. Hoffman talking on the phone in extreme close-up on one side of the frame, while on the opposite side people are milling around in the newsroom in the background, and everything is in focus. There are also frequent scenes in which a television is playing on one side, showing moments from the Nixon White House years, while on the other side Woodward and Bernstein can be seen in contrast, working away on Nixon's downfall.

"It's used in such an interesting way in this movie, but I'm not sure what Pakula was up to with it," Mr. Soderbergh said. "There is no real obvious reason to use it. Maybe he's just trying to create this sense of being totally immersed in the newsroom. Otherwise, perhaps, if you are shooting Redford talking on the phone, he would be kind of isolated. This way, he's part of this larger group."

The film does not rush itself, Mr. Soderbergh noted, but maintains a definite relentlessness. Information is parceled out—sometimes in humorous exchanges of dialogue from William Goldman's script— one classic line after another, "Follow the money" being only the most famous, and sometimes in snippets of chatter during one of the half-dozen telephone scenes.

"It's so smart how they did this," Mr. Soderbergh said. "You get the scene where Redford is working on the phone, trying to get a small piece of information, and then you cut to the scene where you see what happens with that information once he gets it. It's a great narrative device. It's just good storytelling. It implies all the work that went into getting the information while keeping the story moving along."

It's all about the task of luring the audience from one scene to the next.

"I've begun to believe more and more that movies are all about transitions," Mr. Soderbergh said, "that the key to making good movies is to pay attention to the transition between scenes. And not just how you get from one scene to the next, but where you leave a scene and where you come into a new scene. Those are some of the most important decisions that you make. It can be the difference between a movie that works and a movie that doesn't."

And the transitions in *All the President's Men,* he said, are marvels. The movie does not race forward. There are no action scenes, no big dramatic moments. And the plot frequently dead-ends into unresolved cul-de-sacs. But the overall effect is thoroughly gripping.

"The movie so much has the rhythms of real life in it," Mr. Soderbergh said. "Or are we just getting old? I was going to say you don't see movies that often today that just have the small moments in them where things are not accelerated, where people move at a real-life pace. But I'm wondering whether, for some people, their experience of the world isn't like that anymore, whether they're just sort of always overloaded and accelerated and that's how they perceive the world. Maybe, to them, something like the slower scenes in this movie don't feel like real life."

Jason Robards appears on the screen for the first time as the *Post's* top editor, Ben Bradlee, meeting with other editors behind the glass walls of his office.

"Oh God, what a great performance," Mr. Soderbergh said.

That, he said, was another astonishing element of the movie: how many of the biggest stars of the period and finest actors of all time came together and, in this one movie, did some of their finest work.

"One of the things I thought about when I watched this while we were preparing *Traffic* was how it's such a varied cast in terms of the types of actors and what they can do," Mr. Soderbergh said. "Yet the fact is that they all still feel like they're in the same film. They occupy the same universe."

Often, when different kinds of actors are thrown together—matinee idols with classically trained stage actors, stand-up comics next to Method actors—an artificial flavor takes over. Such a mix "would be absolutely crucial to making a movie like *Traffic,* especially since we were shooting in such a fragmented way with so many different locations," he said. "There is always one thing about a movie that I'm about to do that scares me, and that was what scared me about *Traffic:* how could I make sure all one hundred and fifteen actors felt like they were in the same film? And I came to *All the President's Men* for help with that."

Up on the screen Woodward and Bernstein hop in their car and head to the Library of Congress, searching for information. As they drive into the downtown Washington traffic, the slow march of the musical score by David Shire begins to play.

"That's the first music cue in the movie, did you notice that?" Mr. Soderbergh said. "What is it, like, thirty-five or forty minutes into the film? There is really very little music in this movie. The score is unbelievably good, but there is not much of it, like maybe fifteen minutes in the whole film. It's such an important lesson. I really try to be careful about that stuff, about not packing a movie with too much music."

The Watergate reporting has stalled. Woodward and Bernstein are about to be sent back to the metro desk. So Woodward pulls his trump card, walking to a phone booth across from the old Executive Office Building ("We had a shot of that building in *Traffic,*" Mr. Soderbergh said. "It looked more blue in our movie.") and calling his secret source, Deep Throat.

A few scenes later they meet, lonely figures in a creepy, almost-vacant underground garage. The Deep Throat scenes are perhaps the most famous ones in the film. They come to dominate the story, yet there are really only three fairly short appearances by Deep Throat.

"The scenes are just mind-boggling," Mr. Soderbergh said. "Everything about them. The way they're lit. The way they're shot. The dialogue. The sound. Look: this is Gordon Willis at his absolute best."

Woodward wanders through the dark garage, his footfalls hitting like bricks on the otherwise hushed sound track. A droning air conditioner hums in the background. Finally, up against a pillar several yards away, he sees a dark figure (Hal Holbrook) illuminated by the orange flash of a cigarette being lighted. Cold and warm colors mixing again.

"It's just so perfect," Mr. Soderbergh said. At a cursory glance, the scene appears lost in gloom and colorlessness. But there are exceptionally subtle varieties of color and texture.

"In his close-ups Holbrook's got a light right on his eyes, but it's maybe two stops down, at the very edge of perception," Mr. Soderbergh said. It does give the actor the look of an animal hiding in the forest at night, or a vampire. "And there is another light off to the side that just draws a line right around him, highlighting the side of his face. Look at him. He's like a ghost."

But when Mr. Redford appears to deliver his half of the lines, the look is quite different. Though still clothed in gloom, slightly warmer colors illuminate his face. "See, with Redford we get skin tones, but with Holbrook it's just completely monochromatic. Deep Throat is not even human."

The Deep Throat sequences "are so beautifully constructed," Mr. Soderbergh said. "The power dynamic between the two of them is so very well drawn. No, I think they are really the heart of the movie."

Another scene draws Mr. Soderbergh's admiration: the long sequence during which Mr. Redford, sitting at his desk, juggles two phone calls to learn why a $25,000 check from Republican campaign donors has turned up in the bank account of a Watergate burglar.

Besides being a virtuoso piece of acting by Mr. Redford, the scene is intensely compelling and visually interesting, though it draws strength from the most subtle details, Mr. Soderbergh said.

"Just watch," he said. "This is a single take. It must be, I don't know, six or seven minutes long." It is one of the newsroom scenes that uses the dual-focus lens. Mr. Redford talks on the phone, punching back and forth between the two calls, trying to control his growing excitement as he traps his quarry. At the same time, in the background, the newsroom is bustling. People huddle around a television, chat, make their own phone calls.

"You have to watch very closely, but if you look at the edges of the frame you can see that the camera is very, very slowly zooming in on Redford," Mr. Soderbergh said. "It's just so elegant and slow and gradual." And even though it is happening in an inconspicuous way, the tension builds.

"Just amazing," Mr. Soderbergh said.

When the film ended, Mr. Soderbergh stood and stretched. "Well, that was a treat," he said. He wandered back to the projection room, where he had to recover the two film canisters containing the movie. He carried one in each hand and wandered outside into the afternoon sunshine to wait for his driver.

He considered how to explain why a movie like *All the President's Men* works so perfectly. You can dissect individual scenes, but something larger is at work.

Yes, the director, the cinematographer, and the screenwriter were all working at their peaks. And yes, they made exquisite use of technical gizmos. And certainly the film was aided by the cast, in which every performer seemed to give one of the best performances of his or her career.

But something else is going on, too. Something like luck.

"This movie just has the perfect balance," Mr. Soderbergh said. "The perfect balance between all of the elements. Sometimes, if you're lucky, you get that, and sometimes you just don't. You are always hoping for that alchemy to occur where everything in the movie is lifted up, because everything and everyone is working at the highest level. You hope for it, and you work for it, and sometimes you get it. And this is just one of those movies."

HIGHLIGHTS OF STEVEN SODERBERGH'S DIRECTING CAREER AND INFORMATION ON *ALL THE PRESIDENT'S MEN*

■

What They Watched

All the President's Men. Directed by Alan J. Pakula; produced by Walter Coblenz; screenplay by William Goldman; cinematography by Gordon Willis; music by David Shire. With Robert Redford, Dustin Hoffman, Jason Robards, Jack Warden, Martin Balsam, Hal Holbrook, and Jane Alexander. 1976.

Steven Soderbergh's Films

Solaris. With George Clooney, Natascha McElhone, and Jeremy Davies. 2002.

Full Frontal. With Julia Roberts, David Duchovny, and Blair Underwood. 2002.

Ocean's 11. With George Clooney, Brad Pitt, Julia Roberts, Matt Damon, and Bill Murray. 2001.

Traffic. With Michael Douglas, Benicio Del Toro, Don Cheadle, Catherine Zeta-Jones, and Dennis Quaid. 2000.

Erin Brockovich. With Julia Roberts and Albert Finney. 2000.

The Limey. With Terence Stamp. 1999.

Out of Sight. With George Clooney and Jennifer Lopez. 1998.

Schizopolis. With Steven Soderbergh and Betsy Brantley. 1996.

Gray's Anatomy. With Spalding Gray. 1996.

The Underneath. With Peter Gallagher and Elisabeth Shue. 1995.

King of the Hill. With Jesse Bradford and Jeroen Krabbe. 1993.

Kafka. With Jeremy Irons and Theresa Russell. 1991.

sex, lies and videotape. With James Spader and Andie MacDowell. 1989.

7

Ang Lee on
Love Eternal

A ng Lee was, without question, the most passive-aggressive subject in the series. Unfailingly polite and soft-spoken in person, his demeanor and tone of voice reminded one of a Buddhist monk. But there was iron beneath the cowl. Lee was eager to watch a film that had really meant a lot to him as a boy, even though it was almost never seen in America outside of Chinese-American families, a two-and-a-half-hour operatic romance in Mandarin. He was certain that if I hadn't seen the film at least once before we sat down together, I'd spend the whole time reading the subtitles and trying to figure out what was going on. Better, he felt, was for me to watch it once on my own and then again with him. The problem was, he had the only copy of the film we could find, and I couldn't fly into New York to watch it with him until the night before. Lee had one of his assistants call me several times to figure out when I could get his copy of the film and where I would watch it. A close friend of mine was giving a piano recital the evening I arrived, which I wanted to attend, but Lee and his assistant were relentless. Eventually, it was agreed that his assistant would deliver the tape to me at the *New York Times* early the next morning, wait while I watched the movie, then take the tape back to Lee. I had only about ninety minutes between the two viewings, which meant that I watched five hours of Mandarin opera in less than eight hours, a lot more than I ever had before and likely will again. The bottom line: Lee was right. The interview wouldn't have gone as well as it did if I'd been struggling to keep up with the plot instead of listening to him.

■

Ang Lee sat on a swivel chair, his hands folded, a bank of dark monitors before him. "Every time I see this movie, I cry," he said. "It's a little embarrassing. From when I was a little boy until now, I always cry." Sure enough, he just thought about it, and his eyes began to moisten.

The unadorned white space, its paint slightly peeling, is one of the gadget-filled editing suites in the offices of Good Machine, an independent film financing and distribution company where Mr. Lee makes his headquarters. It is in a thick, slightly dingy building near the mouth of the Holland Tunnel, within muted earshot of the cacophonous tumult of Canal Street. Mr. Lee took a videocassette of Li Hanxiang's *Liang Shan Bo Yu Zhu Ying Tai*—which Mr. Lee said is best translated into English as *Love Eternal*—from its blank white sleeve, and with a mechanical whoosh it slid into one of the VCRs.

"I am sorry that this is the only version I have of this film," he said. "It is okay?"

A truck rumbled by outside. Mr. Lee, forty-six, swiveled to face the largest of the monitors, which flickered then burst to light, a Chinese fanfare over the sparkling, gaudy logo of the Shaw Brothers' Hong Kong film studio. It was okay.

"This is a movie I don't always think about, until you asked me to pick one movie to watch," Mr. Lee said. "I think the reason I wanted to talk about this movie is because it reminds me always of my innocence."

It was 1963. Mr. Lee was nine, living in a small town called Hwalian on the east coast of Taiwan, the self-described naive son of a school principal. His was a traditional Chinese household, with servants, Mandarin sensibilities, and a yearning, shared with most of its neighbors, for a kind of dream vision of the old, lost China of the mainland.

"I think that for every movie I make, I always try to duplicate that feeling of purity and innocence that I got when I saw this movie," he said. "I bring in Western drama. I bring in metaphor. I bring in Jean-Luc Godard. Whatever I bring in to my own films, I am forever trying to update and recapture that feeling. I call it juice—the juice of the film—the thing that moves people, the thing that is untranslatable by words."

When watching a favorite film, Mr. Lee said, most directors will inevitably concentrate on the craft, the strategic bursts of directorial inspiration, and indeed he did, too, while watching this film.

"But how a scene was shot, that is minor to me," he said. "It is more the juice, the core emotion, how it moves us. It is whether the whole film works at a deep level. You know, that primo feeling. There is no word for it. But that is what this movie did to me, and ever since, I am always trying to recapture it."

Love Eternal was a stupendously popular, melodramatic version of a Chinese opera that was already familiar to many of the Taiwanese who flocked to see it in the mid-1960s, when it was a recurring favorite across East Asia.

"I was able to recite the whole movie before I ever got to see it," Mr. Lee said. When this film opened to acclaim in Taipei, the entire sound track, music and dialogue, was released on a four-record set, and Mr. Lee's family bought it. But he lived far from the capital, and it took several months for the film to make its way to his coastal town. He spent those weeks listening to it over and over until he could recite the entire movie.

The film became so popular in Taiwan that some claimed to have seen it five hundred times, Mr. Lee said. Lines of its dialogue became part of everyday conversation, the way catch-phrases from a *Saturday Night Live* routine ("You look maaahvalous!") can sometimes permeate American pop culture.

"People would take two box lunches, go to the theater, and watch it all day long," he said. "My parents were watching it often. I remember the third time they went to see it, there was a typhoon coming, and they still left us at home. 'Okay, we're going to see this movie, bye.'" He laughed. "And this was on a typhoon night." The film was popular with everyone, he said, from children to housewives to university intellectuals.

"It was a big hit in China, but particularly in Taiwan," Mr. Lee said. "This is because of the Mandarin culture in the movie. We had escaped from the mainland in the civil war, and we missed that culture. For those of us too young to remember the mainland, we did not really know the old culture. So when we would see it in this movie, we would think, 'Oh, that is China.' When I went back to China to make *Crouching Tiger, Hidden Dragon,* I knew nothing about the real China. I had this image in my mind, from movies like this. So I projected these images as my China, the China in my head."

The China in Mr. Lee's head is a sumptuous fantasyland of rich homes and sparkling streams and forest pagodas, interrupted by the tragic calls to duty of the traditional codes of filial piety and social loyalty. It is the setting of Mr. Lee's *Crouching Tiger, Hidden Dragon,* which had recently become the most successful foreign-language film in American movie history.

Love Eternal is not "the greatest movie ever made," Mr. Lee said. "But there is something so honest and straightforward about it. I cry. I always cry. But I watch it for that feeling, the feeling of the innocence of watching a movie and wanting to believe."

The main purpose of this series is to gain some insight into film artists' creative geography by watching films that had a resonant impact upon them. But it is also an attempt to give people a fresh look at great films from the past, through the eyes of important artists, or to introduce readers to films they might not have seen. For this second purpose, *Love Eternal* may be a problem because it is rarely seen in the United States outside a handful of Chinese-language cinemas or university programs and is unavailable commercially. Only a lucky consumer might stumble across a copy from abroad in some out-of-the-way video shop.

So, in the theory that very few have seen it and very few are likely to see it anytime soon, a fuller description of its plot may be necessary:

Love Eternal is based on a well-known Chinese opera, a fantasy of beauty, grace, and tragedy performed in a heightened mode of theatricality. Le Di plays a young woman from a prosperous family in a small town. She is miserable in her cloistered life. Smart, curious, and eager to learn, she persuades her old-fashioned parents to let her go to school in a nearby city disguised as a boy, as girls were not allowed to study.

On the road, at a streamside pagoda, she meets Ling Po, playing another student heading for the school, and they immediately become friends. After some comic episodes about whether her friend will discover that she is a woman—checking her for a fever when she is sick, asking her to go swimming in the river—Le Di finds herself falling in love.

When she is forced to leave the school and return home, she confesses her secret to a woman who works at the school, and they plot to find a way to bring the couple together. Yet during the long journey back to the streamside pagoda where they met (Ling Po accompanies her on part of the trek home), she repeatedly tries but fails to find the courage to confess her secret. Finally, in a burst of inspiration, she tells him that she has a twin sister at home, and she promises her sister's hand in marriage.

But when Le Di gets home, she finds that her parents have promised her to an even more prominent local family's son. She is devastated but trapped by the code of filial piety. She must obey her father. She has also made a solemn promise to her friend, however, and the code of social loyalty is almost equally binding. Back at the school Ling Po finds out that his schoolmate is a woman and, overjoyed, begins an immediate journey to claim his promised bride.

When he arrives, in the film's most impassioned scene, his song of joy is crushed by the news that Le Di has been promised to another. He immediately begins to show signs of fever and consumption. Making his way back to the school, he dies pitifully in a bloody coughing fit. Le Di, when she hears the news, agrees to go ahead with her arranged marriage, but only if the procession passes the forest knoll upon which her true love's grave lies.

There, she rips off her wedding cloak to reveal funeral raiment and sings an impassioned aria to her lost love. The heavens respond, stirring up a cyclone that sweeps away the wedding party and splits her lover's grave like a coconut. Inside, she sees a ghostly image of her love and rushes to join him. The cyclone buries the grave under a mound of dirt, but a final image shows the lovers reunited, flying through the air across a rainbow bridge to the gate of a heavenly paradise.

"People think that the Chinese films being made now, for the last ten years, are the real traditional Chinese films," Mr. Lee said. "But they are not. Films like this one are the real traditional films. All of these movies today, even mine, are always an attempt to break away from this tradition. I think I only broke halfway, and the other half, I just couldn't stay away."

Mr. Lee is soft-spoken and reflexively self-effacing, blushing frequently when he is caught crying. But he can also be demanding. He sent his assistant out the night before the screening with a copy of the film, insisting that I watch it before we were to see it together.

He also wanted me to get over my initial reaction to what, to Western audiences, would be the most distracting and perplexing things about the film: both of the lead roles, that of the girl and her school boyfriend, are played by women.

"For many years, ten years or more, this was the most popular kind of film, these melodramas," Mr. Lee said. "The woman always played the main male roles, especially if it was romantic. It was a tradition from Chinese opera, where the prettiest man's part was played by a woman. As a compliment, you would say of a man, 'He is so pretty, he looks like a woman.' At the same time, if a woman was supposed to be ugly, a man would play that part. So for ten years no one wanted to see men play men. It was difficult for men to get work. And then around 1970 it all changed, and the martial arts movies began, and it all became very macho and male."

This movie, he said, is one of the pinnacles of that older, feminine style. But while some educated or gay audiences might have seen a homosexual subtext in the story line, to most audiences at the time it was just accepted at face value. "The audience was not confused," he said. "They saw the man as a man, not as a woman pretending to be a man, although at the same time they also appreciate that it was a woman pretending to be a man. Part of the appreciation was watching how well the woman could pretend to be a man."

Having women express romantic emotions for one another was simply easier for the audience to accept. "Men and women, unless they are married, they must never touch, even on the stage," he said. "So because it is two women, there was no sense of lust for the audience.

"Think of it, though: it is a really kinky story. Very sexy. But to audiences at the time, there was no sense of being sexy. It is all pure, sexless, like an all-boys' choir. To have seen a real man expressing romantic feelings for a woman on the screen would have been too strong for the audiences then. China was a very repressed society."

Mr. Lee said he recognized that there was something about the plot of *Love Eternal* that was more than a little reminiscent of *Yentl* (1983), another film in which a girl dresses up as a boy to go to school. *Yentl,* based on an Isaac Bashevis Singer story and starring Barbra Streisand, is set in the world of the shtetl. The similarities between these films is shallow, Mr. Lee said, noting that while the setup for the two stories was similar, the way they played out and the message they imparted were entirely different. *"Yentl* is *Yentl,"* he said.

Modern audiences may find it difficult to ignore that a woman is playing the male lead. The movie continually teases the audience with this. In one early scene Le Di dresses up as a male doctor to convince her parents that she will be able to pull off the deception at school. She looks nothing like a man. Nothing. But her parents are completely fooled. "The whole idea is just too wacky for the parents to realize what is going on," Mr. Lee said.

Mr. Lee smiled as the Shaw Brothers logo spilled across the screen. "Look, look, do you see that?" he asked, freezing the videotape and rolling it back. "Look at this dissolve." As the letters sparkled on the screen, a very subtle shadow rolled over the speckled background, giving it a faint three-dimensional look.

"I always noticed that when I was a little boy," he said happily. He closed his eyes and began to sing along, softly but audibly, to the song behind the opening credits.

"No other Chinese film affected me the way this one did," he said. "I felt it so strongly."

Not until he was eighteen, he said, did he begin to see films from abroad. Fellini's *Roma* was the first.

"It was only then that I realized that movies could do more than tell me a story," Mr. Lee said. Yet in later years, only a few films ever had the same impact on him as *Love Eternal*. Ingmar Bergman's *Virgin Spring* was one, Vittorio De Sica's *Bicycle Thief,* Yasujiro Ozu's *Tokyo Story,* Michelangelo Antonioni's *Eclipse*. Those are the only titles that came to mind, he said. "These are the movies that affect you so deeply that you feel that you are a different person from the one who went into the theater."

No recent film has moved him as deeply. "It is harder and harder to get to me," he said. "Especially after I started making movies. I don't remember when I have cried in a movie theater. If I do, it is because it reminds me of something else. It's not the movie that makes me do it, because I have become too much in the habit of watching how the people do it, to concentrate on the making of the film."

The opening shot of *Love Eternal* is a street scene, shot from far overhead, a long line of storefronts ending at an ornate gate, the streets teeming. This cuts to the shot of a balcony, the beautiful heroine standing at the railing. A chorus sings the introduction: the poor girl is miserable and trapped.

Cut to a closer shot of the girl. She looks out at the passing scene, a nearby pond, the sky. Then she turns and enters the room, where a maid tries to console her.

"Here is how it was always done with the Chinese films," Mr. Lee said. "You begin with the exterior, then the framing; then you go close up to a person, then to what that person is watching, often something in nature, and only then to the internal feeling of that character. You look out the window, you see the moon, then you look down at yourself.

"You go from the setting, to the person, to the looking at nature, to the internal feelings. This was as close as Chinese could get to psychoanalysis. We just didn't go there directly, only through metaphor."

Immediately Mr. Lee began to point out the elements in the plot that were different from those of similar melodramas of the period. First and most central, the parents are depicted as wrongheaded. Unwittingly but unbendingly they make one wrong call after another and end up destroying their daughter's life.

Usually, Mr. Lee said, parents were unerringly wise. Second, the heroine is the smartest person in the movie, the only one who, in scene after scene, sees events clearly. In one important episode she even proves herself wiser in the teachings of Confucius than her male classmates.

This, Mr. Lee said, was probably not done in an attempt to upend the social order, though to some audiences it might have had that effect. More likely, he said, it was simply to heighten the tragedy.

Love Eternal was an opera that originated in a small company in Hwangme, outside Shanghai. Even though the operas were created as full-length stories, it was rare for audiences to see them performed that way. More usually, touring companies would do a kind of music hall revue, beginning with some martial arts acrobatics for the children, then some "mediocre material," he said. Only at the end would they perform a few scenes from an opera.

That is why, he said, the operas were divided into distinct chapters—easily discernible when watching the movie—and each chapter had a name, usually a bit of poetry. In *Love Eternal,* especially popular was the sequence called "18-Mile Escorting," during which the two lovers make their return journey to the pagoda, singing all the way, staring at fish and other creatures that miraculously mirror their inner state.

"It is very operatic; do you see that gesture?" Mr. Lee said, mimicking the graceful way Ling Po twirls a hand fan. "See the way the actresses twirl the fan. It is a certain way of movement, to make it graceful. It is all beautifying, you know.

"Everything in these stories is made more beautiful. In *Crouching Tiger,* in the tavern fight sequence, I referred to this, but using a fan made of metal."

He laughed at this. But in a way, he said, it is the crux of what *Crouching Tiger* was about, for him: an attempt to blend the two dominant genres of Chinese filmmaking, the feminine operatic melodrama, like *Love Eternal,* and the masculine martial arts adventure, and to do it in a way that also integrates Western notions of psychoanalytical character development.

"What I did in *Crouching Tiger* was a little unnatural for the industry," he said. "It is my idea of martial arts films, as I think they should be. But I had no confidence when I was making it. I wanted to appeal to the Asian audiences and to the Western art house audience. I had no idea of it crossing over to the Western mainstream, as it has."

The operatic sequences in *Love Eternal* are the most distinctive, the ones that elicit the greatest response from Mr. Lee. The film splits almost in half, the first portion played almost entirely for comedy and the second portion as tragedy. From the moment the lovers part at the pagoda, the comedy withers and the tears begin to flow.

"Oh, look, did you see that camera move?" Mr. Lee asked. "It was so subtle. Here, let's take another look."

He wound the tape back. Ling Po is escorting Le Di back to the pagoda. Time and again, she has tried to tell her secret to her love, but either Ling Po has proved too dense or Le Di has lost her nerve.

Ling Po crosses a bridge, but Le Di hangs back. For the first time she has second thoughts about whether she should tell her secret at all, because it would mean disobeying her father.

"Here it is," he said. "The tears just swell seeing this. I don't know why."

In the shot Le Di is walking, singing, her arms moving in graceful rhythm with the music. Then she stops and takes two steps backward.

The camera makes a very slight movement away from her—on either a dolly or a track, it is unclear—while equally subtly the lens zooms in on her. She steps back, the camera pulls farther back, but the lens moves forward. It is a slight moment of discombobulation.

"Notice the way the music slows down, and her movements," he said. "I don't know why he does this, but it has the effect of making us realize that something important has happened. And it is a signal to the audience, I think, that something sad is coming."

Throughout the film, in the manner of all traditional Chinese operas, the actresses modulate their movements and even the pace of their lines to match the rhythm of the music. They twirl, pose, speak rapidly as the music pulses, then freeze, pose, and speak more slowly as the pulse slows.

"It is so beautiful, isn't it?" Mr. Lee said, following one such sequence, beating out the rhythmic modulations in the air with one hand while the other swirled gracefully in the air to the melody. "The subtitles are not good. The lyrics are so beautiful here. They are poetry." He began to hum softly.

What many Western audiences—and even some Asian audiences—do not realize is how much martial arts films, which have become so popular in the last quarter-century, owe to the traditions of Chinese opera.

"They are all choreographed in the same way," Mr. Lee said. "Pose, reestablish position, pose again. It is all the same."

In the last minutes of the film, from the death of Ling Po—blood spilling into a pond—until the transcendent ending, with the two lovers flying to heaven, Mr. Lee cried continuously. He shrugged sheepishly about it.

"When I was a boy I would weep so loudly in this movie that other people in the row, who had also been crying, would suddenly get quiet and wonder who was making that noise," he said.

Mr. Lee said it was not until he was rewatching *Love Eternal,* about a month ago, that he realized how similar the film's ending was to the final shot in *Crouching Tiger,* with the girl leaping off the bridge high in the mountain and flying through the clouds.

The scene was in the book that Mr. Lee adapted, but he said he now thought that it was no coincidence that it had appealed to him so much. At some level, he said, he was remembering this scene from *Love Eternal,* the literal flying in escape.

And the themes of both films, he said, are strikingly similar, about lovers who, because of the strictures of filial piety and duty, cannot speak openly about their romantic feelings.

"It is, I think, the great Chinese theme," Mr. Lee said. "For the Chinese audience, it is just in our blood. You must hide your feelings. That becomes the art itself, the metaphor and the symbolism, the use of color and framing.

"It is a way of not saying something but of expressing it anyway. And it is such an emotional outlet, especially for a repressed society. That is the heart of both films, the repressed emotional wish. That is the hidden dragon."

And that was the juice in *Crouching Tiger,* Mr. Lee said, the love unable to find words.

In *The Ice Storm,* he said, the juice came from one word, *embarrassment,* that he tried to weave through the story in a kind of fugue. In his *Sense and Sensibility,* it was the moment of transition, when the two sisters, played by Emma Thompson and Kate Winslet, exchanged personalities, one suddenly becoming more outgoing and impulsive, the other more sober and analytical.

"To me, how people make this and that scene is less important than what makes us make our movies," Mr. Lee said. "What spoke to you and, eventually, whether you transmit that emotion to the audience. The juice, it's indescribable."

He pressed a button and with another whoosh the videotape slid from its mechanical womb.

"The intellectualizing, the analysis—that can come later," Mr. Lee said. "In my movies, I hope that is all in hiding. It is the juice that we want. I think that's what brings us to the movie theater. All the ways and means and heart are just vehicles, ways of peering down through a protection, to reach that juicy part that is very vulnerable and that you can only reach when you are in the dark, in a movie theater, and you are with people."

HIGHLIGHTS OF ANG LEE'S DIRECTING CAREER AND INFORMATION ON *LIANG SHAN BO YU ZHU YING TAI*

∎

What They Watched

Liang Shan Bo Yu Zhu Ying Tai (*Love Eternal*). Directed by Li Hanxiang; produced by Shao Yi Fu; music by Chow Lan Ping; cinematography by Hur Lan Shan and Dai Chia Tai. The screenplay writers were uncredited. 1963.

Ang Lee's Films

Crouching Tiger, Hidden Dragon. With Chow Yun Fat, Michelle Yeoh, and Zhang Ziyi. 2000.

Ride with the Devil. With Tobey Maguire, Skeet Ulrich, and Jeffrey Wright. 1999.

The Ice Storm. With Kevin Kline, Sigourney Weaver, and Joan Allen. 1997.

Sense and Sensibility. With Emma Thompson, Kate Winslet, and Hugh Grant. 1995.

Eat Drink Man Woman. With Sihung Lung, Yu-Wen Wang, and Chien-lien Wu. 1994.

The Wedding Banquet. With Mitchell Lichtenstein, Jeanne Kuo Chang, and Winston Chao. 1993.

Pushing Hands. With Sihung Lung, Bo Z. Wang, and Deb Snyder. 1992.

8

Wolfgang Petersen on
High Noon

olfgang Petersen was undoubtedly the best sport in the series. His was one of the first interviews I did (in a wonderfully atmospheric screening room on the Warner Bros. lot) but the piece kept getting postponed, month after month, by the appearance of other subjects whose installments needed to appear to coincide with the release of their films. In the end, though, I think it was best, because it put several months between his interview and Janusz Kaminski's. Both involved filmmakers who chose a Hollywood movie that they'd seen as a young man living abroad, Kaminski as a teenager in Communist Poland and Petersen as an even younger boy in postwar Germany. The pieces are almost bookends, little love sonnets to the movies about the mysterious and unexpected ways that Hollywood can appeal to those living far away, in vastly different societies. What I also remember most vividly about this interview was the two men from the Academy of Motion Picture Arts and Science's film library who brought over a 16-millimeter print of *High Noon* that had been director Fred Zinnemann's own personal copy. It was one of the treasures of the Academy vaults, and they hovered over it like Secret Service agents monitoring the movements of the president's favorite child.

■

The glimmering ships came sliding out of the North Sea mist and floated, one after another, up to the locks at Emden, a German seaport right at the Dutch border. While the vessels paused for the water level to be adjusted, the hungry townspeople clustered on the shore and waited for whatever treasures the grinning sailors might toss to them.

"It was the late 1940s and I was, oh, maybe seven years old," said the director Wolfgang Petersen, now sixty. "We were really starving back then because it was so early after the war, you see. The only way our parents could get anything to eat was for us to run to where the ships were stopped.

"These huge American ships came in. They were like a spaceship, like a close-encounter thing, and we were crazy about those beautiful ships. On them were Americans with these big smiles on their faces, and they were throwing food down to us. I had never seen before these oranges and bananas and chewing gum. We kids were like little rats down there, hungry, jumping on all that stuff. I have never forgotten that image of America. To us America was something like a paradise. They have so much that they can throw it away, you know. And not only that, but they are good. They give it to you. They like you, even though you were the enemy."

Mr. Petersen was sitting in a small projection room on the Warner Bros. movie lot in Burbank, one corner of a square adobe building with a red-tile roof surrounded by a quadrangle of khaki-colored offices stuffed with conference tables, blackboards, and high-tech gizmos. It was in this very warren that Mr. Petersen finished editing his latest film, *The Perfect Storm*. Now the sounds of excited conversation came from the projection booth as the precious print of *High Noon*—the director Fred Zinnemann's own print, bequeathed to the Academy of Motion Picture Arts and Sciences for safekeeping—was carefully threaded into the projector. Two representatives of the Academy's archives were watching intently as the projectionist did his work, making sure that Zinnemann's irreplaceable print was not damaged.

Perhaps it was natural, Mr. Petersen said, that after these early encounters with Americans and their exotic land of forgiveness and plenitude, he and the other boys of Emden—and later of Hamburg, where Mr. Petersen's family moved—spent their summer hours watching the latest Hollywood films and playing cowboys and Indians in the wreckage of the Third Reich. He loved Hollywood movies, especially the westerns. When he was fourteen, Mr. Petersen took his 8-millimeter camera and, with the help of neighborhood boys, made his own slapdash western. There was a saloon, a poker game, a fistfight, a shoot-out. "I must say, it was very generic," he said.

Even then, there was something about Gary Cooper—tall, weary, a little the worse for wear—that got deep under the young Mr. Petersen's skin. To American audiences, the story of *High Noon* took place in a familiar kind of standard-issue frontier town, stripped down to its genre essentials. But Mr. Petersen caught something else in the shifting eyes and compromised morals of the supporting characters.

High Noon has had champions and detractors since its release in 1952 as something of a comeback vehicle for the fifty-one-year-old Cooper, coming a decade after films like *The Pride of the Yankees* (1942), *Sergeant York* (1941), and *Beau Geste* (1939) had made him one of Hollywood's emblematic faces. Howard Hawks, for instance, frequently derided *High Noon,* asking what kind of hero Cooper was portraying, scampering all over town begging for help from townspeople just because a few bad guys were headed his way. In fact, Hawks said his own *Rio Bravo* (1959), with John Wayne playing a tough frontier sheriff, was to some extent a reaction to *High Noon.* And many saw in the film, either in its stubborn marshal or its mendacious townsfolk, a veiled reference to the anti-Communist crusades and blacklisting of the early 1950s.

But that was not what reached out to Mr. Petersen, an idealistic German boy coming of age in the receding shadow of a lost war. To him *High Noon* was about the world he saw all around him.

"I think this movie was so important to me, and was really one of the reasons that I became a film director, because of the way life was in Germany in the nineteen-fifties," Mr. Petersen said. "You know, the war had ended not so long before and people were trying to forget it, to get on with rebuilding the country. People were not really talking about the past or about responsibility. And then I saw this movie, and it was so clear to me: There is good. There is bad. It was about heroism, you know, about courage. The effect this had on a young boy—what was I? Twelve? Thirteen? Something like that—it was very powerful."

High Noon is perhaps most famous today for its formal structure. It is 85 minutes long, and that is roughly the time span it covers. At the beginning, Will Kane, a retiring marshal played by Cooper, is being married to Amy Fowler, a Quaker played by Grace Kelly, and they are about to go on their honeymoon. Before they can leave, word comes that Frank Miller, a desperado whom Kane was responsible for putting behind bars, is on his way back to town to settle the account. Indeed, three of Miller's gang are already at the station waiting for the noon train.

Rather than running, as his pacifist wife and almost everyone else urges him to, Kane insists on staying to meet Miller. It is his duty. For the rest of the movie, he goes from one person to another, one group to the next, trying to rally support. But one by one, people abandon or betray him. His deputy (Lloyd Bridges) is sulking because he didn't get the marshal's job. His mentor (Lon Chaney Jr.) is upset that a lifetime as a lawman has left him destitute and arthritic. A town business leader (Thomas Mitchell) first seems supportive but then insists that Kane flee for the good of local commerce. Every few scenes, Kane passes a clock that shows that noon is drawing ever closer until finally the marshal is left alone and the noon train arrives.

"I wanted to be like Gary Cooper when I saw this movie," Mr. Petersen said. "He was a true movie star for me in the true sense. No one comes forward to help him, but he doesn't back down. All those townspeople who refuse to help him—they all have good reasons, but still. You know, in Germany, there was absolutely a lack of heroes in the years after the war; people not communicating, just going along, living, not talking about the past. Better not even to think about it, you know? Of course, we as kids could sense that something was not being said.

"And the silence was more horrible. We knew there was something wrong. And when you are twelve, you want to believe in something. You want to believe that there is a good cause and truth and that there is courage in the adults. But to be surrounded instead by this silence, I don't know. That is what this movie said to me. All these townspeople, having reasons not to do the right thing, compromising, being silent. It felt very much like the world I was living in. And then, in the middle of it, this one man, this hero, standing up for what is right, even if he must stand alone. He seemed close to me. I could understand that man. I wanted to be fighting for something good. To stand tall. Not to compromise."

Mr. Petersen said he could trace a direct emotional line from watching *High Noon* and other Hollywood films of the late '40s and early '50s to his current life as one of the leading directors of big-budget studio blockbusters. "After seeing all of these early movies, I decided that I wanted to do this, I wanted to make movies," he said. "I wanted to tell these wonderful stories. And if you start thinking like that, well, at the end of that dream stands Hollywood, because this is the most exciting place to make movies in the world."

The Warner Bros. screening room went dark, and Mr. Petersen leaned back in his chair happily. "This is so good," he said. The credits were rolling, simple lettering over black-and-white images of the three desperadoes meeting on the open range, beginning to make their way to Will Kane's town. Tex Ritter sings "Do Not Forsake Me, Oh My Darlin'." The compositions of the riders and the landscape are very carefully framed, each shot bearing a sense of formal arrangement, the light and the dark of Floyd Crosby's cinematography altogether stark. What was it that Mr. Petersen found so good? The images? The song? The deliberate pacing and the sense of momentum as the men gather and begin to ride faster and faster? "All of it," he said.

He is not a silent movie-watcher. Frequently during the film, Mr. Petersen would gasp in surprise, laugh softly, or say things like "Oh, I love this scene" or "Now we cut to the train station, boom," or he would comment on Cooper's almost eerie ability to let a string of emotions bleed out of his face without seeming to move a muscle.

"This face is amazing," he said. "You see the whole range of emotions on that face. Whatever he feels, you can see it. Oh, this sequence now in the church, it's very typical."

Will Kane has been making the rounds—to the judge, to his angry deputy—and finding no help anywhere. Finally he decides to stop by the church, where a worship service is in progress.

"We have been to the judge and we have been to the deputy, so now we go to the church," Mr. Petersen said. "Let's see how the people in the church react." Kane is embarrassed to stand in front of the families in church and ask for help; his face is a rich mix of decency, desperation, and disappointment. "In this scene are some of the most powerful close-ups for Cooper," Mr. Petersen said. "I think Zinnemann was very good at knowing how to use the close-ups— the real close-ups, the close close-ups—just when they would have the most impact. He saves them just for the most special moments to keep them more powerful. Just like he did with the music."

Dimitri Tiomkin's famous score has been imitated so often that one imagines it suffusing the film, but what is striking is how infrequently music is heard. Long sequences that today would be plastered with wall-to-wall music are allowed to play in silence or with some evocative ambient sound, like the ticking of a clock. Thus, when Tiomkin's score does emerge, it feels all the more powerful.

"I did that also a lot in my film *Das Boot,* working with the terrors of silence, which can be even more effective than the loudest sound effect in the world," he said.

Now, studio executives and many filmmakers are reluctant to work this way, preferring to keep the score thrumming. "There is no will to go to the risk of working with silence anymore," Mr. Petersen said. "And I must tell you that, as I am sitting here talking about it right now, I think I must look to myself to see if I should do more than I have done in my most recent films, because I think that it can be so effective."

Mr. Petersen laughed happily as the parents shooed the children out of the church so they could have a town hall discussion about what should be done. "Now it's time for the democracy, for everyone to have their say," he said.

The arguments fall on all sides. Some want to help; some are afraid, some indignant. "Hmmmm," Mr. Petersen said, watching the sequence of impassioned speeches. "Look, these are great close-ups." The minister is asked what should be done. "He has no answer," Mr. Petersen said. Sure enough, the minister gives a wishy-washy speech and admits he is not sure what the right thing to do is. "Not much help there," Mr. Petersen said.

Thomas Mitchell, playing Jonas Henderson, the businessman who had seemed to be Kane's strongest ally, stands up in front of the group and gives the longest speech, a wonderfully structured piece of misdirection by the screenwriter, Carl Foreman. At first, Henderson seems to be rallying the townspeople to Kane's cause, but gradually, as he goes on, it becomes clear that he is actually leading them in the other direction, and he ends up urging Kane to get out of town before the train arrives.

"So, they all sort of have their reasonable points," Mr. Petersen said. "Everyone gets their say; everyone gets to make their point. But in the end, they don't help him. He is on his own. That's what I really like."

Up on the screen, Lloyd Bridges slinks into the town saloon. The eyes of the cowpokes surreptitiously follow him through the crowded room to the table where he plops down, orders a whiskey, and says leave the bottle. "I like these scenes, really beautifully cast," Mr. Petersen said. "It reminds you how important casting is, not just for the big roles but for everyone. There are a lot of great actors in this film, even in some of the smaller roles that appear only once or twice. Look, Lloyd Bridges is just great in this bar scene, and this guy, the bartender, he's just perfect." Mr. Petersen paused and watched. "A lot of drinking in the movies in those days," he said. Mr. Bridges's deputy slams down one glass of amber liquid after another, and so does everyone around him.

When the moving camera lighted on the bar's piano player, who wiped away his sweat, Mr. Petersen remarked on what he felt was one of the director's underappreciated strategies in the film. Almost everyone who has written about *High Noon* has noted the use of clocks and the sense of real time, but not so many have noticed how meticulously the director played with heat and sunlight.

"The heat, you see there, it's building," Mr. Petersen said as the piano player wiggled his neck in his sweat-streaked collar.

Several times during the film, as Kane walks along the dusty street, the camera takes time to note his shadow. And as midday approaches—and the arrival of the killer's train—the shadow gradually shrinks away. At the same time, there are more scenes of people wiping away sweat or glinting into the hot sun. "It's very cleverly done, and very subtle," Mr. Petersen said. "No one ever talks about it, but you do get this sense of heat building along with the tension, just as it would as you approached noon."

By the end, and Kane's confrontation with the gunmen, the shadows have virtually disappeared.

"Now here comes for me one of the most memorable scenes," Mr. Petersen said. "I was shocked by it as a kid, by the violence and the rawness of it. Of course, by today's standards, it is pretty tame."

Bridges watches as Cooper goes into the livery stable, then follows him inside. Cooper, who by now realizes that no one is coming to help him, stares at his horse, trying to decide whether he should run away. Bridges walks up beside him. "Are you scared?" he asks Cooper. "I guess so," Cooper replies.

Mr. Petersen clapped his hands in delight. "Isn't that great? 'I guess so.' That's so great," he said.

Bridges urges him to flee. Cooper resists. A fistfight erupts.

"It's really well done," Mr. Petersen said. "A very good fistfight. I remember, when I first saw this, my heart was just pounding. I felt so bad again for Cooper, who is considerably older than this younger deputy. This to me is one of the undercurrents of the movie. Cooper is getting old and his marshal here is getting older, so there is this feeling that he can't be this man of action for much longer. This may be the last chance for him. I had a little bit of that feeling in the movie I made with Clint Eastwood, *In the Line of Fire,* where he is the aging Secret Service agent. I was not consciously thinking about *High Noon* at the time, but there is a parallel now that I think of it."

This note of elegy moves Mr. Petersen to the topic of westerns, the great pleasure of his youth, now an all but vanished genre.

"Yes, it's too bad, but I think it's over for westerns," he said. "It's very hard to analyze why this has happened. I think it has something to do with how our world has gotten more complicated. Westerns grew out of simplicity. They were about a black-and-white world, a good-versus-evil world. This kind of simplicity just doesn't reflect the world today. Our society, especially the Americans, lost its simplicity in the nineteen-sixties, when America went into the Vietnam War and all the lines got blurred. What I always identified with the westerns was their very clear simplicity. Yes, I am afraid that is finished. Oh, here is a scene that I don't think Howard Hawks would have liked."

Cooper has retreated to his office. It's only a few minutes to noon, and he sits behind his desk desolate, on the edge of tears.

"So? He is having a little bit of the misty eyes? No, Hawks would not have approved," Mr. Petersen said. "Has Cooper written his will yet? That always got to me, too, because it is so sad. Oh, here we go."

Cooper reaches into his desk, pulls out some paper, and begins to write a last will and testament. This kicks off perhaps the most famous sequence in the film. As the clock ticks and the music gradually builds, Zinnemann cuts back to each of the people we have met during the film, a montage of accelerating speed and volume during which we get to see what all the other characters are doing at that moment.

"This is great parallel editing," Mr. Petersen said. "You get to see how many characters there are in this film. We meet them again, one by one, and what is amazing is how familiar they are to us. There is nothing confusing about them. Why? Because they have all had their little moments during the film."

The cutting becomes more rapid as the music swells and pulses, mimicking the ticking of a clock or the momentum of a locomotive. Then, just when it seems that the music cannot get any louder, it stops dead. Silence. And then, in the distance, we hear the screech of the locomotive whistle.

"What a great pause," Mr. Petersen said. "That silence before the whistle. Once again, he uses silence so well. Zinnemann is a master of these things."

Cooper rises and walks out into the street. The carriage carrying Kelly to the train station passes, but she does not even turn to wave good-bye.

"I hated her here," Mr. Petersen said. "Oh, how I hated her."

And Cooper is left alone in the middle of the shadowless midday street. The camera pulls back and then up into the air. He is the only living thing in sight.

"Oh, I was gone here, this was so strong," Mr. Petersen said. "This poor man. Look, no one is there. Where are the people? They are just gone. Not even a dog can be seen. He is completely alone. People are not even peeking through the windows. They have disappeared, like in a nightmare. This is one of the most effective shots, of this man walking alone down the street. That's what makes this movie a classic, that's what makes this so great."

By now, Kelly has jumped off the train after hearing the first gunshot, unable to leave Cooper, and she has found her way back to his office. Cooper is out on the street; the killers are moving in on him.

"Look here at this shot coming up," Mr. Petersen said. "It shows you how subtle Zinnemann was, yet how effective. There is this shot where there is a gun belt hanging on the wall. Here it comes, boom!"

As Kelly moves toward the office window, we see, to her right, a pistol hanging on the wall.

"You see, he does not even have her look at the gun." Mr. Petersen said. "To the audience, we want almost to scream out, take the gun! Take it! Go help him!" Instead, Zinnemann cuts back to Cooper across the street, where he has taken refuge. One of the killers, smiling malevolently, moves in for the kill. There is the pop of a gunshot and a puff of smoke behind him. The killer falls, revealing, behind him, Kelly framed in the office window, the still-smoking pistol in her hand.

"You see, we wanted her to take that pistol and we did not know if she had even seen it," Mr. Petersen said. "Now, she has taken it. It is like we in the audience willed it to happen. That is how a great director pulls you into the story, makes you an accomplice. She has acted to save her husband, and she is redeemed!"

Back in the projection room, under the careful scrutiny of the academy curators, Zinnemann's *High Noon* print was rewound and placed back in its protective canisters.

"I saw this film, oh, maybe six or seven times when I was young," Mr. Petersen said, walking out into the warm afternoon glare. "Then I saw it again for the first time in a long time a couple of years ago, when I installed a video screening room in my house. I just wanted to check it out. And I loved it again. I just loved it. There is something about this movie, because it meant so much to me when I was growing up. I am not sure if I am still objective enough to know if the film holds up. Maybe it doesn't. It doesn't matter. I just remember what this movie meant to me when I was young. Because it is about memory, you see? It is about Germany in the 1950s. It is about watching an American movie star and identifying with him."

Mr. Petersen made his way through the labyrinth of the Warner lot, passing through the old courtyards where Bogart and Cagney and, yes, Cooper once walked. He paused finally and sat down on a bench beneath a leafy arbor. Over his shoulder nearby, embedded in the wall, was a piece of graffiti-stained masonry with a plaque identifying it as a shard from the Berlin Wall.

"You know, when you grow up and when no one around you seemed to care, where it was all about making money and rebuilding Germany and being ashamed and silent about the past, a movie like this can have such an effect on a young man," he said. "This movie had such an enormous impact on me because I could see what a story can do to you, how it can change your perspective. It was not just entertaining. I was deeply moved by it. And now, here I am, sitting with you on this Hollywood lot, and I am making movies."

Mr. Petersen stood up and began to walk toward his car.

"Always when I talk about this, it is still some kind of a miracle," he said. "If you pursue something with all of your will and all of your strength, there is a way you can make it work. You know, it is not a natural thing that a little boy from Emden should become a Hollywood director and fulfill his dream. That is not what I would say is normal. But you can do it."

HIGHLIGHTS OF WOLFGANG PETERSEN'S DIRECTING CAREER AND INFORMATION ON *HIGH NOON*

■

What They Watched

High Noon. Directed by Fred Zinnemann; written by Carl Foreman; produced by Carl Foreman and Stanley Kramer; cinematography by Floyd Crosby; music by Dimitri Tiomkin. With Gary Cooper, Grace Kelly, Thomas Mitchell, Lloyd Bridges, and Katy Jurado. 1952.

Wolfgang Petersen's Films

The Perfect Storm. With George Clooney, Mark Wahlberg, and Diane Lane. 2000.

Air Force One. With Harrison Ford, Gary Oldman, and Glenn Close. 1997.

Outbreak. With Dustin Hoffman, Morgan Freeman, and Rene Russo. 1995.

In the Line of Fire. With Clint Eastwood, Rene Russo, and John Malkovich. 1993.

Shattered. With Tom Berenger, Bob Hoskins, and Greta Scacchi. 1991.

Enemy Mine. With Dennis Quaid, Louis Gossett Jr., and Brion James. 1985.

The Never-Ending Story. With Noah Hathaway, Barret Oliver, and Tami Stronach. 1984.

Das Boot (The Boat). With Jürgen Prochnow, Herbert Grönemeyer, and Klaus Wennemann. 1981.

Die Konsequenz (The Consequence). With Jürgen Prochnow, Ernst Hannawald, and Werner Schwuchow. 1977.

Einer Von Uns Beiden (One or the Other of Us). With Klaus Schwarzkopf, Elke Sommer, and Jürgen Prochnow. 1973.

Ich Werde Dich Töten, Wolf (I Will Kill You, Wolf). With Ingrid Oppermann, Wolf Roth, and Ursula Sieg. 1971.

Der Eine, Der Andere (The One, The Other). With Hans-Peter Korff and Hurst Uhde. 1967.

9

Harvey Weinstein on

Exodus

If there was one significant departure in the series, it was the decision made on the spur of the moment, during a phone conversation about something else altogether, to ask Harvey Weinstein to take part. Although he had directed, and planned to direct again, Weinstein was most definitely best known as the boisterous, sometimes bombastic co-chairman (with his brother, Bob) of Miramax Films, the single greatest success story of the indie film movement. Weinstein, in his take-no-prisoners struggle not only to get independent films respected by the Hollywood mainstream but included among the regular Oscar winners, had made a lot of enemies in the studios. In the process, he had also turned himself into a Hollywood celebrity in his own right, a boldface name in the gossip columns whose Machiavellian schemings were certain to inspire rage and spill ink. Can a studio chief be considered a creative filmmaker? Certainly. Irving Thalberg created the template. And there is no question that when it comes time to make the most crucial decision of all, whether a film actually gets made or not, that decision falls to the big guy in the corner office.

■

This is what I was afraid of," Harvey Weinstein said, burying his head in his hands. "That the filmmaking wouldn't be as strong as the themes of the piece."

Up on the screen, in one of the opening scenes of Otto Preminger's 1960 film *Exodus,* an epic adaptation of the Leon Uris bestseller about the birth of modern Israel, Ralph Richardson and Eva Marie Saint were sitting at a table on a sun-dappled terrace in Cyprus, sipping cool drinks and chatting about archaeology. The scene goes on and on. The camera does not move. The conversation does not improve. Both of them look as if they would rather be almost anyplace else.

"Oh my gosh, I can't believe how wooden this is," Mr. Weinstein said. "You can't believe Dalton Trumbo wrote this. I am listening to this and thinking my memories of this are so much fonder."

Memories of movies can be weirdly fluid and tricky, especially those that hit you at just the right time in your life. Who hasn't had the experience of returning to a film seen as a child and finding that what was once hilarious or stirring is now sophomoric or mundane? Still, if there was something about a movie that struck you when you were younger, it will probably still be there, if you look hard enough or give the movie time to work on you.

"Who knew Otto Preminger and Jim Jarmusch were cousins?" Mr. Weinstein said with a theatrical moan. "Talk about minimalism. I mean, look at this. These scenes are all just master shots. There is no cutting within any of these scenes. I am sitting here, and I am amazed."

Mr. Weinstein, forty-nine, is in the second-floor screening room at the TriBeCa headquarters of Miramax Films, the independent film production and distribution company he founded with his brother, Bob. Miramax has bedeviled the Hollywood giants over the last decade, frequently dominating the Oscar competition and developing a reputation for creative acumen and business ruthlessness that has made the Weinsteins among the most contentious figures in the movie business. (Miramax is now a Disney subsidiary, though it operates independently and the brothers remain in control.)

"When I was a boy growing up in Queens, one of the great influences on my life was my Aunt Shirley, who loved bestselling books,"

Mr. Weinstein said. "Aunt Shirley loved Leon Uris and gave me all of his books. My favorite was *Mila 18,* which was kind of the prequel to *Exodus,* about the uprising in the Warsaw Ghetto. That's one of the reasons I wanted to watch this movie today.

"As a kid I swore to my aunt that *Mila 18* would be made into a great movie, and the rights to it ended up being owned by everybody but me over the years. Then a year and a half ago I got the rights, and now it's finally going to be made into a movie, and I might direct that movie myself because I swore to my aunt that I would make it."

Mr. Weinstein recalls the pride he felt upon seeing one of the biggest and most admired movie stars of the day, Paul Newman, playing a tough, heroic Jewish commando in *Exodus.*

"Guys like me, we grew up with two kinds of Jews—you know, the Jews who marched into the concentration camp and the Jews who fought," Mr. Weinstein said. "Uris's books were about the Jews who fought. So for us, as young kids, you know, this was the movie where we had our first Jewish hero. I'm sure blacks must have felt the same way when they saw Sidney Poitier" standing up to bigots.

"Suddenly for us there was this new Jewish way of thinking," he said. "Instead of growing up to be a professor, a lawyer, or a doctor, you could grow up to be a soldier, you know, for your people. You can be tough. You can be John Wayne, too."

In the months since Mr. Weinstein had agreed to sit down and watch a movie for this series, several titles had been discussed and rejected. From the beginning he was passionately involved in the decision about which film to watch.

"I just like so many movies," he said at one point. Perhaps something from the French New Wave, or a classic from his beloved Italian cinema? Or maybe something rousing that he saw as a boy, like *The Magnificent Seven* or *The Great Escape*? An early selection, *Spartacus,* was chosen largely because Mr. Weinstein loves its Dalton Trumbo script, but it was rejected for fear that it would be seen by others in Hollywood as a none-too-subtle dig at *Gladiator* (with which Miramax's *Chocolat* was then competing in the Oscar race).

Even as late as the day we were to watch the movie, it was unclear which one he would choose. He burst into the screening room armed with both a 1960 print of *Exodus* and a DVD version of Federico Fellini's *Amarcord,* another favorite.

"I'm really torn," Mr. Weinstein said as he swept through the room, too energized to sit down. "I haven't seen *Exodus* in so long, and it has Paul Newman in it, who is my hero. But *Amarcord* is such a wonderful film, too, and we could talk about my love of Italian cinema. I don't know. Let's see how *Amarcord* looks."

The DVD was cranked up, but the images were very dark and bled of color; apparently the projector in the Miramax screening room was having trouble reading the digital information on the *Amarcord* disc.

"Well, this is no good," Mr. Weinstein said. "I wonder how well a forty-year-old print is going to hold up. Let's give it a try. It can't look any worse than this."

The Fellini film disappeared, and a few minutes later the familiar, haunting melody of the *Exodus* theme filled the room. "It's another great Saul Bass title sequence," Mr. Weinstein said, referring to the flame-licked logo of a group of hands holding up a rifle. Bass revolutionized film marketing in the 1950s and early '60s with a series of title sequences that used a recognizable logo, like the chopped-up silhouette for *Anatomy of a Murder* (1959) or the swirling spirographs for Alfred Hitchcock's *Vertigo* (1958).

"Hey, this looks really great for such an old print," Mr. Weinstein said, settling back in his screening room chair and stretching out his legs. "Let's watch this."

Mr. Weinstein's main interest in the film, he said, was Trumbo's script. "It was with this movie and *Spartacus,* which came out the same year, that Trumbo emerged from the blacklist," he said. "And both of those movies also have Trumbo's great theme, which is the power of the few against the mighty. That really impressed me as a young man, and it's stayed with me.

"In a way I think it's a theme of my life: You can beat the mighty, you can go against the majors, and you can win. There's a Kurt Vonnegut quote from *Cat's Cradle* that's kind of the motto of Miramax." (Mr. Vonnegut wrote, "There is no reason goodness cannot triumph over evil, so long as the angels are as organized as the Mafia.") Mr. Weinstein continued, "*Exodus* has one of those great Trumbo scripts that reminds me of that theme."

Miramax has been known for encouraging fresh new directors, like Quentin Tarantino, and for energizing the careers of a generation of new faces, like Ben Affleck and Gwyneth Paltrow. But Mr.

Weinstein said he was even prouder that Miramax films had been nominated for screenwriting Oscars almost every year for a decade.

"I'll sail right into a controversy," Mr. Weinstein said. "I know that the directors think they're the ones who make the movies, and I don't want to minimize the director's role. But they don't make good movies unless they have a good script. Whoever said film is about collaboration got it right. For instance, look at this movie. I don't think Otto Preminger is a great director by any means. You know, we've been sitting here laughing at some of the things he did. Yet in the end this movie has real power, and that's because of the contributors to it, especially Trumbo's script and great performances from Paul Newman and Sal Mineo."

Austrian-born Preminger's critical reputation has diminished since his heyday in the two decades between the end of World War II and the emergence of the psychedelic generation. If he is widely known at all now, it is probably as the almost cartoonish Nazi thug he played in films like *They Got Me Covered* (1943) with Bob Hope, and Billy Wilder's *Stalag 17* (1953), an exaggerated version of the vain Prussian martinet that was once the domain of Erich von Stroheim.

But at one time he was the famous filmmaker who made celebrated hits like *Laura* (1944) and *The Man With the Golden Arm* (1955), and he nurtured his public image as a visionary tyrant. In the '60s, when his directing career was fading, he became a frequent guest on talk shows, telling stories of Hollywood and adding fresh varnish to his Teutonic persona.

Exodus arrived at a particularly interesting point in the history of American filmmaking. Television had come into its own in the '50s, forcing Hollywood to respond with bigger screen images and longer, more epic productions. At the same time directors like David Lean had proved that large-scale location epics, once the sole province of middlebrow biblical spectaculars, were also wonderful vehicles for exploring sophisticated themes and complex characters. Directors like Stanley Kramer were also using this form to delve into the kinds of social issues that Hollywood had previously considered too disturbing for mainstream audiences.

Based on a beloved bestseller, *Exodus* was not exactly a huge gamble. But it was a gamble. Its heroic celebration of the Jewish struggle to found a nation in the ashes of World War II was also unflinching in the way it addressed issues of anti-Semitism and ethnic violence. Mr. Preminger made it as a big, all-star prestige picture, pure Oscar bait. (It ended up winning only one, for Ernest Gold's majestic score, though Mineo's supporting performance as a bitter Holocaust survivor and Sam Leavitt's cinematography were also nominated.)

"When I was twelve years old this movie blew me out of my chair," Mr. Weinstein said. "Maybe it will pick up later. Let's not give up on it."

The film divides into two sections. The opening sequences, set on Cyprus, are about the efforts of a Jewish commando, Ari Ben Canaan (Mr. Newman), to smuggle Holocaust refugees into Palestine on a decrepit freighter they call the *Exodus*. Richardson plays the essentially kindhearted British commanding officer who must try to stop him, Peter Lawford is his blatantly anti-Semitic adjutant, and Ms. Saint is the American widow of a war photographer who becomes romantically involved with Ari.

Scene after scene is shot in the same stultifying manner: the camera hangs back in a midshot, getting everyone involved in the scene into the frame, and then sits there and watches them talk. Except in one or two instances, the camera never cuts within a scene to a close-up or tries to vary the rhythm of the sequences by moving in on those who are speaking or cutting to reaction shots from other actors.

One scene is emblematic: Mineo's refugee, Dov, has been injured in a fight with British soldiers and is recuperating at an internment camp, where another young refugee, Karen (played by Jill Haworth), tries to treat him. Dov has angrily refused help from the doctors until Karen scolds him, and he allows her to come near. Ms. Saint's character, Kitty Fremont, has witnessed the incident and staggers from the tent, visibly upset by the conditions under which the refugees are living.

"Now that was a well-written scene," Mr. Weinstein said. "He's being tough; she steps forward and stands up to him. The dialogue is great. But look how clumsily it's staged. You can't blame this on Trumbo. I'll bet if you read the script, it comes across perfectly. But this way, with everything shot in a master, never cutting to a close-up, everybody just kind of wandering around in front of the camera, it's deadly dull. Am I going to be the only guy who watched a movie for this series and came away thinking that the theme of the film was great but the artfulness of the moviemaking wasn't?"

Perhaps one reason the movie seemed so great to him as a boy was that it mirrored many of the stories he had heard from his father, who had been a supply sergeant in the United States Army. "He was stationed in the Middle East, and as a Jew he dealt with anti-Semitism," Mr. Weinstein said. "He was in Cairo, and I know that after the war he drifted into Israel and tried to help supply the Haganah, the Jewish underground military organization in Palestine. He would, I guess, borrow some American stuff out of supply depots. As a boy I would see some of these old Haganah guys at reunions."

Mr. Weinstein said he was weaned on stories about how the Haganah and the Irgun, another militant underground group, were able to gather the supplies they needed to take European Jewish refugees into Palestine and to push for the creation of Israel.

"In a way it seems too easy, the way they do it in this movie," he said. "But the thing is, they did do it, and without a whole lot of fanfare. It was the brilliant thing about these small groups of guerrillas, how bold they were and how courageous. I mean, they did it. They stole all this stuff. They pulled it off. That to me was the Israeli spirit. That's what *Exodus* said to me. For the Israelis to become a force in their own area, they had to be tough. You need to have, unfortunately, that kind of ruthlessness."

Whenever there was a scene that promised to unleash some energy, Mr. Weinstein would lean forward and say, "Okay, maybe now the movie will get going."

He said it when Mr. Newman made his first appearance, jumping out of a boat in the dead of night to swim ashore in Cyprus clandestinely. Mr. Newman's presence did immediately perk up the picture. "He's such a strong actor, he can hold your attention even in a crowded master shot," Mr. Weinstein said. And he said it again when the crowded ship of refugees was bottled up in the harbor in Cyprus.

In one scene Karen is standing at night at the ship's railing, telling Dov how one non-Jewish family had sheltered her for a while during the war, and Mr. Newman walks up behind them, stops, and listens. It's a glaring moment of proof of the power of a movie star. Ms. Haworth and Mineo are acting their hearts out in the scene while Mr. Newman just stands there, still as a stone. And you can't take your eyes off him.

"What a horrible thing to do to someone, to ask them to act a scene like that and then put Paul Newman in the background," Mr. Weinstein said. "I mean, for mercy's sake, could we have cut to a close-up? Let her tell her story in a close-up. Oh, my Lord. I don't want to be the guy who criticizes the movie he's watching, but holy cow."

Once again Mr. Weinstein buried his head in his hands.

And then, almost like a miracle, something happened: the movie got good.

It happened so subtly that it took a while to notice, but gradually the refugees arrive in Palestine, and the story opens up. Preminger began to take more time and care with the filmmaking. Dozens of new characters and locations are introduced; instead of hanging back with the camera, Preminger began to move in closer, staging several stirring action sequences, cutting to close-ups and reaction shots in longer, dialogue scenes. And the location work is stunning. The Israeli coast, the fertile valleys, the narrow streets of Jerusalem, the terrace of the King David Hotel: everything is presented with vivid care. It's like a different movie.

Mr. Weinstein gradually became aware of what was happening. "Look, he did two shots in that scene, a close-up cutting to a medium shot," he said. "Where did that come from? Maybe shooting in Cyprus was a pain in the neck. Maybe they shot this part first and ran out of money before they got to Cyprus. I don't know."

But from the minute it reaches Haifa, the movie picks up. The story line splits in half, following the adventures of Karen and the other members of a rural kibbutz while also tracking the urban intrigue in Jerusalem, where Dov and other members of the more radical wing of the Jewish military underground hide from the police and plot the bombing of the King David Hotel.

The mainstream wing of the movement is symbolized by Ari's father, Barak Ben Canaan (Lee J. Cobb), the leader of the kibbutz movement and a historical stand-in for David Ben-Gurion. In the book and movie the more radical wing is headed by Barak's estranged brother, Akiva Ben Canaan (David Opatoshu), a stand-in for Menachem Begin.

Ari and Kitty move back and forth between these two worlds: Kitty because she acts as the audience's on-screen counterpart, learning about the complexities of the politics along with us; Ari because he is not sure in which camp his ultimate loyalties lie.

"You see, what they are showing in these scenes is Uris's version of the history, how the early Palestinians and the Jews did get along together, before they were taught to hate each other's guts," Mr. Weinstein said. "And Newman, who's kind of in the middle, also gets to put forth the philosophy of the Uris books, which is that the Jews have no friends, and that's the way it's always been. Every time in the movie that the question comes up, Newman understands that essentially, in the end, the Jews will have to stand alone."

In perhaps the longest and most emotionally intense scene in the movie, Dov seeks to join Akiva's radical guerrilla group and is questioned about his experiences during the Holocaust. Akiva relentlessly prods him until finally Dov breaks down and confesses that he saved himself at Auschwitz by working on the grave-digging crew. It's the best scene in the movie.

"No question about that," Mr. Weinstein said. "That's a great piece of acting. Sal Mineo is great in this movie. You know, I had a grandmother who lost four brothers and three sisters in the camps, and her mother made it to Israel. I went there on a visit, and I got this lieutenant in the Israeli army to take me into the occupied territories. I never saw such hate like I saw in the eyes of the young Arab kids. They hate the Israeli soldiers. I mean, they really hate them. It's such a damn shame."

Mr. Weinstein sighed and stared back up at the screen. "Man, the movie just really kicked into gear, didn't it?" he said. "It became really good, right? I mean, it's incredible, the difference. I see Jerusalem here, and I feel like going there tomorrow."

A confrontation between Ari and Akiva is particularly vivid, each making his own eloquent arguments for what needs to be done as the United Nations prepares to vote on the partition of Palestine.

"That's writing," Mr. Weinstein said. "That's great writing. Did you hear what his uncle said? 'Terror and violence are midwives. We bring nations into the world.' What a line. That's what makes Trumbo so great. Where are the Dalton Trumbos today? Where are they? I mean, I guess you've got Steve Zaillian, maybe Eric Roth, and probably William Broyles. There are a handful, I guess. But why aren't there more movies that have this level of writing? I mean, this scene is worth the whole movie to me."

Mr. Weinstein was particularly taken with the sequence, a short while later, in which Ari leads a raid on the British military prison to rescue his uncle and other imprisoned commandos. Several teams of disguised soldiers move across rooftops, through sewers, across dusty courtyards. "Look at this Turkish bath they're going through," Mr. Weinstein said. "My lord, it's something. The amount of locations in this one sequence is staggering. There must be fifteen different locations here. And everyone has something interesting to look at."

Inside the jail, the prisoners prepare for their escape: quiet footfalls in stone corridors and tense looks in dark cells. Then an explosion.

"This is a real action movie, you know," Mr. Weinstein said. "This is about something. It has substance. It has real excitement because it's about real people. I mean, as opposed to the junk we're doing today that's called action movies. I'll tell you something, I've been wrestling with this for a long time, whether I should go make some action movies. I don't know, maybe I'd fail miserably. But I just can't believe what action movies have become. When I was a kid, we had *The Dirty Dozen* and *The Great Escape*. What do they have now? Fifty bad ones for every good one. I think I'm just going to try to produce a pure action movie."

He paused and watched the end of the raid. Ari and his uncle are on their way, but both have been wounded. The other commandos blend into the crowd without a backward glance.

"See, these guys, they go through all that, and then they don't even say good-bye," Mr. Weinstein said. "They don't shake hands, nothing. It's like, okay, we did our job. That tells you something about the characters of these Haganah guys. They had to be like that. Not like these action movies today. No story. You don't care about the characters. It's just, let's have one stunt after another stunt."

The film comes to a tragic end, and Mr. Newman's final scene is beside a double grave; two people, a Jew and an Arab, have been killed in fighting after the United Nations vote to create Israel. Standing quietly over the grave, his face awash with pain, Mr. Newman gives another beautiful Trumbo speech, this time wondering whether the Arabs and Jews will ever live together in peace. (The film is not exactly evenhanded. An effete Nazi character is seen basically organizing the Arab attacks on Jewish settlements, and the only fully rounded Arab character is Ari's boyhood friend, who ends up slaughtered for his live-and-let-live attitude.)

When it ended with a caravan of Israeli soldiers moving off and the stirring Gold score cranking up to full bore, Mr. Weinstein sighed.

"It's so sad, so tragic," he said. "The fact that now—what is it?—forty years since this movie was made, and the situation is still so awful. It breaks your heart."

Late morning had morphed into midafternoon. Lunch had been sent up from the TriBeCa Grill on the ground floor—hamburgers all around—and the empty plates littered the screening room floor. "How quickly three hours and forty minutes went, huh, guys?" Mr. Weinstein said, standing up and stretching.

It had been at least ten years since Mr. Weinstein had seen *Exodus*, he said. In many ways, watched again after so long, it did not live up to his vivid boyhood memories.

"You know, while the filmmaking might not have been so strong, you have to admire Preminger in one way because he dealt with this whole issue of anti-Semitism," Mr. Weinstein said. "I mean, who was dealing with this stuff in 1960? This is a little creaky, this movie, but I would be proud to have put this out, for what it did in 1960.

"There are some great scenes. The dialogue is so strong. I don't know. When you're a young Jew living in Queens in 1960, and you see Paul Newman as a Jewish commando, you see women fighting alongside men, you see the commitment. I guess it made Jewish-Americans proud to be Jewish, proud of Israel. It did me."

HIGHLIGHTS OF HARVEY WEINSTEIN'S CAREER AS A PRODUCER AND EXECUTIVE PRODUCER AND INFORMATION ON *EXODUS*

■

What They Watched

Exodus. Directed and produced by Otto Preminger; written by Dalton Trumbo; director of photography, Sam Leavitt; music by Ernest Gold. With Paul Newman, Eva Marie Saint, Ralph Richardson, Lee J. Cobb, Sal Mineo, Jill Haworth, and Peter Lawford. 1960.

Harvey Weinstein's Films

AS A PRODUCER

Chicago. Directed by Rob Marshall. With Renee Zellweger, Catherine Zeta-Jones, and Richard Gere. 2002.

Malèna. Directed by Giuseppe Tornatore. With Monica Bellucci and Giuseppe Sulfaro. 2000.

Shakespeare in Love. Directed by John Madden. With Gwyneth Paltrow and Joseph Fiennes. 1998.

Restoration (co-producer). Directed by Michael Hoffman. With Robert Downey Jr. and Sam Neill. 1995.

Deep End. With Pete Townshend. Originally released in Britain as *Pete Townshend's Deep End*. 1985.

The Burning. Directed by Tony Maylam. With Holly Hunter and Jason Alexander. 1981.

AS AN EXECUTIVE PRODUCER

Gangs of New York. Directed by Martin Scorsese. With Leonardo DiCaprio, Daniel Day Lewis, and Cameron Diaz. 2002.

Chocolat. Directed by Lasse Hallstrom. With Juliette Binoche, Johnny Depp, and Judi Dench. 2000.

The Cider House Rules. Directed by Lasse Hallstrom. With Tobey Maguire and Michael Caine. 1999.

Good Will Hunting. Directed by Gus Van Sant. With Matt Damon and Robin Williams. 1997.

The English Patient. Directed by Anthony Minghella. With Ralph Fiennes and Kristin Scott Thomas. 1996.

Emma. Directed by Douglas McGrath. With Gwyneth Paltrow and Jeremy Northam. 1996.

Prêt-à-Porter (*Ready-to-Wear*). Directed by Robert Altman. With Kim Basinger and Sophia Loren. 1994.

Pulp Fiction. Directed by Quentin Tarantino. With John Travolta and Samuel L. Jackson. 1994.

10

Michael Bay on
West Side Story

At the time that I sat down with Michael Bay in producer Jerry Bruckheimer's screening room he was just days away from delivering what was almost certainly his biggest and most important project to date, Disney's blockbuster re-creation of Pearl Harbor. Some whom I talked to later saw a certain amount of press-agent scheming in Bay's choice of film, *West Side Story*, perhaps a too calculated attempt to broaden his image beyond the macho action movies that had made him one of the most successful directors in Hollywood. Bay denied this, in fact told a detailed story about the effect *West Side Story* had had on him as a young film student, a story backed up by his college professor and creative mentor, Jeanine Basinger. But Bay had become something of a punching bag in Hollywood, reviled by some critics for his fast-cutting style of action, and as the opening of *Pearl Harbor* approached many people were eagerly looking for ways to attack it and its creative team. My feeling is that one need only look at the things that struck Bay about *West Side Story*—the use of color, for instance—to get a hint at how his creative mind works and where those fast cuts and fiery sunsets came from.

■

Michael Bay was just days away from putting the conclusive touches on his latest movie, the $135 million historical epic *Pearl Harbor*, and he had been working pretty much around the clock for a week, his head full of last-minute details about music, sound cues, and the color mix.

"So I thought, yeah, what better way to lose myself than to spend a few hours watching *West Side Story*?" he said. "We're, like, four days away from locking *Pearl Harbor* for good, in terms of final everything, and here I find myself watching this movie and just totally forgetting all about it. I love movies where you can kind of relax and escape."

Mr. Bay, thirty-seven, is six feet two inches tall with light brown hair and movie star looks. He strode into the new screening room at Jerry Bruckheimer Films, in a network of redbrick buildings near the Santa Monica Freeway, and moved quickly to the center seat in the back row, extending his long legs and staring down at the white flickering glare of the screen. When he moves, whether walking across a room or stretching out in a screening room chair, he does it with a very confident, athletic polish.

"What I remember about this movie, and I haven't seen it for a long time, is that you don't necessarily fall in love with the actors or the love story," Mr. Bay said. "It's more about the style and the dance and the energy and the amazing music. So I thought, okay, this is a good way to lose myself at the end of one of the hardest weeks I've ever had, on *Pearl Harbor.*"

Although he started his career making music videos for Tina Turner, Lionel Richie, and others, Mr. Bay has in a few short years become one of the most successful directors of Hollywood action blockbusters, beginning with *Bad Boys* in 1995, a buddy-cop thriller starring Martin Lawrence and Will Smith, and continuing with *The Rock* (1996), starring Sean Connery and Nicolas Cage, and *Armageddon* (1998), a hugely successful science-fiction thriller, starring Bruce Willis and Ben Affleck, about an asteroid streaking toward Earth.

In each case, Mr. Bay worked with the producer Jerry Bruckheimer, as he did again with *Pearl Harbor,* his most ambitious project in both length (2 hours 50 minutes) and scope (stretching from the air war over Europe to the Japanese attack on Hawaii to the responding air raid over Tokyo), and one of the most anticipated films of the summer of 2001. It opened in more than 3,000 theaters and had the lucrative Memorial Day weekend all to itself. No other studio dared go up against this Disney behemoth.

"Do you think people will be surprised that I picked *West Side Story* to watch?" Mr. Bay asked.

He didn't wait for an answer: "I've got to tell you, I have so many different tastes in movies. But people try to pigeonhole you. They say, 'No, he just does action.' Which is why *Pearl Harbor* will show a different side to me. It's more poetic and poignant. Despite the big action scenes, it feels like an epic old love story."

Besides, he said, musicals illustrate what it is that first drew him to filmmaking. And the kind of musicals made in 1961—when Robert Wise and the legendary choreographer Jerome Robbins directed *West Side Story*—have more in common with the blockbuster action movies of today than many filmgoers realize.

"When I was at college, at Wesleyan, I took this course in musicals from Jeanine Basinger, a great professor, a real guru on movies," Mr. Bay said. "Frankly, it was a course that I wasn't really excited to take. I wasn't sure at the time if I wanted to be a photographer or a cinematographer, but that course on musicals really opened my eyes to how far you can push the film medium and where you can take it in terms of cutting and craft. It's strange, but when filmmakers are forced to solve the problems you need to solve to shoot dance, they really find themselves using the film medium to its fullest."

Great movies—the ones that interest him and that he says he tries to make—use the medium to create a world on the screen, he said, an imaginary but convincing place conceived by the filmmaker.

"I love it, the idea of crafting and creating these worlds," Mr. Bay said. "In a way, I think it goes back to my childhood a little bit. When I was twelve or thirteen, I used to make these very elaborate train sets in my bedroom. I just loved going into my imagination and making stories about the little fake town and creating my own little disasters. It was very elaborate; detailed mountains, mom-and-pop stores, houses, trees, golf courses. The idea was to make it as realistic as I could get it.

"I remember one time my parents came into my room to have a serious talk, you know. I was spending too much time locked away with my train sets, and they wanted me to get outside more. I actually made my first movie about one of my train sets. I was doing some glue fires and the buildings caught on fire, and that caught the drapes on fire. I put most of it out, but it kind of wrecked my room. I was grounded for three weeks.

"And then, a few years later, I got a job with Lucasfilm where I was filing artwork in their library. I was filing away the artwork for the *Star Wars* movies, you know, and I remember one day coming across the production designer's blueprints for Yoda's house. That was when I really started to get interested in film, because I could see how they were creating this whole world. It was just like my train sets. Part of filmmaking is that you have to become a magician. You have to create a world, and nowhere is that more important, more essential, than with musicals. That's what *West Side Story* does. Just look at how Robert Wise creates his world."

The film's lush overture fills the small screening room. On the screen an abstract series of lines gradually expands and thickens and transforms itself into the Lower Manhattan skyline. The color keeps shifting from magenta to yellow to blue, all explosively vivid.

"Can you imagine sitting in a theater back then and just watching this?" he said. "How long does this overture go on? It must have been something, sitting there watching it with those first audiences. Can you imagine audiences doing that now? I remember, even when I saw it, I thought, 'This is weird.'"

With a flourish, the overture ends and the camera pulls back to reveal, across the bottom of the screen, the film's title. And gradually, the brightly colored abstract rendering of lower Manhattan resolves itself into a real, overhead shot of the city. The camera glides like a hawk over New York, where a street-gang version of Shakespeare's *Romeo and Juliet* plays out with a beautiful Leonard Bernstein score, lyrics by Stephen Sondheim, and a script by Ernest Lehman. The movie includes several ballads and love songs that have become classics, like "Tonight," "I Feel Pretty," and "Somewhere," and such comic gems as "America" and "Gee, Officer Krupke."

"I haven't seen this film in a long time, not since college," Mr. Bay said. "So what was that, maybe sixteen or seventeen years ago? At that point, I had been seeing a lot of musicals for Professor Basinger's course, about five of them a week, and what really struck me about this movie was how it started with this very stylized introduction and then went into the real world with real shots of New York. This first sequence, the first fifteen minutes, was really amazing to me. Watch how they do this, how they take this real world and introduce dance to it and make you buy it. You know, there's this moment, really early on, where they're walking down the street and they start doing these pirouettes and you're thinking, 'This is really weird.' But you buy it. They make you buy it. That's always the big thing when you are try-ing to put an audience into the world you are creating. You've got to make them buy it."

The camera slides over the rooftops of Manhattan, the familiar images of the Midtown towers and the United Nations gradually blending with more anonymous, densely packed neighborhoods. In contrast to the lush overture, all that is heard now is a distant high-pitched tone, like a cross between a school-yard whistle and the call of a waterbird.

"Here we go," Mr. Bay said. "I love this." With a flourish, the camera careens down into an urban playground where a group of young men lean against a chain-link fence. There is something immediately odd about them. While everyone else in the concrete yard is involved in a chaotic welter of ball playing and activity, these youths are poised in perfect configuration, and they are snapping their fingers in time to the music, as if they are on their own wave length.

When the young men—members of the Jets street gang—move through the playground, they do it with careful choreography, a kind of swaggering dance that ties them together and separates them from everyone else.

"You see the levels of stylization you have going here?" Mr. Bay said. "First, you had those abstract lines and the bright colors and the overture. And then this changed to the real world. And then, after that, you meet these guys and they're kind of in between. They exist in the real world. The real world is all around them. But at the same time they're on a different level, in their own musical dancer's world. Okay, fine. You go along with it. It's interesting. But wait. Watch. Here's where it starts to get weird."

The Jets are going down the sidewalk, moving to the music, and then one of them, then another, and finally all of them break out of their ranks and do graceful pirouettes, extending their arms, spinning and then moving back together in the street gang's swagger.

"It's very bold," Mr. Bay said. "But this is where I think you really start buying it. This is where you really understand and accept the world that's been created for the movie."

Others are introduced, without dialogue: members of a rival Puerto Rican street gang called the Sharks. The dance begins to tell a story. In comical set pieces, the gangs encounter each other, their movements always part realistic, part dance. "They don't say anything, but you're able to follow what's happening through the dance and the staging and you're sort of mesmerized," Mr. Bay said. "It's the whole vibe. The colors, the costumes, the attitude. They're explaining the whole Jets-Sharks turf war to us. Oh, I love that cut."

Three members of the Sharks, dancing forward, swaying from side to side, move toward the camera and seem to run right into it. There is a cut as one of their bodies covers the lens and, just as suddenly, they are moving away from the camera down the street, their backs to the camera. "That's great; it's like the camera moved right through them," Mr. Bay said. "I love dynamic things like that. Look at this, too, how the dancers are really close to us in the foreground while the buildings are looming up in the background. It's very dynamic. Wise was a film editor, you know. You can see it in this movie. See how precise everything is, transition to transition. All these great cuts. Man, I've stolen things from this movie and I haven't even known it."

That's what *West Side Story* is about to him, Mr. Bay said: the energy and dynamism of some of the sequences, especially the gang scenes and the dances, as well as the way the movie creates a universe with its own logic and look.

"They take this real world and they segue you into this fake world, this dance-stylized world, and then they mix the two worlds together," Mr. Bay said. "And later in the movie, just like the Jets have their own world-within-a-world, when Tony and Maria, the two lovers, get together, they have yet another distinct, stylized world that's just for the two of them. It's a world-within-a-world-within-a-world. There are so many levels of stylization, and sometimes they all come together in the same scenes. That's what really excited me about musicals. I know it sounds kind of strange, but you can really let yourself go in musicals."

Even when the opening sequence ends, moving quickly into the film's first song and dialogue scene, the mood continues. Russ Tamblyn, George Chakiris, and the other gang members talk in a rhythmic way. It is not singing, but it is definitely syncopated, like somebody's idea of conversational blank verse recited by a group. And the effect only becomes more pronounced when others in the film— like Simon Oakland's racist cop and Ned Glass's kindly candy store owner— speak normally.

The various levels of reality extend even to the film's sets and locations: a mixture of authentic Manhattan streetscapes and stylized versions of them lighted with the kind of bold colors pioneered by Vincente Minnelli and popular with many musical directors from the late 1940s to the twilight of the musical in the 1960s.

"That's a real location, no question about it," Mr. Bay said during one sequence on a basketball court. Later, in an alley, with a bold, red light on the background wall and a chilly blue emanating from windows to the side, he remarked, "That's a set." Real location, studio set. That was the whole point. The film was creating a world where the two kinds of reality could fit side by side, just as the dancing street gangs mingled with the ordinary people walking down the street.

"What I like about musicals is that they break the rules of cinema," Mr. Bay said. "You know what I'm saying? The old rules of editing where, it's said, you must cut from this to this. You can't cut from here to there. You can't place the camera there; you have to place it here. When I do my action movies, I break the rules, too. That's one thing musicals and big action movies have in common. With both of them, you can break the rules. One of the things that can make them exciting is that you are breaking the rules."

The use of privileged angles puts the camera where, logically, it cannot be—for example, in the middle of what viewers know should be a wall. In musicals, audiences are willing to accept the use of some privileged angles. Viewers understand that the world being presented is not meant to mirror the real world. The same license sometimes works for action movies, Mr. Bay said.

"Like there is this shot in *Pearl Harbor* where the camera follows this bomb all the way from the Japanese plane, falling through the air over the battleship until it crashed through the deck and explodes below," he said.

It is impossible. No camera could do this. But the audience will accept it. In the service of the action, he said, the audience will allow a certain suspension of the ordinary rules of filmmaking, just as it will with musicals. In the case of his plummeting-bomb view, Mr. Bay said, it is done to achieve a heightened reality rather than a musical fantasy world. But remember, he said, hyperreality is a kind of stylization, too.

No matter how realistic it is, the miniature world of the train set is not real, and part of the pleasure comes from knowing this and enjoying the craftsmanship that made it so convincing.

In the rooftop dance in which the Shark men face off against the Shark women to sing "America," Mr. Bay noted the twilight urban setting, the surrounding water towers, and the backdrop of shaded windows. "I really hadn't realized there are so many music videos that were basically stolen from this movie," he said. "It was so influential. I mean, how many commercials and Janet Jackson videos have copied this one scene alone?"

West Side Story won ten Oscars, including best picture, best directors, best cinematography (Daniel L. Fapp), and both supporting acting awards (for Mr. Chakiris's performance as the leader of the Sharks and Rita Moreno's as his girlfriend). It continued a cycle of bigbudget musicals that frequently dominated the Academy Awards from Minnelli's *American in Paris* in 1951 through such later films as *My Fair Lady* and *The Sound of Music* in the mid-'60s. In a way, Mr. Bay said, the big musicals of that era had an audience appeal similar to that of today's big action movies—escapism with high production values.

The doomed lovers in *West Side Story* are the good-natured Tony (Richard Beymer), a former member of the Jets, and Maria (Natalie Wood), the sister of the leader of the Sharks, who try to overcome the gang rivalry to forge a romance. As in Shakespeare, Tony is unwittingly involved in a killing, and the romance withers into tragedy. In this version, though, there is the added, very American angle of racism and ethnicity: Maria and the Sharks are Puerto Rican; Tony and the Jets are Irish and Italian. The Verona for which they fight is a grubby grid of Upper West Side slums.

As Mr. Bay watches *West Side Story* and measures it against his memory, most of his comments fall into four categories. He is struck by Mr. Wise's dynamic cuts, by the vivid use of color, by the differences in texture between the scenes shot on location and those shot in the studio, and by how much, true to his recollection, he finds the central love story and the lead actors uninteresting.

Some of the cuts, like those involving the prowling gangs, clearly excite Mr. Bay. "Oh, man, that's a great cut, so precise," he said at one point. "Another great cut, look at this."

What, he is asked, makes a cut great?

"It's just something that, *pow!,* adds energy or gives you a surge," Mr. Bay said, and is silent for several minutes.

"It's really hard," he finally said. "It's very hard to describe what makes a good cut. I know it when I see it. It's an internal thing."

Like most musicals of the period, *West Side Story* also frequently alerts audiences that it is taking place in an artificial world by using bold and unnatural colors. In many sequences the room walls or building exteriors are lighted with bright red or yellow, and there are strange mixes of colors, like icy blues next to cozy ambers. Sometimes the gangs' colors (blue for Jets, red for Sharks) are used as a symbolic backdrop.

"I don't like too many colors in a shot," Mr. Bay said. "I like blues. Remember that last shot, the one with the door in it?" He was referring to a scene in Maria's bedroom. Its door is made up of a dozen small, colored glass panes, a checkerboard of red, blue, yellow, and green panels. "Too many colors. I would never shoot a scene in that room. Never. I have an aversion to that door. I don't know why. It's just my eye. Fewer colors are just more pleasing to me. Now look at this shot of the alley. This is nice. Not too many colors, and you've got this warm orange next to the cold green. Yeah, this is better."

At the end of the film, when the screen goes dark and the lights come up, Mr. Bay said that his memories of the film were fairly accurate. Again, he found the dance sequences and the scenes of the gangs energizing. And, again, he found the love story uninvolving and the lead performances bland. He was especially put off by Mr. Beymer's Tony, who seems too much the choirboy to be a former gang member and neighborhood legend.

"No way this guy is the cofounder of the Jets," Mr. Bay said.

"When he appears, I find myself starting to zone out. He doesn't look like a tough guy. He's a little too femme for that, you know? I don't buy him in this role. I must tell you, you just can't fake it with acting. I think guys in the audience can sense when you're not a guy's guy. That's why, you know, I was pitched some actors for *Pearl Harbor,* and good actors, too, who are great in other kinds of roles, and I'd have to say to the agents, 'Sorry, I don't really think he's a guy's guy.'"

Overall, though, he felt that *West Side Story* had once again provided him with the escapism that he wanted to distract him from the myriad details of finishing his own movie.

He stood up, collected his empty water bottle and a stack of papers. His jacket was draped over the back of an adjacent chair; he retrieved it and slid it onto his long arms.

"You really think people will find it weird that I picked a musical to watch?" Mr. Bay asked. "I guess it sounds kind of funny. But you know, the thing about filmmaking is that you grow. You grow and you change and your tastes change. Each movie I've made, I did for a specific reason, and each of the last three of them, before *Pearl Harbor,* were popcorn movies. *Bad Boys* basically had no script and it was about the charisma of the two stars. *The Rock* had a kind of outlandish story, but it had very classy actors in it and it was exciting and energetic. *Armageddon* is like a total fantasy for a fifteen-year-old. It's funny—when the critics tried to review *Armageddon,* I mean, relax, it's a popcorn movie. It's not supposed to be taken seriously. It's a fantasy world."

That is true of *Pearl Harbor,* too. It presents a fantasy world—Michael Bay's vision of what it would have been like to be there, with privileged angles and digitally enhanced sound. But it is different, too, he said, because its subject is more serious and its ambitions are higher. It is a gourmet popcorn movie.

"What I love most about movies is creating my own world," Mr. Bay said. "That's what I tried to do with *The Rock* and with *Armageddon.* With *Pearl Harbor,* it's a more realistic world, but it is still creating my own world. The same as they did with *West Side Story.* We had to do some unreal things. We had to mix real footage with digital footage. It's a false reality, but its purpose is to make it feel more authentic."

Mr. Bay remembered his mother's visit to the *Pearl Harbor* set in

Mexico, the same huge water tank where James Cameron filmed much of *Titanic*. On the set, Mr. Bay and his team had constructed portions of Battleship Row, the central cluster of military vessels that were hit by Japanese bombers on December 7, 1941.

"The crew had put up this director's chair for her and put a sign on it that said 'Mom,'" Mr. Bay said. "And she came and sat down and looked around, and it was all really just massive. And she said, 'Oh, it kind of looks like your train set, only bigger.'"

HIGHLIGHTS OF MICHAEL BAY'S DIRECTING CAREER AND INFORMATION ON *WEST SIDE STORY*

What They Watched

West Side Story. Directed by Jerome Robbins and Robert Wise; produced by Robert Wise; screenplay by Ernest Lehman; music by Leonard Bernstein; cinematography by Daniel L. Fapp. With Natalie Wood, Richard Beymer, Russ Tamblyn, Rita Moreno, and George Chakiris. 1961.

Michael Bay's Films

Pearl Harbor. With Ben Affleck, Josh Hartnett, Kate Beckinsale, Tom Sizemore, Cuba Gooding Jr., Jon Voight, Alec Baldwin, and Dan Aykroyd. 2001.

Armageddon. With Bruce Willis, Billy Bob Thornton, Ben Affleck, and Liv Tyler. 1998.

The Rock. With Sean Connery and Nicolas Cage. 1996.

Bad Boys. With Will Smith and Martin Lawrence. 1995.

11

Julianne Moore on
Rosemary's Baby

In many ways, the session with Julianne Moore was the least typical of the series and the most typical of the way most celebrity interviews take place. She lives in Manhattan, and was in California only for a few days, to take part in a press junket for her upcoming film, *Evolution* The studio that released the film, Dream-Works, wedged in a few hours in the middle of a day of interviews for her to watch *Rosemary's Baby* with me in a suite at a Beverly Hills hotel. The interview came sandwiched between a bunch of other, assembly line–style meetings with groups of entertainment reporters from around the country. And we watched the film not in some state-of-the-art screening room but on a regular twenty-seven-inch television and a VCR borrowed from the hotel. She arrived dressed in a simple blue-denim outfit, but looking almost shockingly beautiful. She was happy to be away from the rat-a-tat interviews and eager to watch the film. The studio had set out an array of cinema-style treats—Milk Duds, Three Musketeers bars, Junior Mints—and she grabbed a box of something sweet and sat down on the sofa across from the set.

■

The camera sweeps with a creeping, predatory slowness over the towers of the East Side of Manhattan, sliding up Fifth Avenue along Central Park's billowy treetops and then turning, moving across the Great Lawn and the reservoir, up along the side of the San Remo apartments on Central Park West, then pausing again, dipping and now gliding like a hawk over the pinnacles and protrusions of the Dakota. All the while, the credits of *Rosemary's Baby* appear on the screen in the pretty script you might see on a greeting card or a baby shower invitation. And the music is a woman's voice intoning a lullaby that is at once beautiful and sad, like something a young mother might sing over a baby's grave.

"This used to terrify me, just terrify me," said Julianne Moore, popping a Milk Dud into her mouth and staring at the television screen with happy, fearful anticipation. "It's like a mother's lullaby, only really creepy. Look at the Dakota, how terrifying it looks, and yet normal at the same time. I used to live a block from there on Seventy-first Street. Wow, I love the beginning of this movie."

Ms. Moore was leaning back on a sofa in her suite at the W Hotel in Westwood. She was in the midst of a long weekend of interviews for her latest movie, *Evolution,* a comedy about alien invaders, and the distributing studio, DreamWorks, had set up a VCR, rounded up not one but two copies of the movie (just in case), and set out an array of movie theater candies. "Oh, I didn't know they'd do this," Ms. Moore said. "I brought my own." She pulled a box of Hot Tamales from her pocket.

The credits end ("Written and directed by Roman Polanski") with the camera hovering over the arched West Seventy-second Street entrance to the Dakota. Far below, we can make out two tiny figures moving along the sidewalk toward the entrance.

"This is the first movie that came to mind when I thought of what I wanted to watch," Ms. Moore said. "I think it's the most unbelievable example of female paranoia that exists. I mean, here is a woman who is trapped in a situation in which every authority figure she turns to, every avenue she explores, turns against her. She finds her power not in overcoming the horror of her situation but, in a way, accepting it."

She laughed and popped another Milk Dud.

"The camera work is extraordinary; the acting is superb," she said. "It's a movie movie. And it's just one of those movies that, I don't know, bring you to another place cinematically. Those are the kind of movies I like."

And there is one more thing. "I love devil movies," Ms. Moore said. "I'm not entirely sure why. I don't really like horror movies—I mean, things like slasher movies. People with knives don't scare me. That's almost too realistic to be scary. But I remember seeing this movie when I was a kid called *The Reincarnation of Peter Proud*. I haven't seen it since. It's probably terrible. But I remember it being absolutely terrifying. I think I always found movies about the occult or the devil exciting and scary because they're about people who suddenly find that the world is out of control, that they're in this sort of morass. And let's face it, the devil is a glamorous foe in film."

While Ms. Moore can be very analytical, particularly when discussing the performances in the film and the way Mr. Polanski's direction accentuates them and pulls viewers through the story, more often she is simply caught up in the experience of watching the film again. "Wow, isn't that great?" she will say after a shot that impresses her, or, "Look at that, did you see that?" after an acting moment that strikes her as particularly subtle and difficult. For her, watching *Rosemary's Baby* is a pure pleasure, and watching it with someone else is a cause for sharing the pleasure, not for beating it to death at every turn with analysis.

Wearing a denim jacket over blue jeans and square-toed black boots, she props her feet up on a coffee table. On the screen, the eternally off-kilter Elisha Cook Jr. is showing a young couple, played by Mia Farrow and John Cassavetes, around an old but spacious apartment. The camera glides with them from room to room, pausing to study the threadbare furnishings owned by the apartment's previous occupant, a recently deceased elderly woman. Sometimes all three of them are in the frame, sometimes only one or two. The camera will sometimes precede them into a new room; at other times, it will follow them.

"That's what's kind of lovely about this movie," Ms. Moore said. "You watch a lot of other movies from this period, and the scenes often feel very static or set up, but this one doesn't. It flows, like real life. And when you examine the shots, like this one, they're really pretty complicated. There's a lot of movement and choreography to make them come out looking this unforced and natural. And look how Polanski always keeps people on the edge of the frame.

"It adds tension, but in a subtle way," she said. "You keep wanting to look around the edge of the frame, but you can't."

Ms. Moore, thirty-nine, has become one of the busiest actresses in Hollywood. In 2001 alone, she has already starred in *Hannibal* and *Evolution,* and had finished two more films that were awaiting release, starring opposite Kevin Spacey in *The Shipping News,* Meryl Streep and Nicole Kidman in *The Hours,* and Billy Crudup in *World Traveler* (written and directed by Bart Freundlich, Ms. Moore's companion and the father of her three-and-a-half-year-old son, Caleb).

She appeared in two films in 2000, five in 1999, and four in 1998. In the thirteen years since she won a Daytime Emmy Award as best ingenue for a regular role on *As the World Turns,* Ms. Moore has appeared in thirty-three movies, earning Oscar nominations for *The End of the Affair* in 2000 and *Boogie Nights* in 1998.

Rosemary's Baby, when seen again, evades the quagmire that sinks many older films: it maintains its dramatic power while remaining very much a creature of its period, the late 1960s. It was one of the most eagerly awaited films of 1968, based on the hugely popular novel by Ira Levin and starring Ms. Farrow, one of the era's hottest young actresses.

Many who had read the book went to the film wondering how Mr. Polanski, then known mostly to foreign film enthusiasts for dramas like *Knife in the Water* (1962) and *Repulsion* (1965), was going to handle the story's sexual aspects, and whether he would choose, at the end, to show what Rosemary's baby looked like.

The story of *Rosemary's Baby* was once familiar to pretty much any literate, attentive American, and it has been copied countless times since. Rosemary and her husband, Guy, an aspiring actor, move into an apartment and find themselves surrounded by a gaggle of elderly, eccentric neighbors, particularly Roman and Minnie Castavet (Sidney Blackmer and Ruth Gordon), who live right next door.

At first Rosemary insists that she and a very reluctant Guy befriend the couple, whom she imagines are lonely. Later, when she finds them a little creepy and intrusive, she wants to pull back. But then, mysteriously, it is Guy who insists that they get closer to the couple. After a romantic dinner with him, ending with a strange-tasting chocolate mousse brought over by Minnie (she pronounces it "chocolate mouse"), Rosemary passes out and has weird, frightening dreams in which she is stripped and seemingly assaulted by a demon-like creature.

Shortly afterward, she becomes pregnant and begins to fear that the kooky neighbors are actually devil worshipers who have designs on using her baby in some kind of blood ritual. The truth is even more horrifying: the experience was no dream, and she is carrying Satan's child.

"What's going to be interesting about watching this movie again after so long is to see how Polanski pulls it off," Ms. Moore said. "At the beginning of the movie, it's all about this normal young couple, although there is an undertone of creepiness. But fairly quickly, Guy begins to recede, and we see the movie almost entirely through Rosemary's eyes. She becomes more and more isolated. And since we are seeing the story through her, we share in her growing fears and paranoia."

What really impresses Ms. Moore about the opening scenes is Mr. Polanski's control of tone. "It's great," she said, "because he can keep things creepy yet, at the same time, make everybody appear to be very normal and bustling and happy."

Rosemary meets a young woman in the basement laundry room. She is living with Minnie and Roman, who have kind of adopted her, and she shows Rosemary an ornate, odd-smelling ball necklace that the couple have given her.

"This New York City basement laundry is just so perfect," Ms. Moore said. "And it's just so authentic. Almost every big apartment building in New York has a room in the basement like this, kind of creepy, with that right-next-to-the-boiler feeling. And it's great, too, how Polanski brings in the smells of things. Later, when Rosemary eats Minnie's chocolate mousse, she says that it has a chalky undertaste. He's always making a point of how things taste funny or smell bad. It's another way of pulling you into the story and raising the tension."

Guy and Rosemary first meet their next-door neighbors when, in the very next scene, they join a crowd of people looking at a dead body on the pavement. It is the young woman Rosemary met in the laundry room, apparently a suicide. "She's dead already?" Ms. Moore asked. "Only one scene? That's funny; I had remembered them having a much bigger relationship. I guess the reason you remember it being a bigger part is that Polanski has made it so important in the story."

The audience is introduced to Roman and Minnie out here, on the sidewalk, reacting to the young woman's death. They appear to be almost stereotypical New York eccentrics: he's dressed in a flaming pink suit, and she's, well, she's Ruth Gordon.

"I love her in this," Ms. Moore said. "Because she is so eccentric, and we've all had neighbors like this in New York."

Since we are watching very closely, waiting for the moment when the movie shifts and begins to play solely through Rosemary's perspective, we spot it immediately. And it is very interesting, for two reasons.

The camera is above a double bed, pointing straight down and gradually sliding from left to right. It is dark and late at night, and the only sound to be heard is the ticking of a bedside clock. The camera pans across a sleeping Guy to a close-up of Rosemary's face, wide awake. It is Ms. Farrow's first real close-up in the film. We hear the ticking of the clock, and then the camera moves up toward the wall—the wall that we know separates Rosemary's bedroom from the neighbors' apartment—and she hears faint religious chanting beyond the wall and slips into the first dream sequence. The motif is used frequently throughout the film, the ticking of the clock signaling that the movie is about to move into spooky, usually dreamy territory.

Shortly after, Guy comes home from a day stumping for acting jobs—he has just lost a very important one—and we can tell from the moment he walks through the door that he is depressed. Rosemary doesn't notice it at first because she is afraid to tell him that she has promised Roman and Minnie that they'll come over for dinner.

"John Cassavetes is so good in this," Ms. Moore said. "And it's all right here in this scene. Look, you can tell from the moment he walks through the door that he's depressed. He doesn't say anything, but you can tell by his body language and the way he gets irritated with her chattering in the next room. You see how defeated he is about something. Then you can see him try to rally, to get over whatever is bugging him. But what's great is that he conveys this, but he also conveys a certain vanity, an actor's vanity. He plays an actor, and you can see that in the performance. And it's all done with such great, great subtlety."

During the dinner with Roman and Minnie—the elderly couple prattling on about nothing, the younger couple trying to look interested—Ms. Moore notices something about Rosemary that hadn't struck her before.

"Look at all the dresses they make her wear in this," Ms. Moore said. "They all make her look so childlike. Mia Farrow was already very young-looking and very pretty, but when they put her in these big collars and cuffs, it's so infantalizing."

The next day, after Guy has had a mysterious conversation with Roman that Rosemary cannot quite overhear, and after, much to her surprise, he has made a subsequent visit to the neighbors' apartment, the phone rings. Then Mr. Polanski gives us the first of three famous scenes in which we peer through a doorway from another room as someone, just out of view, talks on the telephone. In this first scene we listen as Guy learns that he has the part after all, since the actor who first won it has mysteriously gone blind. Later, again from Rosemary's perspective, we listen to Minnie making an appointment for her with a well-known New York obstetrician, who turns out to be a Satanist also, of course. The same sort of shot is used as Rosemary learns that one of her best friends, who had been researching witchcraft on her behalf, is dead.

"It is just so tense, and it's all done in the directing," Ms. Moore said. "We're just straining, trying to see around that corner to where they're on the phone, and we can't."

One day Guy suddenly announces that he wants a baby immediately. Rosemary is a little puzzled—he has been acting strangely—but goes along with him and organizes a romantic candlelight dinner. It is at the end of this meal that Minnie provides her chalky-tasting chocolate mousse.

"Just take a look at what Rosemary is wearing," Ms. Moore said. "No more childlike dresses for her."

Ms. Farrow is wearing a sexy bright-red pantsuit, symbolic of the blood sacrifice she is about to become.

Here the movie takes a hard turn toward horror. Rosemary, drugged by whatever is in the mousse, staggers down the long hallway in their apartment. "What a beautiful shot," Ms. Moore said. "Look at her in that red outfit with that big round light hanging in the kitchen like a moon." As Rosemary staggers forward, Guy catches her, and the camera turns and follows them as he leads her toward the bedroom. Another large hanging light dominates this end of the hallway, too, but it's not spherical. It's pointed and sharp-looking. "It's like a knife hanging over her head," Ms. Moore said.

The scenes in which Rosemary half-hallucinates her Satanic ordeal are fairly strong, even by today's standards. She imagines herself nude on a yacht with a group of well-to-do people. Drifting in and out of consciousness, she feels herself lifted and carried into Roman and Minnie's apartment, where she is laid on a kind of altar. Roman, Minnie, Guy, and all of the others are standing around, nude, chanting, and Satan appears out of the shadows. "This isn't a dream," Rosemary screams. "This is really happening!"

Ms. Moore slapped her knees. "Whew, excuse me, but that is absolutely terrifying," she said.

"It's all really happening," she said. "That's what's so great. It validates every paranoia you ever had. Here is a person who says, 'They're out to get me,' and they really are out to get her. People are saying, 'Oh, it's just in your head, you're just imagining things.' But she's not. That's what's so terrifying."

Born in North Carolina, Ms. Moore traveled all over the world, moving with her military family from base to base. For several years, they lived in Alaska, then in her early teens, Virginia, and during her high school years, Germany. "I think I was about fifteen when I first saw *Rosemary's Baby*," she said. "I was living in Virginia and I saw it on television. I just stumbled across it, basically."

When she first saw the movie, Ms. Moore said, she had no intention of becoming an actress. As a young girl, she wanted to be a doctor. "Movies came much later," she said. "I came to acting through books and then theater. Movies came last." And while she loved movies, she said, neither she nor her parents were film connoisseurs.

"I saw a lot of movies in the seventies on television, and beyond that, I saw a lot in the theaters," Ms. Moore said. "Basically, I went to see whatever was playing. Living in Alaska, and then on the base in

Germany, you had only one theater, and they changed the movie every week. So I just went to see whatever was playing. Everything. I remember seeing *Minnie and Moskowitz*, and I saw *One Day in the Life of Ivan Denisovich*, and of course I saw all the popcorn movies, too. It was good, in a way, to just see everything. It teaches you taste."

Shortly after the rape scene, *Rosemary's Baby* abruptly changes tone again. Rosemary is delighted to learn that she is pregnant, and the whole look and feel of the film become cheerier. When Guy comes home and she tells him the news, she is glowing with it.

"The movie changes in tone, and you go with it," Ms. Moore said. She caught herself, noticing something in Cassavetes's performance. "Oh, oh, look, is he crying? Yes, just for a moment. That was beautiful. What a perfect moment. Wow. I mean, how great was that? There were like fifteen things going on at the same time in his performance. He can't look her in the eye; then he starts to cry, and then he says he wants to go tell Minnie and Roman. And that's when you see where his obvious excitement is, that he gets to take the good news to them. There's such tremendous texture in this movie."

For Ms. Moore, the most effective scene comes after a party Rosemary has given for some of the couple's younger friends. She looks terrible and breaks down in tears about the pain she has been suffering. Afterward, Guys berates her for revealing this to her girlfriends.

"It's all played in a medium shot, with no intercutting," Ms. Moore said. "See how they're at different sides of the room, and the camera just sits back and watches them. It's all one take. And it's all very upsetting, because you feel trapped in the argument with them and you can see the tension in their bodies. Polanski is letting the rhythm of the argument control the pace of the scene."

Rosemary is weeping, angry, complaining about the constant pain she has been suffering when suddenly, miraculously, the pain stops. The relief spills across her face.

"This is her best scene in the movie, so far," Ms. Moore said. "Mia Farrow is so good in this, and it's such a hard part. So much of it is reactive. And being passive is always much more difficult."

In the very next scene she is smiling, painting the nursery. "Here we are now; we're happy again," Ms. Moore said. "Polanski keeps yanking us back and forth between cheerful and frightened. You keep getting these little dabs of comedy, all the way through. Ruth

Gordon and the other neighbors are basically played for comic effect. That's how the horror is introduced in this movie, as comedy. It's never the dominant tone, but it's there. It's like in *Macbeth,* you know? Somehow it makes the horror even more horrible."

Eventually, Rosemary realizes that her neighbors are actually Satanists and that her husband is in on it. She tries to escape, fails, and is brought back to her apartment to be drugged again and to have the baby. Afterward, she is told that the baby has died. That night she grabs a butcher knife from the kitchen and finds the hidden entrance to Roman and Minnie's apartment.

"This is the last stage in her becoming stronger and more mature," Ms. Moore said. "We haven't seen her in children's clothes for a long time."

In previous night scenes, Rosemary padded around the apartment in big blue fuzzy slippers. But tonight the slippers have changed to plain beige ones. "Oh, yeah," Ms. Moore said. "Watch out. She's got on the sensible slippers."

Rosemary wanders into Roman and Minnie's living room, crowded with Satanists who gradually become aware of her. On the other side of the room is a black cradle. A few of the people are chanting, but for the most part, it looks like an ordinary cocktail party. No one seems more than mildly alarmed that Rosemary has wandered in with a butcher knife and sensible slippers.

"How spooky is this, huh?" Ms. Moore said.

Rosemary pulls back the curtain on the bassinet and sees her baby for the first time. The camera does not show the child. All we get is Rosemary's stunned, disgusted reaction: "What did you do to his eyes?"

Ms. Moore shakes her head and takes in a loud lungful of air. "That is my favorite line in the movie," she said. "And my second favorite is the next one."

Roman walks over to Rosemary's side. "He has his father's eyes," he says.

Rosemary drops the knife and wanders over to sit and drink a cup of tea, totally bewildered. The baby begins to cry, and she looks up. One of the other women is rocking him quite fast. "You're rocking him too hard," Rosemary says. Despite the other woman's objection, Roman invites Rosemary to come over and rock the baby properly.

"Aren't you his mother?" he says. The crowd of people moves between us and the cradle. And the strange lullaby that opened the movie begins again.

"Oh, it gives me chills," Ms. Moore said. "Because it's so complex, you know. There isn't an easy answer here. It's all gray, all ambiguous. What is she supposed to do? She is his mother. I love movies that have ambiguous endings. I like the end of *McCabe and Mrs. Miller,* where Julie Christie is just lying there smoking an opium pipe. Did she know McCabe was being shot? Was she too drugged to save him? Or did she just let him die? We don't know. I'm always excited by that kind of complexity and ambiguity, and this movie has it. *Rosemary's Baby* is such a great movie. It's all gray."

HIGHLIGHTS OF JULIANNE MOORE'S ACTING CAREER AND INFORMATION ON *ROSEMARY'S BABY*

■

What They Watched

Rosemary's Baby. Written and directed by Roman Polanski. With Mia Farrow, John Cassavetes, Ruth Gordon, Sidney Blackmer, Maurice Evans, Ralph Bellamy, and Elisha Cook Jr. 1968.

Julianne Moore's Films

Far from Heaven. Directed by Todd Haynes. With Dennis Quaid and Patricia Clarkson. 2002.

The Hours. Directed by Stephen Daldry. With Meryl Streep and Nicole Kidman. 2002.

The Shipping News. Directed by Lasse Hallstrom. With Kevin Spacey and Judi Dench. 2001.

Evolution. Directed by Ivan Reitman. With David Duchovny and Orlando Jones. 2001.

Hannibal. Directed by Ridley Scott. With Anthony Hopkins and Ray Liotta. 2001.

Magnolia. Directed by Paul Thomas Anderson. With Tom Cruise and Jason Robards. 1999.

The End of the Affair. Directed by Neil Jordan. With Ralph Fiennes and Stephen Rea. 1999.

An Ideal Husband. Directed by Oliver Parker. With Rupert Everett and Cate Blanchett. 1999.

The Big Lebowski. Directed by Joel Coen. With Jeff Bridges and John Goodman. 1998.

Boogie Nights. Directed by Paul Thomas Anderson. With Mark Wahlberg and Burt Reynolds. 1997.

The Lost World: Jurassic Park. Directed by Steven Spielberg. With Jeff Goldblum and Pete Postlethwaite. 1997.

Surviving Picasso. Directed by James Ivory. With Anthony Hopkins and Natascha McElhone. 1996.

Nine Months. Directed by Chris Columbus. With Hugh Grant and Tom Arnold. 1996.

Safe. Directed by Todd Haynes. With Peter Friedman and Xander Berkeley. 1995.

Vanya on 42nd Street. Directed by Louis Malle. With Wallace Shawn and André Gregory. 1994.

Short Cuts. Directed by Robert Altman. With Matthew Modine and Madeleine Stowe. 1993.

The Hand That Rocks the Cradle. Directed by Curtis Hanson. With Rebecca De Mornay and Annabella Sciorra. 1992.

12

Kevin Smith on
A Man for All Seasons

When I told my editors that I wanted to do an installment with Kevin Smith both because I wanted to get more young filmmakers into the series and because I'd met him before, liked him, and considered him extremely smart about film, they were initially dubious, worried that the director best known for rude jokes about flatulence and casual drug use would go out of his way to pick something vulgar and unsuitable. I assured them that was not the case. But even I was a little taken aback when Smith said he wanted to watch *A Man for All Seasons*. He arrived a little late to his editing bungalow on the CBS Studio Center lot in the San Fernando Valley, dressed in his standard attire of shorts, T-shirt, and a baseball cap. But once he'd shooed some assistant editors out of a room with the biggest viewing monitor and slipped the DVD of the film into the machine, he began unleashing a torrent of comments about a film that meant so much to him. So much did he have to say that the resulting transcript turned out to be the longest of any the series produced.

■

Words, words, words. They come spilling out of *A Man for All Seasons* in great torrents that spin and swell into rapids, a furious river of words. And Paul Scofield wraps his dour face and deep-timbred voice around Robert Bolt's dialogue with such satisfying, calculated calibration.

Kevin Smith laughed and nodded his head. "This language, it's so great," he said, leaning back again in a swivel chair in his baby-blue bungalow on the CBS Studio Center lot, where he was finishing the editing on *Jay and Silent Bob Strike Back,* his latest sex-and-drugs comedy.

In one scene, Mr. Scofield, playing the soon-to-be-martyred Sir Thomas More in Henry VIII's England, argues with his sanctimonious son-in-law over the importance of laws. Will Roper, the son-in-law, wants to cut down any laws that get in the way of defeating the devil's work.

"And when the last law was cut down and the devil turned round on you, where would you hide, Roper, the laws all being flat? This country is planted thick with laws, from coast to coast—man's laws, not God's—and if you cut them down, and you're just the man to do it, do you really think you could stand upright in the winds that would blow then?" Mr. Scofield pauses for just a beat. "Yes," he continues, "I give the devil benefit of law for my own safety's sake."

Mr. Smith's comfortably cluttered bungalow is a stone's throw from Ventura Boulevard and just across a concrete canal from the fenced-in compound where production is under way on the latest installment of the network's *Big Brother* reality series. People on the lot have been warned to steer clear of the compound and not tell anyone where it is. It's a big secret.

"The dialogue in this movie—it pops, you know," Mr. Smith said, snapping his fingers. "Back and forth and back and forth. And let's face it, this is a movie that's pretty much all dialogue."

To Mr. Smith, that's the greatest pleasure, seeing how dramatic momentum can come not from action but from the interplay of words and ideas. "Actually, that's what I try to do in my movies," he said. "That's all I'm good at. I don't even think I try to do it; it's just the only thing I can do. I'm terrible at action, but pretty decent at dialogue. And I always thought that this movie had a lot to do with why I write the way I write. Because this is such a definitive film for me. Lord knows, I love popcorn movies as much as the next guy. The *Star Wars* films were a huge part of my life. But this is one of the first movies that introduced me to the notion of dialogue and character and nothing else really needing to happen."

Mr. Smith, thirty, knows he might seem an uneasy fit for the director Fred Zinnemann's dense drama of ideas and intellectual heroism. Beginning with *Clerks* (1994), a witty and ragtag story about young men working dead-end jobs in a New Jersey strip mall, Mr. Smith has earned a reputation for a kind of cheerful, pop-infused vulgarity that snaps with self-deprecating wit. But while he stresses that he does not claim to be the equal of either Zinnemann or Bolt, he does feel a kind of kinship between their work and his quick-bantering comedies of male immaturity, which reside, as he puts it, in a world of jokes about genitalia and flatulence.

"*A Man for All Seasons* has some beautiful scenes in it, but it is not a visually stunning film," Mr. Smith said. "I only wish I were talented enough to pull off a really talky film that's not visually stunning but still gets the job done. All the flicks I've done, people are always going, 'Wow, he's not a really good visual stylist—his films tend to be about dialogue.' Well, this film is all about dialogue, too, but nobody ever calls Zinnemann on the fact that it's not visually popping because he's so skillful that he's able to tell the story in a way that, despite all the dialogue, it doesn't feel static. I wish I could do that."

The short, thick, bearded Mr. Smith is familiar to moviegoers for the small parts he plays in his own films. (In his latest one, he is the wordless Silent Bob to his co-star Jason Mewes's motormouth Jay.) And as he moved through the suite of offices and into the editing room to watch *A Man for All Seasons,* he looked very much like Silent Bob, right down to the doleful eyes and the backward baseball cap. Once in the editing room, the door closed and the DVD slid into the bank of technical gizmos, he pulled out a pack of cigarettes and began to snap it loudly on his forearm.

"Why this movie?" he asked as he watched the credits roll. "It's been a favorite of mine since I was a kid. The first time I saw it was when I was about thirteen. It would have been 1983. I watched it because I was going to a Catholic school in Jersey at the time, Our Lady of Perpetual Help. I had this teacher, Sister Theresa, who was great, and Thomas More was her favorite saint and she loved this movie. For our eighth-grade production one year, she did an adaptation of Bolt's stage play for us to perform. She chopped out a lot, but we still put it on. I played Cromwell. She picked a guy in the class to play Henry VIII because he had red hair. She was kind of fanatical about the details."

Sister Theresa encouraged her class to watch the film when it was broadcast on a local television station, to introduce them to the story and prepare for the class production. "I watched it and I just fell in love with it in general," Mr. Smith said. "Even though it was on television and interrupted by commercials, it knocked me out. I don't know why Sister Theresa loved it so much. I think it had something to do with the integrity of More. He wasn't one of these fanatical kind of martyrs who wanted to die on the sword. He was a lawyer and tried like mad to get out of dying but in the end found no way that didn't involve violating his faith. But for me, I loved it just because it was so well-spoken and yet incredibly spiritual at the same time. Here's a dude who held one of the highest offices in England at the time but was still able to maintain his faith."

Mr. Smith said his family had just bought its first videocassette recorder, and he made a copy of *A Man for All Seasons* and watched it at least ten more times in the next weeks. "It got to the point where my parents were, like, 'C'mon, move on, watch something else,'" Mr. Smith said. "But I didn't want to. It was the language. It was the story. It was being thirteen years old and admiring somebody who was able to go down for God. Maybe I even felt I could identify with Thomas More a bit. I can appreciate the way More's mind worked, how he was able to juggle the two worlds of the spiritual and the everyday. I mean, it's easy to say we don't want to sin, but it's very hard not to sin. Here's a dude who found a way to do it, to walk the line."

Since then, Mr. Smith said, he has watched the film frequently, often pressing it on some of his young friends. "I must have seen *A Man for All Seasons* fifty times, literally," he said. "Probably more than any other movie. When *Raiders of the Lost Ark* came out, I saw it twenty-five times in the theaters. I just kept going and going. But this movie I've seen at least twice as many times. This movie is like porn for somebody who loves language."

When he is asked, as he often is by young fans, to name his favorite films, Mr. Smith says he always cites the same five: Steven

Spielberg's *Jaws*, Martin Scorsese's *Last Temptation of Christ*, Oliver Stone's *JFK*, Spike Lee's *Do the Right Thing*, and *A Man for All Seasons*. For this article, he said, he chose to watch the Zinnemann film both because of its profound impact on him and because he thinks it is the least seen and least remembered of his favorites.

"Nobody ever talks about it anymore, and it's such a great movie," he continued. "Very few people even seem to know what this movie is about. You say the title and people go, 'What's that about?' Yet it won six Academy Awards, including best picture, best director, and best actor. I guess it's just not sexy enough to be remembered fondly."

During a trip to England, Mr. Smith said, he took time out to visit all the sites related to Thomas More, from the Tower of London to Hampton Court and More's own estate in Chelsea. He wishes someone would write a book about the making of the film, but he's not hopeful. In a way, the movie has become too obscure to generate such treatment.

"Are there really any good men anymore?" Mr. Smith asked. "When you hold somebody like Thomas More up, I don't know, nine times out of ten, maybe nine and a half times out of ten, people will always take the easier route. And Thomas More didn't. Partly, it was an issue of faith, but it was also an issue of character. In terms of films, there are very few characters like Thomas More anymore. Everyone is an antihero now."

The story of Sir Thomas More's battle to satisfy the desires of his petulant king without betraying the demands of his own faith is played, in *A Man for All Seasons,* as a kind of grand verbal jousting match. Mr. Scofield's More is so deeply intelligent and nimble that he seems, at first, to be more than a match for the self-serving careerists and aristocratic pragmatists who surround him.

"Absolutely, it's about smart people playing mind games with each other, but it's never obviously or overtly clever, like in an Aaron Sorkin TV show," Mr. Smith said. "If you watch something like *West Wing,* everyone is so smart, so incredibly clever, it seems like they're all trying so hard. Here, it seems so effortless, so much more natural."

The crisis comes when More is appointed chancellor and asked by the king to acquiesce in the separation of the English church from Rome. The king wants his first marriage declared null, largely because it has produced no male heir, but more immediately because he wants to marry Anne Boleyn. The pope has refused to grant a divorce or annul the marriage, so Henry wants to be declared the supreme authority over the church in England so he can overrule the pontiff. More's faith does not allow him to go along, even though almost everyone around him, including his best friend, the Duke of Norfolk (Nigel Davenport), and his beloved daughter, Meg (Susannah York), urge him simply to hold his nose and go along. Why not? Everyone else is. Why lose your position, your fortune, and your life over such a thing?

In the end, More devises an ingenious strategy. Under English law, he cannot be convicted of treason if he simply remains silent on the subject. In the end, the only way the king's prosecutor, Cromwell, can snare More is by having another witness, an ambitious snipe named Richard Rich (John Hurt), lie under oath that More has uttered treasonous statements. "I am a dead man," More tells the church tribunal. "You have your will of me." And he goes under the ax.

Mr. Smith is the kind of film enthusiast who likes to pepper his ordinary conversation with quotations from his favorite movies. Usually, he said, since many of his favorite films are also well known, people get the references and laugh along with him. "*A Man for All Seasons* is a movie that I quote incessantly, but unfortunately, not many people have seen it, so most of my quotes fall on deaf ears," he said.

Nor does he see it getting any more popular. "You try to get a teenager to sit down and watch this movie," Mr. Smith said. "I've tried. It's not easy."

He tried showing it to Mr. Mewes, his frequent co-star. "That was catastrophic," Mr. Smith said. Even Mr. Smith's wife, Jennifer Schwalbach, who is also an actress, had trouble understanding More's dilemma. "She's, like, 'What an idiot More was, to die for that,' " Mr. Smith said.

He partly attributes this attitude to the world's loss of tolerance for the lone, principled stand—especially when it involves an issue of faith. An audience weaned on prime-time fare has little appetite for More's brand of moral rigidity.

"I think we predominantly have a filmgoing audience that was raised on television," Mr. Smith said. "We like our stuff quick and poppy. We have such a short attention span—very MTV. Today, if this film were even made, it would clearly be an independent film. It would clearly appeal to a small, select audience."

Mr. Smith kept up a fairly steady stream of comments as the film unfolded. Sometimes, it was little more than a word. "Wonderful," he'd say after a particularly compelling moment, or "Look at that." The one word he used most often was *genius,* after a particularly sublime acting moment, either from Mr. Scofield or from Robert Shaw, who plays the king.

"Paul Scofield is just so amazing in this movie," he said. "He's one of those actors who makes me wish I was a more serious filmmaker so I could work with him. But I don't really have a lot of parts for Paul Scofield."

Mr. Scofield's performance in *A Man for All Seasons* stands out for several reasons, Mr. Smith said. One is the overplaying by some of the other performers. Compared with Orson Welles's scenery-chewing as Cardinal Wolsey or Wendy Hiller's pickle-faced turn as More's wife, Mr. Scofield's lead performance is a masterpiece of quiet, thoughtful, underplayed eloquence.

"He is so subtle," Mr. Smith said. "He can communicate such disdain without ever uttering a cross word or going over the top. For instance, he never says outright that he hates Cromwell. But it's always in his voice. You can hear it back there."

By the time Mr. Smith first saw *A Man for All Seasons,* he already knew Robert Shaw, largely for playing Quint in *Jaws.* It was a revelation to hear him tear into Bolt's dialogue and to preen his way through this short but decisive role. "It was kind of, 'Oh, my God, it's Captain Quint as Henry VIII,'" he said.

Shaw's performance, which played the king as a kind of gleefully self-satisfied adolescent, has more than a little ham in it, too. But in his case, at least, it fits the part, Mr. Smith said. "It chews the scenery in a different way than Welles did because he's playing a far more colorful character, so it fits," he said. "Look how he paces back and forth as he talks. It's what children do when they're being petulant. You know it's a great performance because he comes into the movie for one major scene, steals the movie for about ten minutes, and then he's gone. But he's so good that he kind of hangs over the rest of the movie. In a way, he's like the shark in *Jaws.* People talk about him long before he shows up and then, boom, there's Henry."

While watching the film, Mr. Smith frequently anticipates his favorite bits of dialogue. Often, he would say the line aloud just before the actor. "You're very free with my daughter's hand, Roper," Mr. Smith would say, just moments before Mr. Scofield utters the line. Or, "I trust I make myself obscure," just moments before More uses the line to explain his strategy to Norfolk.

Most of the time, though, Mr. Smith was content simply to issue an alert. "Here comes a good line," he'd say. And then he'd glance over to gauge the reaction to it.

When Mr. Smith notes something in Zinnemann's direction, it usually involves either some subtle editing choice or the lack of visual razzle-dazzle. ("There are a lot of highs and wides in this movie, but there are no big pullbacks or big directing moments. It's way too understated for that.")

In the crucial scene between More and the king, for instance, long portions of the sequence are played entirely on Shaw's face, even while Mr. Scofield is speaking—partly because it is his big scene, but also because it's a kind of visual echo of the way everyone responds to the king's presence. He immediately becomes the center of attention.

When Meg approaches her father and says she is worried he will be imprisoned for his stance, More grabs his own cloak and responds, "This is not the stuff of which martyrs are made." Mr. Smith laughed out loud, but a little sadly. "Oh, you are so wrong, Thomas," he said. "Probably the only time he really was wrong."

In Shaw's second and final scene in the film, he is singing to his new beloved, Anne Boleyn (played by a bright-eyed and flirtatious Vanessa Redgrave). He spots a figure across the room that looks to him, and to us, like Thomas More, and hopes that it is indeed his chancellor returned to announce a change of heart. "Thomas! Thomas!" the king cries as he strides across the room.

"Watch this," Mr. Smith said. "This is such an interesting choice. Look how long Zinnemann waited to play the reveal."

We see the other man begin to turn, but the camera cuts back to the king's face before we know whether the other man is actually More. By the time we cut back to him, he has bowed low and his face is hidden. He begins to rise, but the camera cuts again just before his face is revealed, and we watch Shaw's reaction—delight melting into disappointment as the man turns out to be someone other than More.

"Zinnemann holds out so we get the reveal after the turn and the bow, so basically you see it on Henry's face," Mr. Smith said. "Such an interesting choice. This way, it really becomes so much more about Shaw's performance. My guess is that it was an editing decision, like somebody in that editing room really dug Shaw's performance and realized that if they cut it this way that his performance would become the punch line."

Only once does Mr. Smith have a quibble with Zinnemann's direction. It comes in a scene in which More is awakened in his prison cell by a guard carrying a torch. The camera shows the sleeping More's face, then cuts to show the torch approaching. The flickering light is out of focus, as if seen through sleepy eyes. The camera then cuts back to Mr. Scofield, whose eyes open, and back again to the torch, which gradually comes into focus.

"I always thought this was a weird choice," Mr. Smith said. "They do that first point-of-view shot of the torch, like it's More looking at it as he wakes up, but then they cut back to him and his eyes are still closed. The sequence is wrong. How can you have a point-of-view shot of More looking at the torch if he hasn't opened his eyes yet? It doesn't feel right. But it's a minor quibble in an otherwise flawless film."

As surprised as he is that so few people have seen *A Man for All Seasons,* Mr. Smith is just as surprised that Zinnemann rarely turns up on the lists of the top directors.

"He's not one of these directors who you drop his name and people go, oh, that's so Zinnemann-esque," he said. "He's wonderful, and this movie is proof positive, but he doesn't have the enduring reputation that he deserves."

For Mr. Smith, Zinnemann's delicate touch is best exemplified in the crucial scene between More and the king. "Just watch this, where they're sitting on a bench and talking," Mr. Smith said. "There's a lot of tension in the scene because we know that the king wants More to go along with his new marriage and we know that More won't. But mostly, it's just these two guys talking to one another for ten minutes. And as they sit on the bench, there is the slowest of slow dolly movements as the camera gradually moves closer to them. You have to watch the edges of the frame to even see it, it's so gradual. There, can you see it? Wow. It's so slow. But somehow, because of it, the scene does not feel in the least bit static. Genius."

In the climactic scene of More's trial before an ecclesiastical tribunal, Mr. Smith notes again and again the director's restrained approach. More is frequently shot from behind, often little more than a small figure in the middle distance. For historical accuracy, Zinnemann also places neither the king nor More's family in the courtroom with him.

"Imagine how much drama you could cull from cutting to them in any given scene," Mr. Smith said. "I always thought that was really brave. It would have been so easy to play the family card and have these reaction shots of his wife and daughter, tearful and worried. That's how they do it in most courtroom scenes, right? But Zinnemann doesn't do it at all. It's just More and the court, that's it. It's so powerful and restrained. It's all about the language and the arguments."

Mr. Smith draws a distinction in his mind between *A Man for All Seasons* and another film based on a play, Arthur Miller's *The Crucible*. Both are about people who lose their lives over a matter of principle, but it is the issue of religion and faith that sets More's story apart for Mr. Smith.

"My feeling is that there are two kinds of people in the world, *Man for All Seasons* people and *Crucible* people, and the difference is what they are willing to die for," Mr. Smith said. "In *The Crucible*, John Proctor gives his life because he doesn't want to stain his name; he doesn't want to be known as a witch, which is just a handle that someone wants to hang on him. So his martyrdom doesn't really impress me. It's never as dramatically interesting as Thomas More, who lays down his life for his soul. It's not about his identity; it's about his soul. Even Norfolk and Meg tell him: 'Just sign the oath, what difference does it make? Say it with your mouth but renounce it in your head.' That's when More gives that great speech about how you are holding your soul in your hands like sand, and if you begin to open your fingers, even just a little bit, it all begins to spill out."

In fact, Mr. Smith said, he's not sure that people without faith are really able to appreciate *A Man for All Seasons* as deeply as he does.

"It's such an inaccessible movie, in one sense, for people who don't believe in God," he said. "Because the whole time they're watching it, they're thinking More is an idiot. Just take the oath. Why not? But everything comes back to God with Thomas More. He could easily take the oath, but he won't because he feels it would violate his relationship to his God. His vision of himself is based on that relationship. That's so different from John Proctor. In this day and age, try to make a movie about a guy who stands up for what he believes based on his relationship to God. I'm telling you, very few people will turn out."

He added, "I speak from experience."

Mr. Smith is talking about *Dogma,* the comedy he made in 1999 with Matt Damon and Ben Affleck as a pair of renegade angels in New Jersey. It was the director's first real attempt to deal with some of the issues of faith that followed him from his Catholic upbringing, and it caused a brief furor when some religious groups criticized it during its production and just before its release. Once those groups saw that he was attempting to be thoughtful about the subject, the furor subsided, Mr. Smith said.

Has Mr. Smith ever thought of embracing Thomas More head on, eschewing the comedy and doing a flat-out drama?

"You know, there's always the temptation," he said. "But I think I'm too young and insecure at this point to give it a shot. Because if you're not one hundred percent sure of yourself, you end up making something like *Interiors*—you know, that Woody Allen movie? And it has a lot to do about perception. People perceive you as one thing. But believe me, there is many a time I have thought about doing something dramatic. Something with some humor in it, but not jokes. I always thought if I did it, it would be a courtroom drama. I love courtroom drama. But there it is; it's language again. What's a courtroom, after all, but a bunch of people standing around talking?"

HIGHLIGHTS OF KEVIN SMITH'S CAREER AND INFORMATION ON *A MAN FOR ALL SEASONS*

■

What They Watched

A Man for All Seasons. Directed and produced by Fred Zinnemann; screenplay by Robert Bolt. With Paul Scofield, Robert Shaw, Susannah York, Orson Welles, Wendy Hiller, Leo McKern, and John Hurt. 1966.

Kevin Smith's Films

Jay and Silent Bob Strike Back. With Kevin Smith, Jason Mewes, Shannon Elizabeth, Jason Lee, and Ben Affleck. 2001.

Dogma. With Matt Damon and Ben Affleck. 1999.

Chasing Amy. With Kevin Smith, Ben Affleck, and Joey Lauren Adams. 1997.

Mallrats. With Shannen Doherty and Jeremy London. 1995.

Clerks. With Brian O'Halloran and Jeff Anderson. 1994.

Mae Day: The Crumbling of a Documentary. (Also known as *Mae I.*) With Emelda Mae, Kevin Smith, and Scott Mosier. 1992.

13

Woody Allen on
Shane

He was one of the dream targets, of course. Who could contemplate a series like this and not wonder what it would be like to have Woody Allen take part? But I never really thought it would happen, listening to talk about how private he was, how controlling and how press-shy, particularly in the wake of his tabloid scandals of the 1990s. The clincher, I think, was that he had taken up with a new distributor for his films, DreamWorks, which was eager to get him out there again, front and center, promoting his work and perhaps doing a little image renovation. I also suspect, though can't prove, that the studio had something to do with urging the director away from choosing a film by Ingmar Bergman or one of the more difficult, European directors he clearly loved. Whatever the case, I am beholden to whoever urged him to choose an American film, because I think his cogent appraisal of *Shane* is perhaps the single best piece of film dissection that the series produced. And as far as his reputation for being a control freak, well, you be the judge. All I know is that more than any other installment in the series, his resulted in the most questions from friends, readers, and other participants in the series: What was he like? All I can say is that I gave my best shot at an answer in the piece.

■

He came into his screening room walking that Woody Allen walk, slightly hunched, a little distracted, his vigorous fingers carving the air as he spoke. "I hope you don't mind," he said, "but I have prepared a statement."

And he pulled from his pocket a folded sheet of canary-colored paper, the double-spaced letters overlaid with black-ink editing that spilled into the margins. Mr. Allen said he wanted to make completely clear why he had chosen George Stevens's *Shane* as the film he wanted to watch.

"I'll just read this into your tape recorder, if that's okay, and then you can do whatever you want with it after that," he said, settling himself in a plush chair in the back corner of the screening room. "Is it on? Can I start talking?"

He held up the canary sheet and began. "When I was invited to pick a film to view and discuss it with the *New York Times,* I wanted to select an American one," Mr. Allen said. "This is unusual for me, because my affection for foreign movies seems to be much deeper. If I were, for example, to list my ten or even fifteen favorite movies— and I don't say best movies, because these lists are always completely subjective—aside from *Citizen Kane,* all of the films would be foreign. A sampling might be *Rashomon, The Bicycle Thief, Grand Illusion, Wild Strawberries, Seventh Seal, Throne of Blood, The 400 Blows, Los Olvidados,* you get the idea."

He cleared his throat, took a deep breath, and continued: "But I didn't want to do that for this, because I wanted to make sure that the people who read this, at least a portion of them, have seen the movie, so I thought I would stay with an American movie. I hesitated, too, about viewing a comedy, because on a list I might make of, let's say, the ten or fifteen great American films, there'd be almost no comedies. Certainly not from the talking era. And I wouldn't include the silent era, because that is a completely different entity. Silent films to me are a completely different kind of thing. If you were to count silent films, of course, between Chaplin and Keaton you could probably get ten great movies. But if you take films only from the start of the sound era, I don't think that there are too many great sound comedies." Mr. Allen, sixty-five, hunched forward and spoke slowly into the recorder, never looking up from the typewritten sheet. (And it had indeed been pecked out on a typewriter, not printed from a computer.)

He wore khaki pants and a button-down blue shirt, long-sleeved and fastened at the wrist, and despite the sweltering summer afternoon he was perfectly dry, pressed, and unruffled.

"I have a very idiosyncratic view of sound comedies that I wouldn't want to interfere with this," he said. "For example, I wouldn't count the Marx Brothers or W. C. Fields films, I wouldn't put them on my great list, as I don't consider their films great. But they are records of performances by these stupendous comedians, and any five minutes of Groucho or Fields is funnier than most purported or even venerated comedies. And still I wouldn't rank their movies, which I find, you know, choppy and even silly, as great comic filmmaking. I would say my personal view of most sound-era comedies would be considered harsh, and I certainly include my own films in that appraisal. None of them would be on any of these great lists, certainly."

There is a scene in Mr. Allen's *Manhattan* in which Isaac, the character he plays in the 1979 film, reclines on a sofa in his New York apartment and recites into a tape recorder a list of what he holds most dear in the world, from city landmarks to creative works like Flaubert's *Sentimental Education*. It is difficult to watch Mr. Allen read his *Shane* statement into a similar tape recorder without catching at least an echo of Isaac's streaming, punctilious manifesto.

"For whatever reason, I am not enchanted by a huge number of highly respected comedies, whose names I would rather not mention and hurt anybody's feelings," Mr. Allen said. "I do consider *The Shop Around the Corner* a great comic movie, also *Trouble in Paradise,* also *Born Yesterday.* Speaking of *Born Yesterday,* I considered the British version of *Pygmalion* with Leslie Howard and Wendy Hiller, and also the Fellini masterpiece *The White Sheik.* Since I spent most of my life in comedy, in one medium or another, I am not a clean, objective judge. I would prefer not to harp on my highly special preferences and distastes. As musical comedy goes, I do consider *Singin' in the Rain, Meet Me in St. Louis,* and *Gigi* great, and probably *My Fair Lady* would have to be ranked up there.

"In the end, looking over my list of great American films, which include, among others, for final consideration, *The Treasure of the Sierra Madre, White Heat, Double Indemnity, The Informer,* and *The Hill* by Sidney Lumet, I finally settled on *Shane.* This is an odd choice in one sense, because I don't like westerns. I like *The Ox-Bow Incident* and *High Noon* and care a bit but considerably less about a few others, but *Shane,* I think, is a great movie and can hold its own with any film, whether it's a western or not."

Mr. Allen looked up from the piece of paper. "That's the only statement I wanted to make," he said, handing over the typewritten sheet along with the still turning recorder. His editing marks cover the entire statement, words are crossed out, entire clauses inserted from the margins.

He nervously cleared his throat again and stood up, peering back into the projection booth where someone was waiting to crank up the first reel of *Shane.* The cluttered suite of Park Avenue offices where Mr. Allen edits his films and maintains a screening room is completely free of the kinds of blinking high-tech gizmos with which other directors surround themselves. The editing equipment, the upholstered furniture, even the copious collection of vinyl jazz albums that line one entire wall all seem like throwbacks to an earlier, analog era, as well-worn as the love seat where Mr. Allen finally came to rest facing the screen.

"I saw *Shane* when it first came out in theaters," Mr. Allen said. That would have been in 1953, when he was just getting out of high school in Brooklyn. "I didn't rush off to see it," he said, "because there's no western film that I ever rush off to see. I'm not really that interested—and, again, this is purely personal—by rural atmospheres. So when a film begins in a farmhouse or something, it's not the same for me as if it begins in a penthouse. I just like an urban setting."

So just why, then, did he choose *Shane*?

"I thought *The Ox-Bow Incident* was wonderful when I saw it, and *High Noon* is a good western, for me," he said. "But none of them hold a candle to *Shane. Shane* is in a class by itself, because if I was making a list of the best American movies, *Shane* would be on it, and none of these other movies would."

The reason, in large part, is the great skill of Stevens, Mr. Allen said. "I rank him very high. And this is on the basis of a very few things, really. The few of his films that I've liked, I've liked very much. *Shane,* I think, is his masterpiece. I do think he would be right up there with my very few favorite American directors—of the era that I grew up in. Orson Welles is in a class by himself, but then, you know, John Huston and George Stevens and William Wyler."

Mr. Allen remembered enjoying *Shane* from the first time he saw it, but he said his appreciation had deepened over the years. "I've seen it many, many times," he said. "Certainly more than twenty. I've also taken people to see it, people who tell me that they can't stand westerns. Because it's more than a western. It's a fine movie. Oh, there are a couple of weaker spots in it, but they are so minor and forgivable, and what's great about it is so wonderful that you'd really have to be carping to be annoyed at them. To this day, if it was on television this week and I happened to be tuning through the channels, I would stop and see it. I am always riveted."

Mr. Allen frequently describes *Shane* as a lovely film, or a beautiful one, and praises it for its poetry and elegant flow, words not normally associated with westerns. Two of his favorite westerns, it is pointed out, are essentially a long buildup to a climactic confrontation. In *Shane* it is Alan Ladd's reluctant gunfighter strapping his six-shooter back on to do battle for the beleaguered homesteaders; in *High Noon* it is Gary Cooper taking on the killer who has arrived on the noon train.

"Yes," Mr. Allen said, letting the notion sink in for a moment. "But if you were asking me, I would say that *Shane* achieves a certain poetry that *High Noon* doesn't. *High Noon* is beautifully made, but you can see the message of it too plainly, you know, and it's just not as well done. For whatever reason, probably because Stevens himself had some of the poet in him, it infuses that material with a certain poetry that *High Noon* doesn't have. *High Noon* is more like a fine piece of work, you know, whereas *Shane* is sort of a fine piece of poetry."

Mr. Allen leaned over, twisted the volume knob on a console beside his seat, and shouted back to the man in the projection booth. The familiar blast of Victor Young's classic score erupts behind the Paramount Pictures logo, pushing into the classic opening shot of the wandering gunfighter cresting a hill and passing down into the troubled valley where the drama will take place.

The colors in the print are a little bled out, which is a shame, because the images of the craggy peaks of northwest Wyoming, where Stevens shot the film, are among the most beautiful in any western. Did Mr. Allen have any idea where the film was shot? "No idea," he said in a crisp tone that discouraged further discussion. A subsequent question was cut off just as quickly. Was Mr. Allen going to be able to discuss the film as we watched it? "I can't talk and watch the movie at the same time," he said.

Oh.

This was a bit of a problem, as the discussion is pretty much the idea of this series. But he was adamant—polite but adamant. He suggested a compromise: we would watch the film for twenty minutes or so, then switch it off and discuss what we had seen before starting it up again.

Shane glides across the bucolic valley to the remote homestead of the Starrett family, Joe (Van Heflin), Marian (Jean Arthur), and Joey (Brandon de Wilde). He asks to cut through their property, says he's just heading north to "someplace I've never been." When Little Joey absentmindedly cocks his rifle, Shane snaps around like a gunfighter. When some rough-looking men ride up, Starrett at first thinks Shane is one of them. They are the Ryker brothers and their gang, open-range cattlemen who want to chase off all homesteaders. They threaten Starrett and roar off.

By this time, an embarrassed Starrett realizes that Shane was not with them and invites him to stay for supper. Shane, used to the gunfighter's violent life, is entranced by the gentle domestic scene. After dinner, the two men work to remove a stubborn tree stump in Starrett's yard, and Shane accepts a job on the ranch.

The next day, Shane rides into the nearby town to buy work clothes and is humiliated by one of Ryker's hired men, played by Ben Johnson. At a meeting that night, Stonewall Torrey (Elisha Cook Jr.), one of the homesteaders, and others shun Shane for his supposed cowardice. They decide to ride into town together in the future, and are seen doing just that, a glowering sky lighted by lightning fore-shadowing trouble ahead.

"Okay, is this a good place to stop?" Mr. Allen asked. "It is? Fine." He called back to the projectionist.

"I think, first off, you take the film from the beginning, there's that beautiful scenic opening," Mr. Allen said. "The sense of this ranch house that's isolated out there, and then the town, which is one of the great images in American film. It's a town in the middle of nowhere, just a few buildings. I mean, it's just a little general store, a bar, a livery stable, just stuck out in the middle of the wild like that. You have a sense that this is what those western towns really looked like."

Mr. Allen noted the complex tangle of relationships that are economically sketched out, one by one, in the opening scenes. "From the first, because of the way Stevens shot it, you can tell that there is this intense fascination between the kid and Shane; it's almost love at first sight or something," he said. "And it's wonderful the way he snaps around when the kid cocks his gun, because you know, immediately, that you're dealing with a tough guy. It's done so offhandedly. There are certain things that you don't think in words, that you think emotionally. You know, it clicks in some subliminal way. Here, you think to yourself, oh, I would like to have this guy on my side. So that then later, when he does go on Starrett's side, it's so wish-fulfilling.

"And the bad guys are handled in a great way, too. The first word out of Ryker's mouth is that he doesn't want any trouble. At several points during the movie, Ryker tries to be reasonable. So it's not just a bunch of bullies. It's more complex than that."

The connecting threads of the relationships are built one strand at a time. Even the tough guy who humiliates Shane in the bar comes back into play, later, redeemed and nuanced. But through it all, the overriding mystery is the character of Shane himself; quiet, calm, utterly competent, and yet yearning for something. "This guy is not a pushover," Mr. Allen said, "but you have also seen this goodness of spirit that he has. Alan Ladd is an interesting choice for the part because Shane is such a passive character in the whole thing. He's just quiet and passive and nonassertive. And he's a small guy, not a big, beefy cowboy star."

The movie starts up again. Shane and the homesteaders are heading into town. The weather is glowering. Shane, now aware that the homesteaders consider him a coward, wanders back into the bar to confront Ben Johnson. They circle each other, then fight. At first, the homesteaders hang back, fearful. But finally Starrett wades in and the two men take on the entire gang. The Ryker brothers, sensing that the time has come to raise the stakes, send off for a gunfighter. Shortly afterward, Jack Wilson (Jack Palance) rides into town, a reptilian, thoroughly malevolent desperado.

"Watch this," Mr. Allen said, breaking his own rule.

Mr. Palance enters the saloon. A dog looks up, sees him, and slinks across the barroom floor. Mr. Palance begins to walk across the room. We see him only from the waist down. Gradually, he dissolves out of the frame and, almost instantly, dissolves back in a few steps farther along. It's beautiful, but ghostly. He's like an apparition.

"It's one of the most puzzling dissolves I've ever seen," Mr. Allen said. "I can't imagine what it was for. It must have been to cover up a mistake. I can't think of any other reason for it."

Once Mr. Palance is introduced, the film returns to the farm. Shane is trying to teach Joey how to shoot until Marian comes out and stops it. She doesn't want her boy to have anything to do with guns. It's clear, too, that the unspoken relationship between Marian and Shane is deepening, though nothing ever happens between them that's more physical than a handshake.

"So, when we last left off, they were riding into town, and you could tell that Shane had his own agenda to settle the score with these people," Mr. Allen said. "And then they go home and you get the scene of Marian fixing up the two men, Shane and her husband, and it's so obvious that she's attracted to Shane, and it's starting to bother her. When Shane leaves, she asks her husband to hold her. She's getting to where she can't trust her feelings. This is wonderful stuff for a cowboy movie because it's not heavy-handed. It's a relationship that develops with the same subtlety that it would in the most sophisticated kind of urban movie."

And then there is Jack Palance.

"If any actor has ever created a character who is the personification of evil, it is Jack Palance," Mr. Allen said. "We've all read about the size of the horse, how Stevens put Palance on a smaller horse so he'd look even bigger. But when he arrives—the music is great—he's all in black; he's so poetically evil. He looks like he'd gladly kill the guys who hired him if they looked at him wrong. He's just bad news. Serpentine. In our minds, he's set off against Shane, one particularly good, almost too good to be true, and the other is totally evil."

By this point, too, we have come to know Starrett a little better.

"Shane is more sophisticated," Mr. Allen said. "Shane has traveled more. He's drifted around more, seen more different sides of the world. Starrett is more plain. But they're both very nice men, both brave men. The only difference is that Shane is so amazing with a gun. He's got the gift of God or the artist or something."

The homesteaders, hoping to buck up their confidence, organize a Fourth of July celebration. Starrett notices Shane dancing with Marian, and an odd look crosses his face. After the party, Shane and the Starretts head back to their homestead. It's dark. When they arrive, the Ryker brothers are waiting for them. So is Wilson.

"This is a great scene," Mr. Allen said. "Really, from here on until the end of the picture are some of the best scenes I've ever seen in an American movie. And this is one of the best. You have so much going on at the same time, but it's never forced. All these relationships are working at the same time, and Stevens is able to make you feel and understand all of it because he has laid the groundwork so carefully in the earlier scenes. You've got the Rykers, talking reasonable again. You've got the wife worrying about her husband, about their boy. You've got the boy watching this. And then, in the background, without a word, really, you've got Shane and Wilson sizing each other up. And the boy watches this, too. It's directed in the most brilliant way. And when, at the end, Jack Palance backs his horse out of the yard, it's just an amazingly wonderful moment."

The next day, Torrey, the hotheaded homesteader, heads into town. It's too much of a temptation for Wilson. With the Rykers' permission, he picks a fight with Torrey. Standing on the raised wooden sidewalk outside the saloon, looking down at the diminutive Torrey slogging through the mud, Wilson belittles him with a hissing voice, casually puts on his gunfighter's gloves, and outdraws Torrey. There is a moment's pause, Torrey standing there with his useless gun in his hand, until Wilson blasts him in cold blood.

"This may be the best shooting confrontation scene in a cowboy movie ever," Mr. Allen said. "First, it's so beautifully filmed, these guys riding into town, the camera going along with them, and then you get the side view of the town with the mountains and the weather. And then Palance, the personification of evil, lures him into this fight. It unfolds so slowly. And then there's the ritual of it, with Palance putting on that glove. It's just his eccentricity, or something, a part of his artistic process, in a sense. It isn't a simple thing, where he just shoots Torrey. There's this whole ritual that goes with it. And it's always so shocking when you get this three- or four-second pause before Palance pulls the trigger, because it's clear that he doesn't have to shoot. He's already beaten him. There's never been a shoot-out in a cowboy movie to equal it, in terms of evil against innocence."

Torrey is buried at the graveyard on a hill overlooking the town. Some of these shots are the most stunning in the film: the small cluster of mourners around the open grave, the tiny town in the distance, the towering mountains all around. That night, back at the homestead, the Rykers pass word that they want to meet with Starrett back in town. He knows it's probably a trap, but he also knows he has to go. His chances are slim, but he has come to realize that the Rykers' increasing violence can be defeated only by more violence.

Shane appears. He has his gunfighter's clothes on again, his six-shooter strapped on his waist. He announces that he, not Starrett, is going into town. They quarrel, then fight, tumbling all over the dusty yard until, up against the remains of the stump over which they labored in the opening scenes, Shane knocks Starrett unconscious, says good-bye to Marian, suffers Joey's withering disdain, and heads into town.

"Shane doesn't want to get back into gunfighting," Mr. Allen said. "He's been trying the whole movie to put it behind him. But he knows that the only way to put an end to the violence in the valley is for him to do it. That's what makes the film great in my eyes. He knows. He's got to go in there and kill them. And sometimes in life— it's such an ugly truth—there is no other way out of a situation but you've got to go in there and kill them. Very few of us are brave enough or have the talent to do it. The world is full of evil, and rationalized evil, and evil out of ignorance, and there are times when that evil reaches the level of pure evil, like Jack Palance, and there is no other solution but to go in there and kill them."

And so the famous climax plays out. Shane makes his long ride into town, Joey running after him. Shane confronts Wilson, pure good versus pure evil, and outdraws him. Then, when the Ryker brothers pull guns on him, Shane shoots them, too, but not before one of them wounds him.

Afterward, Shane gets on his horse and tells Joey that he's not coming back to the ranch. Shane realizes that the era of the gun-fighter is ending, but he also knows that he can't be anything else. And so he rides off. "Come back!" Joey calls. But Shane does not come back. The last shot, a mirror of the opening image, has Shane riding over the crest of a hill. Except this time he is heading out of the valley. And it is twilight. And he is hunched over in the saddle. Wounded? Dead? Or simply sorrowful?

"I don't like to think that he's dead," Mr. Allen said. "Just that he's wounded. I hate to think that he dies in the end. I think they probably are pointing to the fact that he's dying because, you know, he's ascending. But I don't like to think that he's dead yet."

And Mr. Allen stood, stretched, turning the lights on one by one.

"Everything pays off," he said. "The relationship between Shane and the kid pays off in spades. But also between Shane and Marian, between the husband and wife. And when Alan Ladd takes control and tells Starrett that he's not letting him go into town, it's like, you know, you always hope in life that there's somebody who will take that kind of control, who will fight your battles. It's really only in the movies that it happens, though. The moment you really want to see, and that you can never see, is the next morning when the people come into town and see that both Ryker brothers and Wilson are dead. You don't get to see that. And you want to. You want to see how they react when they see what Shane has done for them.

"Because the truth is, most people are not comfortable with vio-lence. So they find themselves at the mercy of armies or groups of policemen or vigilantes. You always hope, in that situation, that either a Shane will appear or that you will somehow become like Shane. I use the example of Michael Jordan. He's the guy who knows that the ball game has to be won in the last six seconds, so he goes out there and quietly wins it. That's what had to happen here. I keep referring to Shane as the artist. You see, that's what he is. Shane is the guy who has brought this gunfighting to the level of art."

HIGHLIGHTS OF WOODY ALLEN'S DIRECTING CAREER
AND INFORMATION ON *SHANE*

∎

Mr. Allen has also acted in films by other directors, notably *Play It Again, Sam* (1972), directed by Herbert Ross from Mr. Allen's screenplay.

What They Watched

Shane. Directed and produced by George Stevens; screenplay by A. B. Guthrie Jr. With Alan Ladd, Jean Arthur, Van Heflin, Brandon de Wilde, Jack Palance, Ben Johnson, and Elisha Cook Jr. 1953.

Woody Allen's Films

Hollywood Ending. Starring Tea Leoni and Treat Williams. 2002.

The Curse of the Jade Scorpion. Starring Woody Allen, Helen Hunt, Dan Aykroyd, and Charlize Theron. 2001.

Small Time Crooks. Starring Woody Allen, Tracey Ullman, and Elaine May. 2000.

Sweet and Lowdown. Starring Sean Penn and Samantha Morton. 1999.

Celebrity. Starring Kenneth Branagh and Judy Davis. 1998.

Deconstructing Harry. Starring Woody Allen, Judy Davis, Kirstie Alley, and Mariel Hemingway. 1997.

Everyone Says I Love You. Starring Woody Allen and Goldie Hawn. 1996.

Mighty Aphrodite. Starring Woody Allen and Mira Sorvino. 1995.

Bullets Over Broadway. Starring John Cusack and Dianne Wiest. 1994.

Manhattan Murder Mystery. Starring Woody Allen and Diane Keaton. 1993.

Husbands and Wives. Starring Woody Allen and Mia Farrow. 1992.

Alice. Starring Mia Farrow and William Hurt. 1990.

Crimes and Misdemeanors. Starring Woody Allen, Martin Landau, and Anjelica Huston. 1989.

Radio Days. Starring Mia Farrow, Julie Kavner, Michael Tucker, and Dianne Wiest. 1987.

Hannah and Her Sisters. Starring Woody Allen and Mia Farrow. 1986.

Purple Rose of Cairo. Starring Mia Farrow and Jeff Daniels. 1985.

Broadway Danny Rose. Starring Woody Allen and Mia Farrow. 1984.

Zelig. Starring Woody Allen and Mia Farrow. 1983.

Stardust Memories. Starring Woody Allen and Charlotte Rampling. 1980.

Manhattan. Starring Woody Allen, Diane Keaton, and Mariel Hemingway. 1979.

Interiors. Starring Diane Keaton and Mary Beth Hurt. 1978.

Annie Hall. Starring Woody Allen, Diane Keaton, and Tony Roberts. 1977.

Love and Death. Starring Woody Allen and Diane Keaton. 1975.

Sleeper. Starring Woody Allen and Diane Keaton. 1973.

Bananas. Starring Woody Allen and Louise Lasser. 1971.

Take the Money and Run. Starring Woody Allen and Janet Margolin. 1969.

What's Up, Tiger Lily? Starring Tatsuya Mihashi, Susumu Kurobe, and Woody Allen. 1966.

14

Denzel Washington on
Ordinary People

A s in many of the pieces in the series, the title of the film Denzel Washington chose to watch, *Ordinary People,* Robert Redford's Oscar-winning study of a Waspy family in the Midwest, was something of a surprise. But again, as in most of the installments, the answer became clear as we talked about the film. In this case, Washington was in the initial stages of preparing for his first film as a director, *Antwone Fisher.* On one level, he was interested in watching the work of an actor making his directorial debut, as Redford did in the film. But more pertinently, Washington was to play a psychiatrist in *Antwone Fisher,* and found that as he imaged the film he kept returning to memories of Judd Hirsch as the suicidal Timothy Hutton's counselor in *Ordinary People.* Where this piece was different from most of the others in the series is that others chose a film that had a profound impact on them when they were young. Washington wanted to watch it only partly because of the fond memories he had of it. More important, he wanted to watch it because it had a direct bearing on where he was creatively at that moment.

■

When Denzel Washington was growing up, the son of a minister, he was not allowed to go to the movies. As a young man, after he had turned to acting and moved to Manhattan, he went through the usual phase of fairly regular moviegoing. But then he moved to Los Angeles in the early '80s and became established as a top star, and once again he found himself seeing fewer and fewer movies.

"When you make them and you're in them and you're around them all the time, it's nice to get away from it, you know?" Mr. Washington said. "But just recently, since I've decided to put on this other hat, I've been watching more movies again. And it's nice. Except I'm looking at them in a new way now."

The other hat Mr. Washington has decided to put on is that of director—which is why he was wandering around the Columbia Pictures lot in Culver City in early September, before the terrible events of the 11th had altered the national landscape. Being a director also enabled him to obtain a plush basement screening room in the legendary Irving Thalberg Building and to persuade Paramount Pictures to send over a print of the movie he had decided to watch: Robert Redford's *Ordinary People*.

Mr. Washington walked into the screening room with a duffel bag in one hand and a naval cap on his head. He sat down with a sigh in one of the big, upholstered chairs in the screening room's back row.

"This is a film that I've been meaning to look at for a while," Mr. Washington said. "Partly, it's because I remember seeing it back when it came out and really liking it. But it's also because of the subject matter. In the film I'm directing, the story is partly about the relationship between a psychiatrist and his patient, who's a troubled kid, just like in this movie. I've always been a fan of Redford's work, both as an actor and as a director. So I knew I needed to see this movie again. It's been sitting there on my table at home. When this came up, I thought, all right, this is great. I'll get to see it on the big screen. That's even better."

Most of the actors and directors who have taken part in this series have been longtime students of filmmaking, the kind of avid moviegoers who have seen just about everything and have very strong feelings about the history of film and the types of movies they love. So this was a bit of a twist, watching a film with someone who was not a fanatic, but who was revisiting a film seen years ago and trying to watch it through new, self-consciously analytical eyes.

"I saw it when it first came out and, you know, I was like everyone else: I thought it was a wonderful film," Mr. Washington said. "It was a very thoughtful examination of this troubled family, and I remember enjoying the way all of the relationships were so layered and complex. I wasn't surprised when it won all those Oscars. But I don't know that I've ever seen it in its entirety since it came out."

Robert Redford was at the pinnacle of his acting career in 1980, when *Ordinary People* was released in theaters. Coming off a decade in which he starred in films that included *The Sting, All the President's Men, The Candidate,* and *Jeremiah Johnson,* he was probably the biggest movie star in Hollywood. So some people back then may have thought there was a little bit of ego-run-amok in the announcement that he would also try his hand at directing.

But *Ordinary People,* based on a novel by Judith Guest and adapted for the screen in a tensely understated script by Alvin Sargent, was immediately recognized by critics and audiences as the work of a very assured, thoughtful, and ambitious filmmaker.

It won four Oscars that year—for best picture, for Mr. Redford's direction, for Mr. Sargent's script, and for Timothy Hutton's career-making performance as the troubled central character. Also nominated were Mary Tyler Moore for her lead role as the boy's icy mother and Judd Hirsch in the supporting one of his acerbic analyst.

"It was Hutton's film debut, wasn't it?" Mr. Washington asked. "And he certainly had the role, didn't he? Of course, he also had the advantage of being new to us. And there was that really interesting piece of casting with Mary Tyler Moore, who was America's sweetheart and all, but playing this very forbidding character here."

The projectionist poked his head through the screening room door and asked if we were ready to begin. Mr. Washington looked over and nodded. "Sure, let's go," he said.

"I half remember there was some scene with Mary Tyler Moore," Mr. Washington said. "Not a scene, really. Just a moment. It's where she's standing at the closet in her bedroom. I remember being very frustrated or tense about it. I wanted her to explode or something; I can't remember. I'm really curious now to see what it was."

The film begins with a black screen, the credits appearing in white block letters, unadorned. There is no music. And then, very slowly, a classical melody is played on a piano, one gentle note at a time. It is the Pachelbel Canon. With a gradual fade-in, we see a series of postcardlike scenes from a prosperous, upper-middle-class suburb of Chicago: broad lawns leading to redbrick Colonial facades, church steeples, leaf-strewn parks (it is clearly autumn), and, finally, a fancy private school.

"They seemed to have everything, didn't they?" Mr. Washington said. "What did they have to complain about?" He laughed.

The music builds, not so much in tempo as in richness, until an unseen chorus takes over the melody. Then we move inside the private school and see that the singing is coming from an actual chorus of teenagers, one of whom is Timothy Hutton as Conrad Jarrett, the bedraggled hero of the story.

The Jarretts have the classic upscale American life. Cal Jarrett (Donald Sutherland) is a white-collar type who works downtown. His wife, Beth (Ms. Moore), is a bright-faced, crisply dressed house-wife with an emotional coating hard and brittle enough for an M & M. Conrad, however, doesn't look so good. He is gaunt, distracted, nervously twitching. We do not know it immediately, but the family has recently suffered the death of an older son, named Buck, in a boating accident on Lake Michigan.

"It's funny, the way they use the music here," Mr. Washington said. "It's so simple. Just that piano at first, one note at a time. When I've been thinking about my movie, when I see it in my head, the music I hear is just a very simple piano and not much else. Did I have this score somewhere in the back of my mind? Could be; I don't know." He thought about it for a few seconds and then shook his head. "No, no, I don't think so," he said. "The music I've been hearing is more like *Eyes Wide Shut*—you know, with that same, single note over and over again? But this might have had something to do with it, too. Who knows?"

Mr. Washington had recently finished acting in two movies back to back, playing a very, very bad cop in *Training Day* (a performance that was to win him his second Academy Award) and then a distraught father who takes over a hospital emergency room to get medical attention for his son in *John Q,* released in early 2002. Much of the time, he said, he has been too wrapped up in his roles to pay a whole lot of attention to what his directors were doing.

That was certainly the case, he said, with his Oscar-nominated performance in Norman Jewison's *Hurricane* in 1999. (Mr. Washington won the Oscar for best supporting actor for *Glory* in 1989.) But during the shooting of both of these most recent films, he said, knowing that he was about to direct his own film, he paid close attention to everything: the way the director interacted with the crew, the choices about lighting, the kinds of problems that arose and how they were dispatched.

Mr. Washington was watching *Ordinary People* just days before heading off to begin shooting the untitled Antwone Fisher story, based on the life of a Cleveland youth who survived an abusive childhood and a stint in a brutal reform school before joining the navy and coming to the caring attention of a naval psychologist. The production shifted in mid-October from Ohio to San Diego for Mr. Washington to shoot its military scenes.

A spokesman for the actor said this week that Mr. Washington was deeply immersed in directing his first film and didn't want to pull himself out of it to see if the intervening weeks—and particularly the events of September 11—had changed his perceptions of *Ordinary People*. (One of Mr. Washington's earlier films, *The Siege*, released in 1998, was eerily prescient about the terrorist attacks, its plot also involving Islamic fundamentalists in New York.)

In early September in the screening room, Mr. Washington silently watched the opening scenes of *Ordinary People*, his head leaning on his hand and his long legs stretched out.

In the film, the young Conrad has come home from school. His parents have engaged in some casual chatter. But it is obvious that something is amiss; people are treating Conrad like damaged goods, and his mother seems to give him only the minimum attention necessary. Cal's attempts to get his son to talk are met with polite resistance. Everything feels awkward. But when they are all going to bed, Conrad in his room down the hall from his parents, Mr. Washington suddenly sat straight up.

"Did you see that cut?" he said. "Did you see how Redford had them turning out their lights at the same time?"

Indeed, that is what happens: Conrad reaches over and clicks off his bedside light; there is a cut and we are in his parents' room, watching as Cal clicks off their light.

"I'm really noticing things like that now," Mr. Washington said. "You see, it's a visual way of tying the two scenes together, so fluid and yet so logical. It pulls you through the story. Having something like this, one light going off and then a cut to another light going off, can connect you from one scene to the next. That's one way a director can keep you involved in the story."

Scenes of daily life play out on the screen. The Jarretts go to a local theater production with another couple. Conrad rides to school with friends, though he seems oddly alienated from them. There are references to his being psychologically unstable and to a recent suicide attempt. His father urges him to see an analyst who has been recommended. He says he will but doesn't seem to mean it. The real story is played out between the lines, in fumbling pauses and eloquent body language.

"Look at this," Mr. Washington said. "It's *American Beauty.* Am I right?"

The family is seated around the elegant dinner table; formal, silent, nothing but the sound of the clicking of cutlery to fill the emptiness. The staging is remarkably like that in the dinner scenes of *American Beauty,* the Oscar winner for best picture in 2000, in which the juxtaposition between the formality and the dysfunction is played for dark comedy. Here, it is used symbolically. For one thing, the silence underlines the family's inability to communicate. But the placement of the actors also puts them in their proper emotional places: Beth and Conrad at opposite sides of the table, Cal seated between them.

"Look at how Sutherland is underplaying here," Mr. Washington said. "It's a very emotional moment, but he's hanging back, not playing for the emotion. It makes it all even more powerful."

In the next sequence, Conrad finally decides to seek out the analyst, Dr. Berger. Conrad is combative, resistant. Dr. Berger studies him. The doctor's appeal—both to us and, after a while, to Conrad— is that it is only in those encounters between analyst and patient that the real issues of the story can be openly discussed and its secrets revealed. In the other scenes, the issue of what is causing Conrad's pain is either avoided or belittled. But here, in Dr. Berger's office, the truth can be addressed.

Mr. Redford's move to directing with *Ordinary People* presaged a generation of stars who became directors, including later Oscar winners like Warren Beatty (*Reds*), Clint Eastwood (*Unforgiven*), Kevin Costner (*Dances With Wolves*), and Mel Gibson (*Braveheart*). But more tellingly, the film harks back to a time when very simple, character-driven stories could be made by big studios rather than relegated to the smaller world of independent film. "Even back then, I think this movie was unusual in that regard," Mr. Washington said.

The story of the Jarretts is a tragedy, but it's also a psychological mystery. In the opening sequences, we gradually learn the relevant facts. Buck and Conrad had been on their boat when a storm caught them off guard. The boat overturned. Buck, the more popular older brother, the apple of his mother's eye, drowned. Conrad survived but couldn't cope, and tried to kill himself. Now, as the movie opens, he is back from the hospital, his wrists covered with angry scars, trying to pretend that everything is normal again.

There are several scenes between Cal and Beth, Mr. Washington noticed, that seem to go on a little too long, but deliberately so. The pauses in their conversation last a few beats too long. Either that, or they nervously step on each other's lines. It's awkward. We can feel the tension in it. "Yet no matter how long the scenes go on, Redford always finds a way to get you out of it and into the next scene," Mr. Washington said. "It's his editing choices, mostly."

One scene takes place at a neighborhood cocktail party. We see several snippets of banal chatter, lots of activity and noise. Then Beth happens to overhear Cal telling someone that Conrad is seeing a therapist. Boom. There is an immediate cut. Suddenly, we are in the car with Cal and Beth, silently driving home. Cal is oblivious, but Beth's jaw is rigid and an icy fury pours from her eyes.

It's that cut, from the noisy party to the silent car, from the bright indoor lights to the dark drive home, that makes a jarring grab for your attention. And it is the context of the cut, from Cal's talking about Conrad's treatment to Beth's icy anger, that snaps it into immediate clarity. Although nothing is said, we in the audience are vividly aware of why Beth is angry, almost as if we could read her mind, and we tensely anticipate the emotional explosion that is to come.

"It's editing choices like that that pull people through a movie," Mr. Washington said. "And in this scene, it can take you right inside a character's head. Did you notice anything else about these scenes? There is no music. None. I don't think there's been any music since the opening credits. Interesting, isn't it?"

He remembered Ms. Moore's performance, Mr. Washington said, and knew she was good. But when he thought back about watching the film, it was always Mr. Hutton's performance that jumped to mind.

"He's got the role—there's no question about it," Mr. Washington said. "But Mary Tyler Moore, she's really doing something here. Can you feel it? I wonder why she didn't win the Oscar. Do you think it's because she played such an unsympathetic character, or maybe the voters somehow got it into their heads that she's really like this? I don't know, but she got robbed. In these scenes, I really believe what her character is doing. I like her behavior. It feels so true."

The very next scene lets him amplify on this and bring to mind something that has also been on his mind as he contemplates the start of production on his own film.

Beth and Conrad run into each other in the hallway outside their bedrooms. They startle each other and immediately feel awkward. The chatter is nervous and ill timed, nothing but banalities. Soon they hardly seem even to be listening to each other. But Conrad has come out of a session with Dr. Berger and is trying, reluctantly, to reach out to his mother. Beth, however, has a frozen smile on her face and seems as if she'll jump out of her skin if she can't get away from him.

All this is revealed in the clipped, emotionless way they talk, not in the dialogue, and in the nervous movements and the body language. Beth can barely look at her son. She fusses with a potted plant. She opens her bedroom door, gets halfway through it, seems to want to run inside and slam it shut. But he keeps talking, won't let her go.

"For her to go over there and touch that plant and move it around, it's so perfect, it conveys so much," Mr. Washington said. "Just her body language—it's so evocative. I'd be curious to ask Redford if they did a lot of rehearsing on this film. It feels rehearsed to me. By that I mean it feels like they've worked out a lot of things, like the plant or the business with the two doors in the doctor's office. That's the kind of smart stuff that can come out of a good rehearsal period."

Mr. Washington repeatedly referred to the restrained use of music in the film. It is heard only during a few brief stretches. There are two main themes, Pachelbel's melody and a warmer piece by Marvin Hamlisch. The music somehow seems to symbolize Conrad's emotional relationship with other people, notably his mother and Jeannine (Elizabeth McGovern), the girl with whom he strikes up a friendship in school.

"Notice how they used the music in this scene," Mr. Washington said at one point.

Beth is standing behind Conrad, and there is a moment, a brief moment, where she reaches out to him—really the only moment in the movie when she seems to make an effort to overcome her aversion to him. When Conrad says something that angers her, the mood is shattered and, with that, the music stops. Just as with the editing cuts, Mr. Redford uses the music, and the lack of it, to highlight the characters' internal emotional life.

"He's up to something with the lighting, too," Mr. Washington said. "Look at the shadows on the wall. Am I right? There's something different about the way this room looks."

He was referring to a scene in Dr. Berger's office, a setting that has become familiar through several scenes.

"It's something here about, I don't know, the changing of the seasons?" Mr. Washington said. "The room is darker than it was in earlier scenes; the shadows in the room are in different places. Maybe it's just that it's getting dark earlier. Fall is turning into winter, and he's telling us that with the lighting. Or maybe it's that the sessions are lasting longer. Conrad is beginning to open up, so he's staying longer. I don't know. But I really think he's trying to tell us something here."

Mr. Washington is also struck by the subtle way the focus of the story shifts from Conrad's problems to the relationship between Cal and Beth.

"I was wondering, a while back, why we had that scene of Donald Sutherland jogging through the park," Mr. Washington said. "But now we know. It was the transition. We needed that scene to move the story out of Conrad's head and into Cal's head."

The theme of the story, he said, is that those who reach out for help and try to heal their pain—like Conrad and then Cal—are granted at least a chance of peace. Others, like Beth, who continue resisting and refuse to reach out, are the story's real victims.

Conrad has his revelations, of course, in the story's climax in Dr. Berger's office, another scene that offers one of the movie's few musical moments. Distraught over the suicide of a friend from his days in the hospital, Conrad is ready, with some calculated prodding from Dr. Berger, to realize why he feels so guilty and where his anger is actually directed.

But the story does not end there. It goes on for another entire reel. Because what is revealed in the wake of Conrad's recovery is that the seed of the family's problems was not in Conrad's head.

"You think the story is about Conrad and his problems, but then you realize that he's fine and it's the parents who are screwed up," Mr. Washington said. "That's the real revelation in this movie. Dad realizes it and gets some help. But Mom isn't interested. She can't face it. The story starts out seeming like it's Conrad's tragedy, but then it turns out it's really Beth's tragedy. She's the one who's left alone at the end."

Finally comes the scene Mr. Washington had been waiting for. Cal and Beth have had their late-night confrontation around the dark dining room table. Quietly and sadly, Cal tells her that he can't understand her aversion to Conrad and doesn't think he loves her anymore. Without a word, she walks up the stairs, opens the closet in her bedroom, and takes down a suitcase. The music is playing again, the same, simple piano melody.

"This is the moment I was thinking of," Mr. Washington said. "We can't take our eyes off her. We want to know how she will react."

Suddenly, the music stops—abruptly, right in the middle of a line of melody—and although she says nothing, the breaking of the melody mirrors a kind of break in her spirit. She gasps quietly, clutches herself. And then she goes away in a taxi. Not a word is spoken.

Ordinary People was only one of the movies that Mr. Washington had planned to revisit as he prepared to direct. Sometimes he focused on films, like this one, featuring an analyst and patient. Other times, he simply watched the work of directors he admired. "I've been looking at a lot of Martin Scorsese films," he said. "I think I've seen *Goodfellas* about eight times, and I've watched Milos Forman's *Ragtime* about a half-dozen times. I've been watching some Kurosawa, too."

So what has he taken away from watching *Ordinary People* again after more than two decades?

"Keeping it simple," Mr. Washington said. "Keeping it focused. Using everything, whether it's the music or the editing or the lighting, to carry the audience through the story and to get inside the characters' heads."

He stood as the lights came up and pulled the cap back over his head.

"I feel kind of bad for Mary Tyler Moore," he said. "Well, I guess you can't let everyone off the hook."

HIGHLIGHTS OF DENZEL WASHINGTON'S ACTING CAREER AND INFORMATION ON *ORDINARY PEOPLE*

■

What They Watched

Ordinary People. Directed by Robert Redford; screenplay by Alvin Sargent; produced by Ronald L. Schwary; original music by Marvin Hamlisch; cinematography by John Bailey. With Donald Sutherland, Mary Tyler Moore, Judd Hirsch, Timothy Hutton, and Elizabeth McGovern. 1980.

Denzel Washington's Films

Antwone Fisher. Directed by and starring Denzel Washington. With Derek Luke. 2002.

John Q. Directed by Nick Cassavetes. With Anne Heche. 2002.

Training Day. Directed by Antoine Fuqua. With Ethan Hawke. 2001.

Remember the Titans. Directed by Boaz Yakin. With Will Patton. 2000.

The Hurricane. Directed by Norman Jewison. With Vicellous Reon Shannon. 1999.

The Bone Collector. Directed by Phillip Noyce. With Angelina Jolie. 1999.

The Siege. Directed by Edward Zwick. With Bruce Willis. 1998.

He Got Game. Directed by Spike Lee. With Ray Allen. 1998.

The Preacher's Wife. Directed by Penny Marshall. With Whitney Houston. 1996.

Courage Under Fire. Directed by Edward Zwick. With Meg Ryan. 1996.

Devil in a Blue Dress. Directed by Carl Franklin. With Tom Sizemore. 1995.

Crimson Tide. Directed by Tony Scott. With Gene Hackman. 1995.

Philadelphia. Directed by Jonathan Demme. With Tom Hanks. 1993.

The Pelican Brief. Directed by Alan J. Pakula. With Julia Roberts. 1993.

Much Ado About Nothing. Directed by Kenneth Branagh. With Kenneth Branagh. 1993.

Malcolm X. Directed by Spike Lee. With Angela Bassett. 1992.

Mississippi Masala. Directed by Mira Nair. With Sarita Choudhury. 1991.

Mo' Better Blues. Directed by Spike Lee. With Spike Lee. 1990.

The Mighty Quinn. Directed by Carl Schenkel. With James Fox. 1989.

Glory. Directed by Edward Zwick. With Matthew Broderick. 1989.

Cry Freedom. Directed by Richard Attenborough. With Kevin Kline. 1987.

A Soldier's Story. Directed by Norman Jewison. With Howard E. Rollins Jr. 1984.

Carbon Copy. Directed by Michael Schultz. With George Segal. 1981.

15

John Travolta on
Yankee Doodle Dandy

John Travolta, another actor who (like Kevin Costner) has taken his share of hits from the entertainment media, turned out to be a real treat. He couldn't have been more friendly or accommodating, and I don't think anyone could read his reaction to watching *Yankee Doodle Dandy* and come away with the idea that he'd held back emotionally. What I like most about the piece, though, is that it illustrates something that is often overlooked: the importance not only of mentors and role models, but of close personal relationships in the shaping of an artist's creative life. And Travolta's deep sense of connection with James Cagney, apparent throughout the piece, forces us to rethink some of Travolta's most memorable roles through a new prism.

■

John Travolta sat quietly in a square, well-cushioned chair along the back wall of his home screening room. He had just finished watching *Yankee Doodle Dandy*, a glossy Warner Bros. biopic about the legendary George M. Cohan, a movie that's been dear to him since he was a little boy in New Jersey dreaming about a life on the stage. Mr. Travolta rubbed his eyes as the screening room door swung open and his wife, Kelly Preston, arrived with their eighteen-month-old daughter, Ella Bleu, on her hip.

"Someone wants to say good night," Ms. Preston said, to which Mr. Travolta offered a broad, brave smile. But she was not fooled, squinting instead into her husband's red eyes. "Have you been crying?" she asked.

Yes, he had been crying; there was no use denying it. He nodded sheepishly. The movie that had meant so much to him as a boy, he discovered, still had the power to reach into his heart. And now, in the wake of the terrorist attacks of September 11, what had once seemed corny, flag-waving jingoism in the screen saga of the man who wrote "You're a Grand Old Flag" and "Over There" instead came across as almost eerily in touch with the current national mood.

"How often does a movie really evoke that level of emotion, you know?" Mr. Travolta said, taking a deep, steadying breath. "And continually, throughout the piece, unabashedly so. I just love it. It's the bomb. Especially at this time, especially now. There were a couple of moments, especially toward the end of the movie, where it really reflected the kinds of emotions I'm feeling about the current situation. I mean, you could sing that song, 'Over There,' and it would still hold up. It sounds like it could have been written today, doesn't it? It's eerie."

Mr. Travolta turned in his seat, raised his arms like a tenor in an opera house, and began singing softly: "Over there! Over there! Send the word, send the word, over there!" He rose from his seat in the dark room and began to sing louder and with more emotion. "That the Yanks are coming! The Yanks are coming! They're drum, drum, drumming everywhere!"

A wide-screen smile slowly spread across his face. "Can you imagine if I had done that when I was on the Jay Leno show, just stood up and started singing that song?" he said, referring to his appearance in late September. "It would have created such a moment. Wouldn't that have been something? Wow. Because I think this attack on September eleventh—and I want to choose my words very carefully—this attack was on the intellectual center of our nation, on New York, which has never been attacked. So it has brought everyone together, finally, in this zone, made everyone a little more patriotic."

Mr. Travolta, forty-seven, lives on a tree-filled, Mediterranean-style hillside estate on the West Side of Los Angeles, a guardhouse at his gate and a line of beautifully restored cars lining the sloping drive. Inside, his home is filled with pictures, many of him—as a boy, as a young man in the mid-'70s television series *Welcome Back, Kotter,* during his first wave of film success after the release of *Saturday Night Fever* (1977), and then later, after his comeback with *Pulp Fiction* (1994), when he became a bigger star than ever. There are also plenty of pictures of Ms. Preston, Ella, and their nine-year-old son, Jett.

In display alcoves in the screening room, and just down the hall near the dining room, are pictures of some of the dinner party guests who have been at the house. They cluster together inside their shining frames, well fed and beaming happily: Tom Hanks, Marlon Brando, Tom Cruise, Dustin Hoffman, and a dozen others.

"I really had a hard time choosing between which of three films to watch," Mr. Travolta said before the screening as he made his way down the hall into what appeared to be a library. The three movies that have had the greatest impact on him, he decided, were Claude Lelouch's 1966 film *A Man and a Woman,* Bertrand Blier's *Going Places,* from 1974, and *Yankee Doodle Dandy.* But he settled on that one, Michael Curtiz's 1942 musical, because of the way it resonates through his life.

"*Yankee Doodle Dandy* was my favorite film as a boy, and I want to see if it still holds up for me," Mr. Travolta said. "I happened to see one short section of it a while ago, while flipping through the channels one night, and it still touched a chord with me. As an adult, I was leaning more toward Lelouch and Blier. But then I thought, no, overall this was such an inspiration to me through my whole life and career that it was just the most valid choice."

Mr. Travolta said he was five when he first saw *Yankee Doodle Dandy* in 1959. To him, then and now, the heart of the film was the central performance of James Cagney as the cocky, cantering George M. Cohan. (Cagney won his only Oscar for the role, one of three the film won out of eight nominations.)

"They had what they called the 'Million-Dollar Movie' on television in New York at the time," Mr. Travolta said. "They would show the same movie, every day, for a whole week. And it was during one of those weeks that I saw *Yankee Doodle Dandy* for the first time."

He was immediately entranced, he said, watching the film several times that first week alone. In subsequent years, Mr. Travolta said, he has seen it at least thirty times.

"It was Cagney, really," Mr. Travolta said. "He just really appealed to me, for the positiveness of his personality and his charisma and the way he made me feel that, with work, I could do the things he was doing in the movie. I guess I was attracted to his spirit, but also the story, because it was about a showbiz family, which is what I am from. His family in the movie reminded me a little bit of my own family, so I identified with that. In my family, we were all actors, singers, dancers. And there was something about the patriotism in the movie that struck me as a child. Jimmy Cagney made you feel patriotic in that movie. So it's the right kind of movie to watch just now, actually. I get chills just thinking about it."

"Are we ready?" he asked. Then he clicked a button on the table beside him, and with a faintly audible whir, shades slowly drew across the room's tall windows, closing off the last of a magenta sunset. A screen emerged from the ceiling on the far wall, slowly covering a bookcase and flashing to brilliance with the old black-and-white Warner Bros. shield logo.

"Cagney was forty-two years old when he did this movie, and it was absolutely a departure for him," Mr. Travolta said. Although Cagney had appeared in musicals before, most notably *Footlight Parade* (1933), working with the choreographer Busby Berkeley, and had begun his career as a vaudeville hoofer in the 1920s, by 1942 he was firmly entrenched in the public mind as the swaggering gangster anti-hero of hits like *Public Enemy* (1931) and *Angels With Dirty Faces* (1938). The sense of menace that Cagney conveyed with his coiled-spring posture and the distinctive cadence of his rapid patter made him one of the most imitated and iconic performers of the prewar years.

"So many actors in our profession keep it a secret that they sing and dance," Mr. Travolta said. "It's not that they want to keep it secret—more that they don't get a chance to do it. But here Cagney was a hoofer and a vaudevillian, and he was desperate to show that he could do this other stuff."

Mr. Travolta said he heard stories about the making of *Yankee Doo-dle Dandy* from Cagney himself, whom he befriended in the last years of the actor's life. In 1980, when Mr. Travolta was starring in *Urban Cowboy*, he arranged through an intermediary at one of the studios for an introduction to the reclusive Cagney, retired from the screen since 1961 and living on a farm in upstate New York.

"I know he was born in 1899, so he was eighty-one years old when I met him," Mr. Travolta said. "I went up to a house he had here at the time, up in Benedict Canyon—this was in addition to his farm in New York—and he was just sitting there in a chair. I sat down and held his hand and I said, 'I just wanted to tell you how much I love you and how much you meant to me,' and I started to cry. And he, being Irish, started to cry, too. And so we just sat there and cried about my love for him."

Mr. Travolta broke into a fresh laugh of delight.

"I told him how he became this figure in my childhood, because I loved his movies, and because my mother, when she wanted to get me to do something, would tell me that Jimmy Cagney was on the phone and he said I should do it," Mr. Travolta said. "You know, she'd say, 'Jimmy Cagney says to clean your room.' And I was so afraid that maybe he was on the phone because, you know, my mother was an actress and it was plausible to me that maybe she knew him. 'Jimmy Cagney says, "Brush your teeth,"' and I'd run to brush my teeth. Anyway, I told him this story and he was very touched, so we struck up this relationship, and I guess I saw him three or four times a year until he died in 1986.

"He was a modest guy. He really was. He didn't like braggadocio. He played all these characters who were cocky and bragging, but he didn't like that in other people. So you had to be careful around him. If you said anything that even slightly seemed to be complimenting yourself, he would call you on it."

On the screen Cohan is basking in an ovation from the footlights on a Broadway stage, the curtain sliding down as he smiles and bows. In his dressing room, he receives a message that President Franklin D. Roosevelt wants to see him in the White House, immediately. And it is there, in a late-night tête-à-tête with the bespectacled president, that Cohan recounts his life on the stage in flashback.

What is most apparent in the opening minutes of the film, and sporadically throughout it, is the weird similarity between the national mood depicted on the screen and the one that the country is now experiencing in the weeks since September 11. *Yankee Doodle Dandy* was released in the months after Pearl Harbor as America was stirring itself to patriotic fervor and preparing for war with Japan and Germany. At the time, Cohan was a half-forgotten figure, a composer and a performer who had made his name on the stage in the last years of the nineteenth century and the first two decades of the twentieth, but whose sentimental style had long since been subsumed in a tidal wave of jazz. But suddenly, the flag-waving author of "Over There" found his outdated sentiments back in vogue.

In one montage sequence in the middle of the film—just after the *Lusitania* has been sunk by a German submarine, drawing the United States into World War I—Cohan speaks over images of newspaper headlines, sidewalk crowds, marching bands, and army recruiting depots. "It always happens," Cohan says. "Whenever we get too high hat, too sophisticated for flag-waving, some thug nation decides we're a pushover, all ready to be blackjacked. And it isn't long before we're looking up mighty anxiously to be sure the flag is still waving above us."

Mr. Travolta raised his hands to his cheeks in astonishment. "Did you hear that?" he said. "That could have been written today."

Once Cohan begins to tell his life story and the film moves back to the nineteenth century, Mr. Travolta becomes even more embroiled in the drama. A first scene shows an old provincial theater where Cohan's father, played by Walter Huston, has just finished an afternoon performance. "This is exactly the kind of show they would have been putting on back then in a theater like this," Mr. Travolta said. "Look at the gaslights. Look how huge this set is. They really did this right, didn't they? And the movie, it already has an emotional quality to it, don't you think? Very rich."

Part of the appeal of the film to the five-year-old John Travolta—especially in these early scenes, when young George joins the family act and has his first success in a national tour of *Peck's Bad Boy*—was to imagine himself in the role, going out on the road as a preteen performer.

"Oh God, yes," Mr. Travolta said. "My parents let me start performing when I was seven, so it was about two years after I saw this movie for the first time. I remember they were doing a lot of productions of *Gypsy* around that time, and I wanted to audition for it and go on the road so much. Whatever was going on in showbiz, I wanted to be a part of it."

Mr. Travolta's mother, Helen, had been an actress and a singer on the radio with a group called the Sunshine Sisters and was a drama teacher in suburban New Jersey when John was growing up. His father, Salvatore, had been a semipro football player but was a co-owner of a tire store in John's youth. Both of John's brothers and two of his three sisters also pursued careers in acting, dancing, and singing.

Cohan quickly grows into a teenage member of his family troupe, now known as the Four Cohans, with his father, mother, and sister, Josie (played by the actor's own sister, Jeanne Cagney). Cohan is portrayed by Cagney as brash and brilliant, endearingly cocksure. When a blustering theater owner insults Cohan's bride-to-be, a hopeful young singer, Cohan responds with a kick in the pants that turns into a big, slapstick gag: the manager crashes through a curtain, upsets some workmen, and causes a whole cascade of objects to crash to the ground around him.

"Today, they wouldn't know how to do a scene like that," Mr. Travolta said. "I'm sure it's a simple thing, written in the script, but they came up with this elaborate way of doing it, as a big stunt. Today, they wouldn't trust it enough. The point is that Cagney and the director know that at this point, the audience really wanted to see this guy get his just deserts because he'd hurt Mary's feelings. So they wanted to get the bad guy and knew that the emotion would be big enough so that it was worth doing as a big stunt. And they also knew that the only way they could do it, with the kind of naive approach that the story required, was to have Cohan kick the guy in the butt and then let the comedy of the slapstick do the work. Today, I'm afraid, filmmakers wouldn't be so clever about it."

The director, the Hungarian-born Michael Curtiz, was one of Warner Bros. prime workhorses in the 1930s and '40s, usually given the best material and the studio's top stars. A short list of some of the enduring films he made in those years would include *The Cabin in the Cotton* with Bette Davis (1932), *Captain Blood* with Errol Flynn (1935), *Four Daughters* with John Garfield (1938), *The Sea Wolf* with Edward G. Robinson (1941), and, of course, the jewel in the studio's crown, *Casablanca,* in 1942.

Mr. Travolta, however, is drawn to *Yankee Doodle Dandy* less for its directorial flourishes—which, frankly, can seem more than a little clunky today, it being at heart a fairly formulaic and sentimental biopic—than he is to the figure at the film's center, Cagney.

"He was an original, totally distinctive," Mr. Travolta said. "It was something about his confidence. He had that in every role. He never seemed to do anything uncertain. I remember, a few years ago, Tom Hanks said to me, 'Where do you get your confidence from?' He was talking about how I would take on so many different types of roles, unabashedly. So I understand that feeling of confidence. It's very appealing."

As Cohan begins his composing career, the movie becomes essentially a kind of greatest-hits parade, showing no doubt highly fictionalized versions of how Cohan came to write "Harrigan," "Yankee Doodle Dandy," "Give My Regards to Broadway," "Mary," "45 Minutes from Broadway," and others. And there are two grand-scale set pieces in which Cagney gets a chance to sing and dance onstage, show-within-a-show scenes from two of Cohan's biggest stage successes.

When Cagney, dressed as a jockey about to run in the English Derby, breaks into "Yankee Doodle Dandy," Mr. Travolta is transported.

"It's delightful to hear him sing it," Mr. Travolta said. "It's magic." The actor's eyes begin to swell with tears, and his voice grows husky. He holds his fist against his clenched lips as he watches Cagney go into his first big dance number, a stiff-jointed, hip-pivoting, tap-clattering burst of energy that makes the thick-torsoed and short-legged Cagney bounce like a pinball around the stage, a fireplug that's come to life with infectious physical athleticism.

"How great is that?" Mr. Travolta said between sharp intakes of breath. "It's so classic." He cleared his throat, wiped his eyes, took a few seconds to compose himself.

In some ways, he said, Cagney's idiosyncratic dancing style is appealing in a way that's inexplicable, like much art. Certainly, Mr. Travolta said, the classically trained dancers of the day, or the more graceful screen dancers like Fred Astaire, probably did not consider Cagney's frenetic jittering to be true, accomplished dancing. But there is something about the bravado, the showing off, that makes it so pleasurable. A dancer like Astaire was always trying to do impossible things, to wow the audience with his unreachable gifts, Mr. Travolta said. But in *Yankee Doodle Dandy*, Cagney always seemed more reachable.

"One just entertained you and the other, Cagney, inspired you to want to do it," Mr. Travolta said. "At least, it did me. It is so magnetic, so powerful and magical and spiritual. In some ways, it was very simplistic. But it was the sort of thing that you could get up and try to imitate it. It seemed accessible. Actually, believe it or not, that was the key to the success of *Saturday Night Fever*. Because everybody who came out of the movie thought, 'Hey, I can do that kind of dancing.' That's the gift. Just like Cagney gave us in this movie. We were able to inspire people to get up and dance again."

In a later scene, Cohan's parents and sister are at a small, provincial railroad station when they receive a telegram from George, now a big success on Broadway. He is offering them jobs.

"That scene looks hokey, but it's really not," Mr. Travolta said. "Things like that really happen to people in show business. I've had scenes like that in my life, you know, where you get cast for something or get a job in summer stock and it happens just like that. The call comes and you get your mother on the phone and say, 'Mom, I just got cast in this movie,' and she yells out for your father, 'Dad, come here, John's going out to L.A.' It seems hokey, but it really does happen."

The scene in which Cohan lets his future wife (Joan Leslie) hear the song he has written for her, "Mary," made Mr. Travolta particularly aware of Cagney's acting choices. "It's great how he's mixing the tea in the background while he talks to her and while she's playing the song for the first time," Mr. Travolta said. "It gives him something to play against while he's doing the scene. He's talking to her, but he's also fussing with the tea. It wouldn't have been nearly as interesting if he was just standing behind her while she played the piano. Oh, and now, look: he's going to take his first sip of tea at precisely the right moment. There's a pause in the music. A close-up. And there he goes. Wow. The timing, it's fabulous."

Mr. Travolta is convinced from the performances in the film—particularly from Cagney, Huston, and Leslie—that the actors knew they were working on a film that would be good. "You can tell that they just knew it," Mr. Travolta said. "There's an energy that actors get when they have good material, and you can feel it in this movie.

I've had the good fortune, several times in my career, where I could feel it. *Pulp Fiction. Primary Colors. Civil Action.* You just know you've got the words. They're in your pocket, and this movie has that kind of energy, where they knew they were making something good."

At the height of his career, Cohan owned a string of theaters, had several shows running at once, and saw his "Over There" become the anthem for America's involvement in World War I. But after the war, as the movie tells it, Cohan kept writing the sweeter stuff that was popular before the war and found himself out of step with the Roaring Twenties. So when Cohan's father dies—a wrenching scene that also brought tears from Mr. Travolta ("I have a story to tell you about Cagney after this, but if I try to tell you now I'll start crying again")—Cohan decided to travel the world and then retire to a remote farm, where he gradually sank into obscurity.

"It's funny, you know, but I never really thought about it," Mr. Travolta said. "This is exactly what Cagney did. He retired when he was only sixty-two years old and lived most of the rest of his life on a farm, staying out of the spotlight. It's almost like he was doing the Cohan thing all over again. You never really know how much art influences people and their personalities, the roles they play. This certainly was the highlight of his career. I wonder. You know, that story I was going to tell you about Cagney? Well, you know the scene where Cohan is at his dying father's bedside? I had a scene just like that with Cagney."

Mr. Travolta's voice began to falter again. "He was in bed and he had his leg amputated because he had diabetes, and I sat by his side. It was almost exactly like the scene in the movie. This is something very few people know. I snuck into the hospital where he was in upstate New York. It was so hard to see him with his leg gone. I just stood by his bed. He tried to make out like he had a lot of energy and was going to rise above it, but it was in the next few days that he died."

Mr. Travolta was weeping now, tears pouring down both cheeks. "It was so obvious when Cagney was smiling at his father during that scene that he was just trying to be cheery for his dad. And that is what was so great. He balances the emotion. So that when it releases at the end of the scene, when he breaks down in tears, it pays off. Very smart Very smart acting. And then the kiss on the forehead at the end. Just brilliant. I mean, how memorable is that? I'll tell you what it is. It's perfect."

HIGHLIGHTS OF JOHN TRAVOLTA'S ACTING CAREER AND INFORMATION ON *YANKEE DOODLE DANDY*

■

What They Watched

Yankee Doodle Dandy. Directed by Michael Curtiz; screenplay by Robert Buckner and Edmund Joseph; produced by Hal B. Wallis and Jack L. Warner; original music by George M. Cohan, Ray Heindorf, and Heinz Roemheld. With James Cagney, Joan Leslie, and Walter Huston. 1942.

John Travolta's Films

Domestic Disturbance. Directed by Harold Becker. With Vince Vaughn. 2001.

Swordfish. Directed by Dominic Sena. With Hugh Jackman. 2001.

Lucky Numbers. Directed by Nora Ephron. With Lisa Kudrow. 2000.

Battlefield Earth. Directed by Roger Christian. With Barry Pepper. 2000.

The General's Daughter. Directed by Simon West. With Madeleine Stowe. 1999.

A Civil Action. Directed by Steven Zaillian. With Robert Duvall. 1998.

Primary Colors. Directed by Mike Nichols. With Emma Thompson. 1998.

Mad City. Directed by Costa-Gavras. With Dustin Hoffman. 1997.

Face/Off. Directed by John Woo. With Nicolas Cage. 1997.

She's So Lovely. Directed by Nick Cassavetes. With Sean Penn. 1997.

Michael. Directed by Nora Ephron. With Andie MacDowell. 1996.

Phenomenon. Directed by Jon Turteltaub. With Kyra Sedgwick. 1996.

Broken Arrow. Directed by John Woo. With Christian Slater. 1996.

Get Shorty. Directed by Barry Sonnenfeld. With Rene Russo. 1995.

Pulp Fiction. Directed by Quentin Tarantino. With Samuel L. Jackson. 1994.

Look Who's Talking Now. Directed by Amy Heckerling. With Kirstie Alley. 1993.

Look Who's Talking Too. Directed by Amy Heckerling. With Kirstie Alley. 1990.

Look Who's Talking. Directed by Amy Heckerling. With Kirstie Alley. 1989.

Urban Cowboy. Directed by James Bridges. With Debra Winger. 1980.

Grease. Directed by Randal Kleiser. With Olivia Newton-John. 1978.

Saturday Night Fever. Directed by John Badham. With Karen Lynn Gorney. 1977.

Carrie. Directed by Brian De Palma. With Sissy Spacek. 1976.

16

Brian Grazer on
Blazing Saddles

*S*uper is a word most often uttered in connection with either heroes or models. But in Hollywood, there is a tiny group of extremely influential people whose names have risen from the small print at the bottom of the movie ads to become celebrities and brand names in their own right. These super-producers command the top producing fees, the biggest budgets, and the closest relationships with A-list directors and actors. Jerry Bruckheimer is one, of course, and, for very different reasons, Scott Rudin. And certainly Brian Grazer is on this short list. Yet the creative role that these producers play remains largely mysterious, perhaps as idiosyncratic as that of directors. Sitting down with Grazer was an attempt to see if the passions and the same sense of being profoundly affected by a film were the same in one of these super-producers as they had proved to be in directors and actors. The bonus was that not only did Grazer pick a surprising and interesting film, but he used it to write a kind of mini-history for a brand of comedy that took root and flourished in the quarter century in which he's been working and prospering.

■

Brian Grazer sat behind the sleek executive conference table in the headquarters of Imagine Entertainment, enthusiastically working his way through a Cobb salad.

"I saw *Blazing Saddles* when it first came out, and I thought it was the funniest movie I had ever seen in my life," Mr. Grazer said. "I just thought it was gut-splitting, shocking, hysterical. At the time, Mel Brooks was new to me. I hadn't seen any of his other movies. And I thought the movie was just the most extremely funny thing I had ever experienced. Based on seeing it, I changed the course of my life."

A cassette of this 1974 comedy had been slipped into a VCR attached to the big-screen television set at one end of the conference room, and Mr. Grazer was staring at the buttons on one of the various remotes arrayed around him, trying to figure out how to fire up the movie. The offices of Imagine, the film and television production company that Mr. Grazer founded with the director Ron Howard in 1986, are on the seventh floor of a modern office building in the middle of downtown Beverly Hills, and the distant groan of traffic could be heard below along Wilshire Boulevard.

Mr. Grazer, fifty, said he had considered many films when trying to decide what to watch for this series. "Movies that have a real emotional resonance for me are usually the very intense dramas," he said. "Movies like *Midnight Express* or *Battle of Algiers.* For me, comedies are hard to see more than a couple of times because you know where all the jokes are. So at first, it didn't occur to me to do a comedy. But then I thought, when I think about what film has personally been important to me, it really has to be *Blazing Saddles.* I've only seen it a half-dozen times or so, but when I first saw it, it really had an amazing impact on my life and on the kind of movies I've made."

Indeed, almost all of the movies selected for this series to date have been the kind of intense, serious dramas to which Mr. Grazer alluded. The only other comedy was *The Graduate,* Mike Nichols's seminal 1967 classic, and that was selected by Mr. Grazer's longtime partner, Mr. Howard. And even among comedies, Mr. Brooks's smart, vulgar, scattershot satire of racial politics and the American western is not likely to be at the top of many critics' lists of the best film comedies of all time.

But Mr. Grazer—a prolific veteran producer who has worked with most of the biggest stars of the last two decades, from Tom Hanks to Arnold Schwarzenegger to Jim Carrey, and who knows a thing or two about making comedies—says that *Blazing Saddles* really played a more prominent role in the shaping of American comedy in the last quarter century than most people realize.

"It was the birth of a certain type of comedy that I call shock comedy," Mr. Grazer said. "The comedies that preceded it were more gentle and earnest. This one was aggressive and in your face, and dealing in a very smart and startling way with the most intense social issues, from racial bigotry to sexuality. It was really shocking, and it did everything to wow you or stir you up or mix you up, to take you off balance, every single moment. It subverted all of your expectations. And Mel Brooks brought to it a kind of smart, sketch-comedy sensibility that he brought with him from his work on Sid Caesar's *Your Show of Shows* in the 1950s. He just put an R rating on it, took it to areas where you couldn't go on television.

"I think you can make the case that *Blazing Saddles* really revived that whole brand of smart sketch comedy and no doubt played a role in the emergence of *Saturday Night Live* a few years later. Anyone, including myself, the Farrelly brothers, anyone who has been making comedies over the last twenty years—I know *Blazing Saddles* has got to be someplace in their heads. It's all about being smart, the visceral, emotional hit of being funny in a very smart way. It's like an adrenaline hit. It goes right into your bloodstream."

Mr. Grazer has produced more than three dozen films since *Night Shift*, the 1982 Ron Howard comedy about two men (Henry Winkler and Michael Keaton) running a call girl ring out of the New York City morgue.

The film he had in release at the time—*A Beautiful Mind*, also directed by Ron Howard, which went on to win the Oscar for best picture—was a psychological drama about the unraveling of a brilliant mathematician (Russell Crowe). But even a cursory look at Mr. Grazer's résumé shows that comedies do dominate. They have helped make him one of the most prominent and powerful producers in

Hollywood who, along with a few others like Jerry Bruckheimer and Scott Rudin, can consistently command the top fees, attract the top stars, and see their names featured prominently above the titles with other creative artists.

"I grew up in the Los Angeles area, out in Northridge, over in the San Fernando Valley, and I was going to law school when I first saw *Blazing Saddles*," Mr. Grazer said. "I immediately decided that I wanted to be a writer and producer. I went to the U.S.C. film school and then I kind of stalked Mel Brooks. I called him and called him and called him, and finally he agreed to meet me. He spent a few minutes with me. He couldn't have been nicer. I went back and wrote my own screenplay and then begged him to read it. I became so sycophantic.

"My script was a kind of Faustian trade comedy about a woman who wants to be a soap opera star and, to get there, agrees to sell her baby's soul to the devil. The baby grows up to be this guy who has really bad luck all his life, the worst luck, but in a funny way, you know, the way Woody Allen might have done it. It never got produced. I still have it in a drawer someplace. Anyway, I kept begging and he agreed to read it, and we talked about it for a while. Each of these handful of meetings with Brooks lasted just a few minutes, but it was enough to make me feel that I could do this kind of work and still be a human being, you know?"

Mr. Grazer stared again at the remotes, pressed a couple of buttons. Nothing happened. He shrugged, handed it to me. I tried a couple of buttons, too. "Play" seemed a good bet. But no. He reached over and clicked on the intercom. A few seconds later, an assistant bustled into the room, smiling apologetically, and clicked a button on the front of the VCR. Immediately, the movie roared to life.

"We can make it louder," Mr. Grazer said. "I like it kind of loud."

The Warner Bros. shield logo fills the screen, followed by a whip crack, a fire burning it away, and the first bars of an absurdly grandiose song along the lines of something Tex Ritter might have done in a 1950s western: "He rode a blazing saddle, he wore a shining star . . ." The images of red-rock buttes and arid plains are drawn directly from the iconography of the American western, the sweeping camera pans channeled almost directly from John Ford. "There is this false reverence in the opening song that is so funny," Mr. Grazer said. "It really alerts you, right away, that the director really had a vision for what he was after."

The ridiculously heroic lyrics match the grandiloquent richness of the camera work and the straight-faced seriousness with which the song is sung. "It's always difficult to get the tone right in these kinds of movies," Mr. Grazer said. The camera finally works its way down to a crew of black railroad workers, pounding in rails under the watchful eye of their white cowboy bosses.

"It used to be the common wisdom that you lit a comedy differently from the way you lit a drama," Mr. Grazer said. "That's why so many older comedies look overlit. It was a way of signaling the audience that it was a comedy. But this one is lit so richly it looks just like you'd expect from a real, traditional western. This is just a distillation of the kind of look audiences had become accustomed to after so many years of John Ford and Howard Hawks movies. The audience back then was aware of this, subliminally, and it added to the comedy."

A duel of wits arises between the black workers and their white overseers, filled with the nastiest racial epithets. At least, it would be a battle of wits, except that the bigoted white bosses are presented as bumbling morons, easily manipulated by the smooth, handsome leader of the black rail crew, Bart (Cleavon Little).

"Listen to this language," Mr. Grazer said. "You just couldn't say this kind of stuff on the screen in those days. And you certainly couldn't do it today. No way. This movie was a kind of singular moment where it was somehow all right to have this kind of racial language in a movie. The secret is that somehow, in the spirit of this movie, there is affection for the characters. Plus you can tell that Cleavon is just playing with these guys. That's what makes it work. They call him racial names, but you can tell that he's so much smarter than they are, so much hipper. You're seduced into being on his side. He's so beautiful and elegant compared to the stupid people around him."

In a way, it was a parody of the whole idea of hipness as played out against the backdrop of the most conservative and traditional of movie genres. Just as black musicians of the early decades of the twentieth century developed their own jargon, to signal one another that the joke was really on the whites—that they were bound together in this alternative world of hipness that the whites all around them were too square to grasp—so does Mr. Brooks flatter the audience by making it part of Little's hip world.

He's actually making fun of Slim Pickens and the other white cowboys, even though they don't understand that; his black coworkers understand it, and so does the audience.

"This is so subversive, so undercutting of the conventional stakes of movies, especially back in the early seventies," Mr. Grazer said. "That's one of the main things this movie taught me, the use of counterpoint. Even though the situation puts Little in the position of a victim, Brooks gives him power and nobility that the white characters don't have, so you know that you don't have to feel sorry for him. Even though on the surface he's being degraded, you know that he's going to prevail. You can sense it."

It was common for *Your Show of Shows* to include parodies of popular films of the period, like *From Here to Eternity,* and there is a clear connection between their approach and that of Mr. Brooks, who was one of the television show's legendary staff writers. What Mr. Brooks was doing in *Blazing Saddles,* though, was to parody not a single film but an entire genre—the traditional, pre-Peckinpah western—and even more unexpectedly to use it to address issues of race and sex that really had no place in the old westerns and that were very difficult for mainstream Hollywood films to approach in any form in the racially charged and sexually liberated world of the late 1960s and early '70s.

Mr. Brooks was able to raise these subjects by the canny way he manipulated the story's tone, Mr. Grazer said. "That these white bigots are so stupid somehow excuses them, or lets you watch them without taking offense," he said. "And almost everyone in this movie who is an authority figure is an idiot, including Mel Brooks, who plays the corrupt governor. In scenes where they are talking about doing really horrific things, like killing innocent people, they spend most of their time talking about extraneous things, as though life and death don't matter. It's so absurd."

Although *Blazing Saddles* is essentially a joke film, built around a series of interconnected sketches, it is also deceptively rich in plot: immediately after Bart is arrested by his white overseers and sent away to be hanged, we are introduced to the chief villain, Hedley Lamar

(Harvey Korman), who is distinguished from the other whites in the film in that he is actually smart enough to understand what's going on around him. That is what makes him evil. The others are just too stupid to get it.

Lamar is the governor's right-hand man and is also in charge of building the railroad. But when the shortest route promises to take the tracks through the small, peaceful town of Rock Ridge, Lamar plots to send his thugs in to chase the settlers away.

Mr. Grazer is delighted with the way Slim Pickens plays the scene in which he describes to Lamar how he and the others will roar into town, shooting and pillaging. Pickens bounces up and down on an imaginary horse, giddy with delight. "He thinks he's being so strong and powerful, but really he looks just like a little boy," Mr. Grazer said.

The anachronisms are everywhere. Outside Lamar's window is a gallows presided over by actor Robert Ridgely, dressed up like a medieval hangman. "This one is a doozy," Ridgely says, kissing the forehead of a man in a wheelchair with a noose around his neck. "Ah, yes," Lamar responds. "The Dr. Gillespie killings."

Even Lamar's own name (so similar to that of the seductive screen siren) is chosen for its joke value. The governor keeps referring to him as Hedy Lamar, to which Mr. Korman must respond, testily, "That's Hedley." Finally, the governor slaps him affectionately on the cheek and says: "What difference does it make? This is 1874. You can sue her."

The movie constantly moves back and forth between fidelity to the tired conventions of traditional westerns and undercutting them by mixing in ridiculous and incongruous elements. "It's like there's no center," Mr. Grazer said. "Brooks is just coming at us from all sides, from every genre and time period, mixing together all sorts of tones. The mix is very absurd and then very serious, until you don't know where you stand. It's all about the joy of breaking with conventions, while at the same time nostalgically embracing them."

When Bart is taken to Mostel's gallows, Lamar comes up with a plan to send him into the town of Rock Ridge, certain that the appearance of a black sheriff will be enough to tear the town to pieces.

The way the town is introduced in the film is a perfect example of the way Mr. Brooks used comic counterpoint, Mr. Grazer said. First, there is a slow, loving shot of the main street, which looks exactly like hundreds of other frontier towns in countless cowboy movies. A chorus begins a mock-serious song that tells us all about "the peaceful town of Rock Ridge," the camera gliding across the storefronts. A few of the townspeople are introduced.

But as the song proceeds, the melody picks up speed and the lyrics become more and more ludicrous, comic bits of visual humor undercutting the seriousness of the tone of the music and images, until it ends in the church. All of the townspeople are gathered there (everyone in the town is named Johnson, from the incomprehensibly drunken Gabby Johnson to Howard Johnson, proprietor of the town's ice-cream shop, featuring just one flavor), and it turns out that the song we have been hearing was being sung by the parishioners like a fractured hymn. It ends with a graphic, vulgar epithet.

"If you didn't have this song, it would look like hundreds of other towns in westerns, but this song takes it in a different direction," Mr. Grazer said. "Everything is against the way you've been conditioned to know it. And the jokes are relentless. Some are in the lyrics; some are visual things. They're constant. Not all of them connect, but they don't have to. They're coming so fast, and so many of them are so great, that you can't do anything but sit back and wait for the next one. Every fifteen seconds you get a comic hit, a shot of adrenaline. It's relentless."

In watching the film this time, Mr. Grazer is particularly struck that Mr. Brooks frequently used a silly bit of visual slapstick to get out of one scene and into another.

"I love this; it's just an amazing shot," Mr. Grazer said. Little is seated astride a golden horse, perfectly matching his suede outfit. There is a close-up of his saddle, which bears a Gucci logo. And as he rides across the desert landscape, ringed by craggy mountains, theme music of big-band jazz blares on the sound track. Just as the incongruousness of this is sinking in, the camera pans over and there is Count Basie's entire orchestra—music stands and all—sitting out in the middle of nowhere, playing away.

"You know what this makes me think of?" Mr. Grazer asked. "Do you remember how they had Burt Bacharach suddenly showing up in that first *Austin Powers* movie? That comes from the same place that this scene came from. The more you look, the more you see places where *Blazing Saddles* has influenced the comedies that came after it."

And then comes the big campfire scene.

Even at the time, it was the one scene that almost everyone who watched the movie talked about, gleefully juvenile while at the same time being so smartly constructed. "To me, this was the big take-away from this movie," Mr. Grazer said. That's movie industry talk for the big scene or big moment that sticks with audiences after they see a movie, the thing they talk about when they describe the movie to their friends. It's a simple enough scene. All it took was the will to do it.

A flickering campfire out on the open plains is surrounded by a couple of dozen cowboys, each with a tin of steaming beans in front of him. They shovel in the beans, taking huge, comic gulps. At just about the moment the audience makes its initial, sophomoric link to childhood jokes about the effects of eating too many beans, something blasts across the sound track.

It is a rude sound, and it is not the rustling of the wind across the sage. No, it is just what you think it is. And it is not one vulgar rip, but a whole string of them, playing out one after the other, like jazz musicians passing along the melody. Each burst is introduced by a cowpoke rising a few inches from his fireside log. There are low rumbles, high squeaks, titanic blasts. And it goes on and on and on.

"That's the big payoff of the joke: it keeps on going," Mr. Grazer said. "In how many more movies have filmmakers tried to get laughs out of doing something that's unexpected and that crosses the taste line? To me, this is what made this the first mainstream American shock comedy."

Mr. Brooks comes at the audience from both sides, goofy lowbrow humor along with smart references to previous films and established stereotypes. When Madeline Kahn appears as an initially villainous seductress, the fact that she is clearly not the blond bombshell she imagines herself to be is enough to carry the joke; audiences that are aware that she is a direct spoof on the dance hall singer played by Marlene Dietrich in *Destry Rides Again* (1939) can get an extra jolt of enjoyment. "You don't need to know that to get the joke, to enjoy the scene," Mr. Grazer said. "But if you do know that, it adds something. Throughout the movie, the humor is very layered that way."

Another thing that Mr. Grazer said he definitely learned from

Blazing Saddles was the effectiveness of giving a power to his comic heroes. It came from watching how Mr. Brooks handled not only Little's supremely confident hero but also his drunken sidekick, the Waco Kid, played by Gene Wilder.

"Most of the time, comedy comes out of a character's foibles or frailties," Mr. Grazer said. "But what Mel Brooks did here is, he gave his heroes a power. Gene Wilder is a washed-out drunk, but he's also really fast on the draw. In all of my comedies, I try to give the hero some sort of power. In *Liar Liar*, Jim Carrey was a really good lawyer. In *The Nutty Professor*, Eddie Murphy was a brilliant scientist. It's easy to be funny and be bumbling, but to be funny and have power at the same time, that's more difficult. But it makes the humor more poignant, and it helps give you a vehicle to resolve things at the end of the movie, to do whatever needs to be done to make the story turn out right."

At the end of the movie, of course, Mel Brooks throws all logic and convention out the window. The climactic street brawl between Lamar's thugs and the townspeople, led by Little, ends with the camera floating high into the sky and then turning to reveal that this is all taking place amid the hangarlike soundstages of the Warner Bros. lot in Burbank. The fight bursts through the wall into a stage where Dom DeLuise is directing a campy musical scene. Lamar flees out a studio gate, hails a cab, and says, "Drive me off this movie." Little pursues him down the traffic-choked street on horseback.

Eventually, they end up at Grauman's Chinese Theater where after a shoot-out Lamar collapses onto the cement footprints. And then, to add a further level of absurdity, Little and Mr. Wilder go into the theater to "see how the movie turns out," and it is *Blazing Saddles* that is being shown. They are somehow sucked back into the film, except Mr. Wilder takes a bucket of popcorn with him.

"It is just amazing, just brilliant," Mr. Grazer said. "The movie goes completely anarchic. This is where Brooks throws out all the rules and says: 'That's it; there are no rules anymore. I've covered everything; I've picked on everybody. Now I'm going to be an anarchist.'"

The film ended, and this time the remote's "Stop" button successfully turned off the television. Mr. Grazer pushed aside the last of his Cobb salad, walked over, and turned up the lights.

"As I look inside the scenes in this movie, I can see the rules and the axioms that I've been using to make myself successful, to be able to produce comedies," he said. "The use of counterpoint. The layering. Giving your hero a power. If the context is to see a thing in a certain way, you suddenly do the opposite thing Anytime you're inside a scene in a comedy, you should do the opposite of what's normal or expected, whether it's in the casting or in the material."

The sound of traffic was growing louder on Wilshire Boulevard, the evening rush hour just beginning to kick in.

"It's okay to go against convention," Mr. Grazer said. "All of your characters don't have to be likable. You don't have to have movie stars for audiences to connect. Studio guys are always saying the characters have to develop; they have to have an arc. But they don't. They don't. All you have to be is smart about it. That's what Mel Brooks was. That's my take-away from this movie after twenty-five years. You approach a movie like he did, with complete confidence. He's trusting you, as an audience, to understand the language of movies. He's trusting that you know what these references mean. And his confidence is contagious."

HIGHLIGHTS OF BRIAN GRAZER'S PRODUCING CAREER AND INFORMATION ON *BLAZING SADDLES*

■

What They Watched

Blazing Saddles. Directed by Mel Brooks; produced by Michael Hertzberg; screenplay by Andrew Bergman, Mel Brooks, Richard Pryor, Norman Steinberg, and Alan Uger; cinematography by Joseph Biroc; original music by Mel Brooks and John Morris. With Cleavon Little, Gene Wilder, Madeline Kahn, Harvey Korman, Slim Pickens, and Alex Karras. 1974.

Brian Grazer's Films

8 Mile. Directed by Curtis Hanson. With Eminem and Kim Basinger. 2002.

A Beautiful Mind. Directed by Ron Howard. With Russell Crowe and Jennifer Connelly. 2001.

Dr. Seuss's How the Grinch Stole Christmas. Directed by Ron Howard. With Jim Carrey and Taylor Momsen. 2000.

Bowfinger. Directed by Frank Oz. With Steve Martin. 1999.

Mercury Rising. Directed by Harold Becker. With Bruce Willis. 1998.

Liar Liar. Directed by Tom Shadyac. With Jim Carrey. 1997.

The Nutty Professor. Directed by Tom Shadyac. With Eddie Murphy. 1996.

Apollo 13. Directed by Ron Howard. With Tom Hanks. 1995.

The Paper. Directed by Ron Howard. With Michael Keaton. 1994.

For Love or Money. Directed by Barry Sonnenfeld. With Michael J. Fox. 1993.

Housesitter. Directed by Frank Oz. With Steve Martin. 1992.

My Girl. Directed by Howard Zieff. With Macaulay Culkin. 1991.

Kindergarten Cop. Directed by Ivan Reitman. With Arnold Schwarzenegger. 1990.

Parenthood. Directed by Ron Howard. With Steve Martin. 1989.

Spies Like Us. Directed by John Landis. With Chevy Chase. 1985.

Splash. Directed by Ron Howard. With Tom Hanks. 1984.

Night Shift. Directed by Ron Howard. With Henry Winkler and Michael Keaton. 1982.

Wes Anderson
on *Small Change*

The idea that started the project to include only well-established artists who did not need to be introduced to readers resulted in a series dominated by actors and directors who'd been at it for years, often decades. The result was that unless some young film-maker, like Quentin Tarantino, had been able to transform himself into a household name, they were unlikely to be invited to take part. As the series progressed, though, this began to feel a little limiting. A certain voice—a younger, less battle-ravaged voice—was missing. Wes Anderson, admittedly, was a borderline case by that early rule. I am not sure that he'd become quite a household name. But he had definitely emerged as perhaps the most admired and distinctive young directing voice in years, and based on just three films. Plus, I had to meet him. His mother, the estimable Texas Anderson, had been our real estate agent when I was the *New York Times* bureau chief in Houston. And I'd listened to stories about him long before I had any notion of covering Hollywood.

•

"Why did I pick this movie?" Wes Anderson asked himself, slouching against the wall in the glass-lined lobby of an office building on the Paramount Pictures lot, a sultry black-and-white portrait of Dorothy Lamour peering over his shoulder. "I don't actually have an answer for that."

Mr. Anderson, it turns out, is the sort of person who tells you—a little sheepishly—that he has no answer to something, and then spends the next two and a half hours giving you one.

A slanted, self-deprecating smile spread across his face. Tall, bony, and professorial, he leaned his forehead down so that he had to tilt his eyes up a bit to look straight ahead. "One thing is, I'm a big François Truffaut fan and this is the most unpretentious movie that I can possibly imagine," said Mr. Anderson, thirty-two.

He is referring to *L'Argent de Poche*—or *Small Change,* as it was released in the United States in 1976 (some other English-speaking countries saw it as *Pocket Money*)—a short, gentle, and studiously improvisational comedy about schoolchildren in a small French town. The documentary-like ensemble piece, teeming with life, arrived amid one of the most fertile periods in Truffaut's career.

"It almost looks like the kind of movie that would be projected on a sixteen-millimeter projector in a school library, or something like that," Mr. Anderson said. "And also, there's something about the fact that I am about the exact age as a lot of the kids in the movie. Even though it's taking place in France and I grew up in Houston, it's my exact childhood period."

In less time than it took a director like, say, Stanley Kubrick to make just one movie, Mr. Anderson burst out of the energetic Texas film community with the cult favorite *Bottle Rocket,* first a short film in 1994 and then a feature in 1996. He followed it with a second Houston-based comedy, the widely celebrated *Rushmore* (1998), and then assembled one of the best casts in a recent American film— Gene Hackman, Anjelica Huston, Ben Stiller, Gwyneth Paltrow, Danny Glover, etc.—to make his latest film, *The Royal Tenenbaums.* Along the way he also helped turn two of his closest childhood friends, the brothers Luke and Owen Wilson, into bona fide movie stars.

Still more of a critics' darling than a mainstream force, Mr. Anderson has a visual approach and storytelling style—a distinctive and, to its fans, beguiling combination of the quirky and the formal—that has received much critical attention, although it has mostly eluded those trying to pin Mr. Anderson down. Some clue, it seems, lies in a film as unprepossessing and unpremeditated as *Small Change,* with its small, acutely observed moments of everyday life.

"People talk about how the early French New Wave movies were so free, and the camera was so liberated and everything, especially in comparison to the films that came before them," Mr. Anderson said. "But not like this. In *Small Change,* the camera is even more free. I think Truffaut makes a kind of point of not obsessing about anything involving light, or anything like that. The whole movie had a real documentary feel to it. It makes you realize how meticulous some of those earlier New Wave movies really were."

Mr. Anderson says he tends to go on jags, immersing himself in the work of directors. He'll see one film by a particular director, and it will lead him to try to see as many as possible of that director's other works as quickly as possible. And sometimes, he finds, a director's sensibility will elude him at one point in his life and then unexpectedly strike home years later.

"You have to be ready for them," he said. "That was the experience I had, for instance, with Luis Buñuel. The first Buñuel movies that I saw were some of the last ones—you know, *The Discreet Charm of the Bourgeoisie* and *That Obscure Object of Desire.* I watched them when I was first in college and I didn't get them at all. I just didn't respond to them. And then, three years later, I saw one of his earlier films—I think it was Jeanne Moreau in *Diary of a Chambermaid*—and I suddenly understood his sense of humor. So I went back and started watching all of his films, and finally I arrived back at the ones that I'd started with, except this time I loved them. I got them, you see. I was ready for them."

In retrospect and with cold objectivity, it is apparent that *Small Change* is, in many ways, a minor-key Truffaut effort, especially compared with masterpieces like *The 400 Blows.* Yet seeing it when Mr. Anderson did—as an undergraduate at the University of Texas, when his filmmaking sensibility was beginning to blossom—was part of what has made the film so important to him.

"I think I saw it first on video," he said. "It struck me at once, you know? It's very wistful and sweet and sad. The first Truffaut film I ever saw was *400 Blows,* and that had a huge impact on me. But there's something about this one, too. And when you do something like this—pick a movie to watch for an article—you want to pick something that you want to proselytize about, in a way. And you're also picking a kind of brand to put on yourself. Oh, he's the guy who picked *Shane* to watch, or he's the one who watched a Roy Rogers movie. I was a little nervous to pick a French movie, because it can make you sound a little too, well, you know. It might not go over with some people."

Mr. Anderson walked around the corner and into a ground-floor screening room that had been set aside for the viewing. He settled himself toward the back of the theater, in one of the broad, upholstered chairs, facing the exact middle of the screen.

The film starts, with appropriate simplicity, on the shot of a girl standing outside a shop in what we are informed is the village of Bruère-Allichamps. The name of the shop, according to the sign above its door, is The Center of France, and the girl scampers inside to buy a postcard, then runs to an island in the middle of the main street to inscribe it. The tall monument behind her, which is also featured on the postcard, marks the exact geographical center of the nation. And it is in this way, quietly but with obvious symbolism, that Truffaut alerts us that his subject will be nothing less than the heart of France as reflected in its children.

As the postcard drops into a postal box, the scene shifts to another village: the girl's hometown, Puy-de-Dôme, where the main action will take place. Happy, screeching schoolchildren run wildly through the streets on their way to school as the credits roll.

"I haven't seen this in about five years, I'd guess," Mr. Anderson said. "I had a laser disc of it for a while and used to watch it a lot. And I think I screened it for the crew when we were making *Rushmore.* They let me have access to a screening room at Disney, and I screened it with a few other movies for the crew, just to get the feel of it."

Maurice Jaubert's happy, energetic music plays over the credits, not quite drowning out the sounds of childish ebullience. Mr. Anderson's own idiosyncratic musical choices have been noted by critics, so it comes as no surprise that he has made a study of Truffaut's scores.

"I had always thought that Truffaut had these two main guys as his composers, Georges Delerue and Jaubert, and I tried to get my hands on copies of all of his sound tracks," Mr. Anderson said. "It was only when I really looked at them that I realized that the music he was using from Jaubert was recycled from films in the twenties and thirties. I've been trying to gather this stuff up. I loved these scores so much in the Truffaut movies that I thought maybe there were some other Jaubert pieces that Truffaut hadn't used. But I'm finding that it's very hard to put your hands on them."

The giggling children are still scampering through the streets.

"Do kids in French villages really run to school in packs?" Mr. Anderson asked. "I don't know, but it feels natural, doesn't it? There's something about these shirts and sneakers that the children are wearing. It's all the same kind of stuff that we were wearing right around the same time, in the mid-seventies. Although our streets in Texas didn't look like this, obviously, the way they're dressed really reminds me of the way me and my brothers would have dressed back then. And I really like them running to school, you know? I like the feel of it. It could come across as a little precious, but it doesn't, does it?"

One by one, in the opening scenes at the school, the characters are introduced: a pair of lovelorn schoolteachers, a new student from an abusive household, a class clown, a precocious girl, and so on. "Oh, these are the Deluca brothers," Mr. Anderson said. "They're great. I love them in this movie. They're always up to something."

The camera glides in and out of groups of people, focusing on one child and then another, cutting to a different classroom, its gaze sliding in and out of conversations and stolen glances. Nothing about the film seems fussy. The camera is where it is.

"That's what's so great about this movie," Mr. Anderson said. "There are all of these threads, all of these people and story lines, but it also feels very free, as though we can join any character at any moment. There are some characters who have just one scene or just one moment, and then a few who kind of continue throughout the whole movie and have their own developing stories. But when they're introduced, they're all introduced in the same way, so you're never sure who is going to turn out to be important and who's making their only appearance. It's very rare to introduce characters that way, yet it doesn't feel like a stunt the way Truffaut does it. It feels very natural."

Julien, the new student from an abusive home, is shown standing in the school courtyard, his scraggly hair obscuring his face. "Now, this is one of the stories that we're going to follow, but he's introduced in the same way as everyone else," Mr. Anderson said. "His story is probably the darkest thing in the whole movie, but it's never really heavy. Nothing is. The whole movie has a real lightness to it."

A Truffaut film featuring a troubled child inevitably begs comparison to *The 400 Blows* (1959) and his other autobiographical films, in which the young director transformed his difficult youth into art. What intrigues Mr. Anderson is not just how differently Truffaut treated childhood trauma in *The 400 Blows* and *Small Change,* but how the entire tone and sensibility had shifted in the intervening decades into one that is lighter and more forgiving.

"This movie has so much innocence," Mr. Anderson said of *Small Change.* "In *400 Blows,* the character of Antoine, who is really Truffaut, is not so innocent. We are on his side, it is not his fault, but he's a lot more complicated and troubled and angry, as Truffaut himself must have been, than Julien or any of the children in *Small Change.*"

Mr. Anderson remembered that as a college student he stumbled across a huge volume of Truffaut's scripts and letters in the University of Texas library. He devoured it and can vividly remember many passages.

"There is one of Truffaut's letters that is amazing and so funny and sad," Mr. Anderson said. The young Truffaut was writing to one of his closest friends, who had entrusted the future director with his books and other valuable things, which Truffaut had promptly sold and kept the money.

"There is a letter of apology from Truffaut that is so overstated," he said. "The language is very flowery, and you get the feeling that, in this relationship, Truffaut felt himself to be intellectually superior and was the dominant personality between the two. But at this point, he was clearly guilty and kind of vulnerable and exposed, and he was trying to maintain the upper hand in their relationship at the same time he couldn't be more guilty. What's interesting is to see how this kid, who came from such a brutal background, went through all of this and came out, in the 1970s, with this humane, gentle attitude about it all."

Several times during the film, Mr. Anderson remarked on the

quality of the children's acting, most of them simply recruited off the streets in the village where the movie was shot. There have been important child actors in all of Mr. Anderson's films, and he has strong feelings on the subject.

"Both *400 Blows* and this movie had such great kids in them," Mr. Anderson said. "I love working with children. They're so surprising, you know? But the casting process is very involved. It takes a long time to really figure it out with them. But then once you get going with them, you can see which ones really snap to it and are completely natural. Some people can just do it and some can't. Plus, they haven't had any experience, so they haven't had a chance to fall into any habits, good or bad. What I've found that's interesting, though, is that the ones who can do it can just do it, right from the beginning. I don't think I've ever seen one improve over the course of making a movie. Either they can do it or they can't. It's odd."

There is also something about the quality of the children chosen by Truffaut: they are attractive and personable, but not plastic or pretty. "They're more appealing than an average kid would be who you'd pull off the street, but they're not like TV kids," Mr. Anderson said. "I have thought about this movie a lot. It's not like, when I was working, I'd think, 'Oh, I wonder how Truffaut would have done it.' But these images have definitely come to me when I'm working. And also the casting. When you see these kids, they don't look like TV kids, yet they're very appealing. That's always something I'm trying to capture."

The scenes float past without any sense of rhythm or purpose, just captured snippets of daily life. The camera visits one child, then glides over to another. Life is going on all around it. In one scene, students are walking into a classroom. One unaffectedly steals a look into the camera, then continues on.

"Now, he could easily have shot that over again," Mr. Anderson said. "Normally, you don't have your actors glancing into the camera as they walk by. But in this movie, it's all right because the whole movie feels that way. The things happening in the movie seem like they're really happening in real life, and in real life a kid might do something like that. In some movies, it would ruin everything. But here, it feels like Truffaut doesn't have to make an effort to cast a spell.

It's all so natural. That's part of why it's so documentary feeling. We really feel like we're in a real French school with real French kids and that we're watching real life unfolding."

Several times, Mr. Anderson pointed out an awkward camera placement or shakiness in a camera movement. "Clearly, Truffaut is a filmmaker who knew how to make a smooth, polished film," Mr. Anderson said. "He made *Story of Adele H.* around this same time, and that feels nothing like this. Like here—see how that camera is shaking and a little crooked? And Truffaut just keeps going. It's part of his strategy for this film. He wanted to get a certain spirit, a naturalness, and that's how he did it. Plus, I think he shot this movie very, very quickly."

Two scenes in the film drew the most comment from Mr. Anderson.

In the first, one of the most famous passages in the movie, a toddler crawls out onto a windowsill in an apartment building, eleven stories above the grass and hedges. As horrified passersby watch from below, the toddler clambers over a low railing and plummets through the air, landing on a fluffy bush with a soft thud and a broad smile, totally unhurt.

"You just know, during all of that, that nothing really bad is going to happen to the kid," Mr. Anderson said. "It just wouldn't fit the tone of the movie. And when the kid falls, you can tell that it's a dummy falling. It's so odd in a movie that's been so realistic. And then he lands and he's smiling and unhurt, and it's—I don't know, what is it? It's not realism. Maybe it's magic realism. But somehow it fits perfectly in the movie."

A short while later, two schoolgirls are wandering down the town's main street, past some shops and a sidewalk cafe. The camera follows alongside them, listening in on their conversation. When they go into a shop, the camera lingers outside, listens to another bit of chatter from a passing pedestrian, then continues to follow the girls down the street. When they go into the cafe, again the camera lingers outside, listening in on first one and then another of the conversations taking place at the sidewalk tables, and then rejoining the girls when they emerge.

"There's not really anything happening in this scene," Mr. Anderson said. "There's no particular agenda that we can see. And the way we move through different groups of people—hearing parts of different conversations, sometimes overlapping—it's very much the way Robert Altman works. And then, in the end, the whole scene turns out to really have been about nothing. It doesn't further any of the story lines at all. It's just a little slice of everyday life, like a punctuation between two more substantial scenes."

It becomes clear as the movie unfolds, drawing us in and out of so many lives, that at least one reason that Mr. Anderson chose it was to revisit so many of the influences that Truffaut had on his work, beginning with the use of children and continuing through the intricate ensemble structure. Even the narration (by Alec Baldwin) that Mr. Anderson used in *The Royal Tenenbaums* has its antecedent in Truffaut. "I love the way he uses narration, like the beginning passages of *Jules and Jim*, remember how he was talking so fast? And it's a narrator who's not a character in the story. In so many movies, he uses narration and letters or books. *The Story of Adele H.* was practically all about letters."

When Truffaut did the credits for *Two English Girls*, another of his '70s efforts, he used multiple copies of the book from which the film was adapted in a checkerboard pattern on the screen. In *The Royal Tenenbaums*, every major character has written a book, and when each is introduced, a copy of the character's book is shown on the screen, just as in *Two English Girls*. "Actually, in that one, Truffaut also showed his written notes from preparing the script," Mr. Anderson said. "All we did was steal the way he had the covers arranged."

Even more, though, than the way Mr. Anderson's style mirrors Truffaut's, what becomes apparent while watching *Small Change* is how different the two directors are. While Truffaut's film feels entirely improvised and ungoverned by fussy filmmaking rules, Mr. Anderson's is formal and calculated and entirely fussy.

"In this movie, it's almost like Truffaut is saying, 'We're not going to have any rules here,'" Mr. Anderson said. "I obsessively make rules. I have weird, pointless rules. I want the movies to be like math, almost. But only in the aspect of the camera and the cutting and how the music is used and things like that, not when it comes to the performances."

His camera operators know there are certain types of camera moves that he does not allow. In *The Royal Tenenbaums*, the entire film is shot using the same 30-millimeter lens. Why? Mr. Anderson shrugged. "I need it to be that lens," he said. "If it's another lens it's like, that isn't right, that's not shaped right."

Another rule: Whenever something is placed on a tabletop, the camera moves directly overhead and shoots the object looking straight down. "It got to the point where they didn't even have to ask me," he said. "They knew it was a tabletop scene, so they'd set up the camera over the table. 'Oh, here it comes, another standard Wes tabletop shot.' It's more for me, I think, than it is for the movie. It feels right to me that way. But the ultimate effect is that it unifies the movie."

Most immediately noticeable, though, is the way his characters are framed. Whether there is one character or a handful, they are always smack in the middle of the screen.

"In the movie we just did, everybody is in the dead center of the frame for almost the entire movie," Mr. Anderson said. "Even when you have nine people in a shot, they are obsessively arranged so you can always see all nine of them. No one is obscuring anyone else. I even had one shot where there were thirteen people, and I wanted to pull straight back and reveal even more people at the edges. But in doing that, I found, some of the people got blocked. So I had Bill Murray and Owen Wilson and one other guy kind of lean forward unnaturally as the camera pulled away, just so they would clear themselves and remain in the shot. I have to admit, I think perhaps it's more meticulous than is really healthy."

Nothing could be further from the sensibility of *Small Change,* in which characters peer into the camera, block out one another, and seem to wander around the frame at will. That's it, Mr. Anderson said; that's the mystery of how one filmmaker can so fundamentally influence another and yet make films that are stylistic opposites.

"One thing I do feel a total connection with this movie about is the way the actors are free," Mr. Anderson said. "Except in weird cases where I have actors leaning so they can stay in a shot, when I have actors playing a scene I try to make it so they are as free as possible. That's where I intersect with *Small Change.* Maybe my actors have to hit a mark, but there aren't too many obstacles in the way of them being able to do what they want to do."

Many of the filmmakers who have taken part in this series have sadly remarked, at some point while watching a movie that has meant so much to them, that the film could not be made in Hollywood today. Too expensive, too quirky, too dark—whatever the problem, they seemed almost wistful about what it must have been like to work at the studios when such movies could be made. But Mr. Anderson just shrugged when asked if he felt that way about *Small Change*. The question didn't apply, he said.

"They didn't make this movie in Hollywood," he said. "The reason you couldn't do this movie today is that François Truffaut died."

HIGHLIGHTS OF WES ANDERSON'S DIRECTING CAREER AND INFORMATION ON *SMALL CHANGE*

■

What They Watched

Small Change (*L'Argent de Poche*). Directed and produced by François Truffaut; screenplay by Suzanne Schiffman and François Truffaut; cinematography by Pierre-William Glenn. With Claudio Deluca, Franck Deluca, Sylvie Grizel, Sébastien Marc, Marcel Berbert, and Corinne Boucart. 1976.

Wes Anderson's Films

The Royal Tenenbaums. With Gene Hackman, Anjelica Huston, Danny Glover, Ben Stiller, and Gwyneth Paltrow. 2001.

Rushmore. With Jason Schwartzman, Bill Murray, Olivia Williams, and Brian Cox. 1998.

Bottle Rocket. With Luke Wilson, Owen Wilson, Robert Musgrave, and Ned Dowd. 1996.

18

Sissy Spacek on
To Kill a Mockingbird

Sissy Spacek I would place in the same category as Woody Allen—the kind of interview subject who was crucial to the series, to validate it and to exemplify it. When I started out, and made a wish list of the actresses I most hoped would take part, she was at the very top, alongside Meryl Streep and Jodie Foster. (They both turned me down, or at least their handlers told me they did.) So to get Spacek to agree to take part, and to have her choose a movie that I also happen to love very much and watch often, was one of the high points of the project for me. She also turned out to be warm, open, and gracious, and extremely generous in talking about what *To Kill a Mockingbird* meant to her in her own life, in the racially charged Texas town where she grew up. I'd really grown to love Texas in the time I was there, so this was also a chance for me to revisit those emotions.

■

Sissy Spacek remembers wandering down to the drugstore in Quitman, the small East Texas town where she grew up, and picking out an empty cigar box that she could use to hide her treasures. "I think I had a couple of school pictures of secret boyfriends, stuff like that," Ms. Spacek said. "I took it out in the backyard and buried it, but I used my feet to measure where I did it. I even made a map. But when I went back to dig it up, my feet had grown and I never could find it again. It's still out there, I guess."

Ms. Spacek, fifty-two, was sitting in the middle row of a small screening room in a glass tower on Park Avenue, the light from the opening moments of *To Kill a Mockingbird* (1962) playing across her familiar freckled face. Behind the film's credits, the camera moved across the worn, dirty contents of a child's cigar box. There were some marbles, a couple of carved figurines, a broken watch, a pocket knife. Elmer Bernstein's score began as a series of single notes, as if pecked out on the piano by a child using one finger.

"That whole idea of these kids with their little secret box and all the trinkets in it, it really spoke to me," Ms. Spacek said. "I couldn't help but think about my own cigar box. And I remember the way the whole movie plays through the eyes of the children. I just remember seeing their dirty little fingernails and their dirty faces and the way they're running around, playing in the courthouse. I used to go down and play in the courthouse, too, and it looked a lot like the one in this movie. I'm sure the county records have never been the same since."

Based on the Pulitzer Prize–winning novel by Harper Lee—her only published book—*To Kill a Mockingbird* is the story of Atticus Finch, a humble and impeccably decent lawyer in a small southern town at the height of the Depression. A middle-age widower (played by Gregory Peck in his only Oscar-winning role), Atticus is seen primarily through the eyes of his two children, a son named Jem (Philip Alford), making his first tentative steps toward maturity, and the story's narrator, a daughter named Jean Louise (Mary Badham), or Scout.

"I think they captured so well how children are drawn to what is mysterious and scary, the way they concoct stories to test and frighten themselves," Ms. Spacek said. "I'm sure I saw this for the first time in a movie theater, probably the Gem Theater in Quitman, where they had a separate entrance for the blacks, who had to sit upstairs in the balcony. And downstairs in the courthouse, I remember, they had separate bathrooms for 'colored women' and 'white ladies.' I wandered into the 'colored' bathroom once, just because I wanted to see what it was like in there, you know, and there was this big black woman who looked at me and said, 'What are you doing in here?' I ran out as fast as I could."

After gaining her first national attention with a supporting role in a 1972 Lee Marvin thriller called *Prime Cut*, Ms. Spacek very quickly became one of the top female stars of the decade, widely regarded as one of the most fertile periods in American filmmaking. She worked with Terrence Malick in *Badlands* (1973), Brian De Palma in *Carrie* (1976), and Robert Altman in *Three Women* (1977) before winning an Oscar as the country singer Loretta Lynn in *Coal Miner's Daughter* (1980).

In more recent years, she has largely played supporting roles in films like Oliver Stone's *JFK* (1991), Paul Schrader's *Affliction* (1997), and David Lynch's *Straight Story* (1999). That history gave the flavor of a full-fledged comeback to her current success in the small, independent film *In the Bedroom* (2001) for which she has won a Golden Globe as best actress and her sixth Oscar nomination.

As a child, Ms. Spacek said, *To Kill a Mockingbird* spoke to her because it evoked so many feelings and images from her small town. "I thought it was a children's movie when I first saw it," she said. "And I was overwhelmed with the familiarity of the world that they lived in. Not until later, when I saw it as an adult, did I understand the deeper dimensions of it. It's so rare to have a film hold up over so many years, and to have seen it from two such different perspectives, yet to have it work for you on both levels so deeply."

Not only the film's director, Robert Mulligan, but also its screenwriter, Horton Foote, and its producer, the future director Alan J. Pakula, came to the movies from the world of 1950s live television, and *To Kill a Mockingbird* has something of the feel of the urgent, naturalistic black-and-white dramas of that period. But *To Kill a Mockingbird*, like many of the best films of the early 1960s, is also a bridge between the kitchen-sink theatricality of live television and the emerging, rougher style of acting and storytelling that took root later in the '60s and then flourished in the '70s. It is also a story about remembering, so it is no surprise that watching it evokes a flood of memories for Ms. Spacek, who says the words "I remember" more often than any others in the course of the screening.

"It was definitely the first movie that came into my mind when I thought about what movie to watch," Ms. Spacek said. "It's my favorite film of all time. Number one, absolutely. I did think a little bit about that scary movie *Night of the Hunter,* which I also love and which had a big impact on me. I remember we had this *Reader's Digest* condensed book of the novel on which it was based, and I would sneak looks inside, where there were these creepy drawings, like one of a dead woman sitting in this Model T at the bottom of a lake. But in the end I thought, no, I should stick with my first favorite."

In the film's opening narration, the voice of the adult Jean Louise remembers her childhood as the camera sweeps across her dusty neighborhood, and her younger self, Scout, as she is called, makes her entrance on the end of a swinging rope, like Tarzan. It was hot back then, she tells us, and everyone was poor, and the days lasted twenty-four hours but seemed longer.

"I remember back when there seemed to be more than twenty-four hours in the day," Ms. Spacek said, laughing delightedly at such small details as a tree fort, a rope swing, and the long line of sun-scorched clapboard houses in the Finches' neighborhood. "Look at how Mary Badham plays these scenes," Ms. Spacek said. "She's always holding on to something or sliding down something or twisting on something. It's so evocative, so childlike. And she is just the cutest thing. We all wanted to be her back then. She was just such a little tomboy who always spoke her mind and wasn't afraid."

The first scenes introduce Atticus, a gentle presence greeting one of his impoverished law clients and reading the morning paper while the children scamper around him. Jem refuses to come down from his tree fort unless Atticus "agrees to play football for the Methodists," and he complains about not having a gun of his own. Scout twists and stretches and swings and looks on.

"The crazy thing is that most boys his age did have guns back then," Ms. Spacek said. "I can remember feeling very left out because I didn't have a gun and all my brothers had one."

Instead of ordering Jem out of the tree, Atticus simply says, "Suit yourself," and turns his back. In a scene a short while later, Atticus goes into Scout's bedroom to kiss her good night, and they talk about how someday Jem will get Atticus's watch ("It is customary for the boy to have his father's watch") but Scout will inherit her dead mother's earrings and pearl necklace.

"He's such a wonderful father," Ms. Spacek said. "I knew that even when I saw the movie as a child. I think every little kid wanted to have a relationship with their parents like this. You know, he didn't insist that they always fall into perfect step. They got to be little individuals. Jem could stay up in the tree if he wanted to. Scout was this scrappy little kid, and he let her be herself. He didn't try to break their spirit."

The staging of the bedside scene between Atticus and Scout, Ms. Spacek said, is indicative of the subtle but calculated way that Mulligan leads audiences through the film and builds to the movie's many emotional high points. The scene begins with the camera peering into Scout's bedroom through an open window with lace curtains hanging down. Why begin by forcing us to look through the gaps in the lace? It's very pretty, for one thing, Ms. Spacek said, but it also subtly makes the point, which becomes important later, that the window is open.

After Atticus has kissed Scout good night and left the room, the camera again takes up its position looking through the lace. We eavesdrop as Scout and Jem in the next room have a quiet conversation about their mother, what she was like, whether they miss her, whether they even remember her. Except now the camera gently glides to the right and we see that Atticus is sitting there, silently, on a porch swing, listening to them through the open window. For an actor the temptation must have been great to react somehow, Ms. Spacek said, to milk the moment. But Mr. Peck resisted, and his face remains contemplative, impassive.

"Isn't that great?" Ms. Spacek said. "As far as acting goes, this film really is a study of less is more. Because it's so powerful this way. It conveys so much. Dignity. Character. Integrity. Atticus Finch is such a heroic man."

The movie slowly eases into its story, first giving us a look into children's world of play. The arrival in the neighborhood of a new boy, Dill—an orphan spending the summer with his Aunt Stephanie, who lives next door to the Finches—inspires Jem to regale the newcomer with the neighborhood's creepiest legend, that of the ghostly, perhaps murderous Boo Radley. He lives unseen in the biggest, scariest house on the block, a captive of his dour parents, who have kept him locked up since an incident many years earlier when he was said to have stabbed his father with a pair of scissors.

Stay away from the Radley house, Dill is warned, especially at night when Boo is said to sneak out sometimes and prey on whatever crosses his path. So, of course, the children spend their days and nights working up the courage to do things like stand on the Radley porch or race up and touch its front door. "We had a haunted house in our neighborhood, too," Ms. Spacek said. "There was this woman who lived there and it was always dark, and I remember my mother bringing me there one time."

Up on the screen, Jem is leading Scout and Dill on a late-night excursion to sneak into the Radleys' yard and peer through their windows.

"Kids always know all of the secret passages and short cuts in a neighborhood," Ms. Spacek said. "I can remember when me, my girlfriend, and her dog, Queenie, used to go out at night in our pajamas and walk through the nearby graveyard. Oh, I would have gotten into trouble if I got caught. And we almost did get caught one night because the night watchman, whose name was Shorty, saw Queenie running around. That was pretty scary and exciting. In a way, it's a lot like what these kids are doing in the movie. You know, you have fun by putting yourself in harm's way because you know, in your heart, that you're really safe. Just like we all knew it wasn't really a haunted house."

Seeing the children on the screen in these scenes—sitting in the gloom behind a shed, lighted only by a distant streetlight, the chirp of insects filling the summer air—has always had the power to evoke memories of her own summer nights, Ms. Spacek said.

"That was the best time of the day, the very best time," she said. "It was dark, or just getting dark, and you were always having the most fun just when you knew you were going to be called inside at any moment. You didn't want it to end. When you were called in, you'd say, 'Oh, we'll pick it up again tomorrow.' But you never could. It was never the same the next day. So it became this magic hour, when it was just getting dark and you had to speed up your play because you knew it was about to end and it would be gone forever."

The opening sequences of *To Kill a Mockingbird,* from Dill's arrival to the late-night raid on the Radley house, are actually a bit of a feint (or so it appears until the last ten minutes). The meat of the story involves Atticus's agreeing to defend a black farmer, Tom Robinson, charged with the rape of a dirt-poor white girl, Mayella Violet Ewell.

The shift is heralded by the almost simultaneous arrival in the story of Bob Ewell, Mayella's racist and abusive father and the chief villain. He and Atticus have several confrontations, usually with Ewell blustering and Atticus refusing to lose his temper. At one point, Ewell goes so far as to spit in Atticus's face.

"There's an awful lot of spit in this movie," Ms. Spacek said. "Back earlier, when they were sneaking into the Radley yard, they spit on the gate hinges to stop them from squeaking. Then Dill's aunt spits on her handkerchief to clean off his face. And now I guess, in those days, spit solved a lot of things."

Of course, it is not childhood but prejudice that is the subject of *To Kill a Mockingbird,* particularly racial bigotry. And it is presented through two interrelated themes, both enunciated by Atticus to his children: Do not prejudge others and do not use your power to harm the innocent.

Repeatedly during the movie (and actually, many more times in the book) Atticus must gently remind Jem and Scout that they should not be too quick to judge anyone else until they've had a chance to "walk around in his shoes for a while." Time and again either Jem or Scout makes the mistake of jumping to a conclusion about someone around them, whether it's a poor client trying to pay off his bill to Atticus, a country boy smothering his lunch with maple syrup, or ghostly Boo sitting in the dark just down the street.

And then another time, when talking with Jem yet again about getting a gun, Atticus makes the point that it is a sin to use a gun or any power to harm an innocent creature. He uses the metaphor of shooting a mockingbird.

When a rabid dog wanders into the neighborhood, the Finches' housekeeper, Calpurnia, calls Atticus and he rushes home with the sheriff. It's the payoff scene for all the conversations about getting a gun. Jem is sure that his father is skittish about guns, maybe even afraid of them. So he is stunned when the sheriff hands Atticus the rifle and asks him to shoot the mad dog. Atticus comically fumbles with his eyeglasses. ("I wonder if that was in the script," Ms. Spacek said, "or did Gregory Peck come up with that?") Then Atticus raises the rifle and downs the animal with one clean shot. The flabbergasted Jem realizes he has misjudged his own father. "What's the matter, boy?" the sheriff says. "Didn't you know your father was the best shot in the county?"

Late one night, when the sheriff is called out of town to investigate reports of a lynch mob, Atticus must go down to the jailhouse to stand guard on his client, Tom Robinson. He sits outside on the stoop, reading by the light of a standing lamp that he has brought from home. The children follow after Atticus, a mirror image of their earlier late-night excursion into the Radley yard, but this time it is not child's play. A line of cars approaches the jail and grim-faced men emerge from them, intent on a lynching.

"I love him sitting there with that lamp," Ms. Spacek said. "I just love that there is the adult world, where these real things are happening, and there is the children's world, where they make up stories and scare themselves, and neither one really understands the other."

When the children rush forward to protect Atticus, he orders them home. But Jem, the only one who begins to really understand what is at stake, refuses. And before the matter can come to a climax, Scout inadvertently diffuses the situation by talking to one of the mob's leaders about his son, a schoolmate. "Don't you know me, Mr. Cunningham? It's me. It's Jean Louise Finch. I know your boy, Walter. He's a good boy. Tell him I said hey."

When the scene is over and the mob has withdrawn, Ms. Spacek wondered about Scout's scene. "I think maybe that speech went on too long," she said. "Did it go on too long for you?" And then she laughed. "It's amazing they were able to make this picture without us," she said.

And then she fell silent as the camera pulled back. The mob had left. The children had gone back home. There was Atticus, sitting on the jail stoop in the lamplight, a lone figure in a gloomy world. From inside the jail came the voice of Tom Robinson. "Are they gone?" he asked. "They're gone," Atticus said. "They won't bother you anymore." All the while, the camera stayed back, as if watching the scene from several dozen yards away.

"Isn't that nice, the way they pulled back?" Ms. Spacek said. "It's so much more powerful. You can see how alone they really were, and him with that silly lamp."

The trial of Tom Robinson, which takes up much of the middle section of the film, is the longest sustained sequence in the movie, and it is intensely frustrating to watch. Witness after witness makes clear that Robinson is innocent of the crime; if anything, he is a victim of having been too sympathetic to Mayella, his accuser. But it is also abundantly clear that no amount of evidence will be sufficient to protect him because it would mean taking the word of a black man over the word of two whites.

It ends, inevitably, with Robinson's conviction. But there is a coda.

As Atticus, alone on the courtroom floor, gathers his papers and prepares to leave, he is watched from above by the black spectators—segregated in the courtroom balcony, just as they were in the Gem Theater—and none of them have left their seats. The two Finch children are up there, too, having watched the trial as guests of the black minister. Jem is devastated by the miscarriage of justice, but Scout is still not fully aware of what has happened. She looks around, a little puzzled. Slowly, one by one, the black spectators rise to their feet as Atticus makes his way out of the courtroom. "Stand up, Miss Jean Louise," the minister says. "Your father is passing."

A half-choked sob escaped from Ms. Spacek. "Oh, that gets me every time," she said. "Every single time." She paused for a few moments, collecting herself. "What a great character Atticus Finch is," she said. "Did you see? He didn't even look up as he left the courtroom. He didn't know they were standing up for him. That's not why he did it, for the approval. To think that there might be people in the world like him. A great film moment. A great, great film moment."

When, in the movie's surprising closing scenes, Scout understands that Boo Radley is yet another person whom she wrongly prejudged, the two seemingly disparate story lines come together with a satisfying, emotional snap. (The hint comes earlier, when we learn that the objects in the children's cigar box during the opening credits were actually anonymous gifts that the children had discovered in the knothole of a tree in the Radley yard.)

That, essentially, is what happens in *To Kill a Mockingbird*: the children's play world and the adult real world crash into each other. The stories of Tom Robinson and Boo Radley, a pair of mockingbirds, intersect through the lives of children testing the waters of maturity.

"It's just poetry," Ms. Spacek said. "When I first saw it as a child, I guess it was that first sequence, with the cigar box, that just swept me away. Now, I guess really it's still the simplicity that astounds me, and the depth of it. It's so moving. 'Stand up, Miss Jean Louise. Your father is passing.' Everyone should have a dad like that.

"I love that it is in black and white. I love that it has a kind of a theatrical quality yet remains very realistic. And the acting—I think Gregory Peck is just great. He's kind of the anchor."

She sat forward in her seat as the final swells of music drifted away, Mr. Bernstein's simple score having grown during the course of the movie into something lush and rousing. She was thinking about the segregated seating in the Gem Theater where she first saw the movie and also about one of its scenes. Atticus is visiting the Robinson shack on the wrong side of the tracks, and Jem, left behind in the car, stares through the window at a black boy, about the same age. They study each other silently.

"I remember a moment when I was a girl, about their age, and I went with my mom out to this black woman's house who was doing some reupholstering work for us," Ms. Spacek said. "Whenever we'd go out there, I'd play with her kids. We'd stay outside. It was hot in the summer and dusty, and we were always thirsty. And I remember how one time they opened up the lip of this well that they had, and pulled up this big bucket of water and they took out a dipper and passed it around. We took turns drinking from it. It went from kid to kid. I remember thinking it was the sweetest, coolest, most wonderful drink of water I ever had. It was a real important moment in my life. I didn't realize it then, but it was."

She brushed back her hair and stood up.

"There are wonderful things about the South," Ms. Spacek said. "Wonderful things and terrible things. And this movie illuminates both of them." She grabbed her bag, slung it over her shoulder, and wrapped a scarf more tightly around her neck. It was cold and dark out on Park Avenue.

"If more people were like Atticus Finch," she said, "the world would be a better place."

HIGHLIGHTS OF SISSY SPACEK'S ACTING CAREER AND INFORMATION ON *TO KILL A MOCKINGBIRD*

■

What They Watched

To Kill a Mockingbird. Directed by Robert Mulligan; produced by Alan J. Pakula; screenplay by Horton Foote, based on the novel by Harper Lee; original music by Elmer Bernstein; cinematography by Russell Harlan; edited by Aaron Stell. With Gregory Peck, Mary Badham, Philip Alford, Brock Peters, Robert Duvall, and James Anderson. 1962.

Sissy Spacek's Films

Tuck Everlasting. Directed by Jay Russell. With Alexis Bledel. 2002.

In the Bedroom. Directed by Todd Field. With Tom Wilkinson. 2001.

The Straight Story. Directed by David Lynch. With Richard Farnsworth. 1999.

Blast from the Past. Directed by Hugh Wilson. With Brendan Fraser. 1999.

Affliction. Directed by Paul Schrader. With Nick Nolte. 1997.

The Grass Harp. Directed by Charles Matthau. With Piper Laurie. 1995.

JFK. Directed by Oliver Stone. With Kevin Costner. 1991.

Crimes of the Heart. Directed by Bruce Beresford. With Diane Keaton. 1986.

'Night Mother. Directed by Tom Moore. With Anne Bancroft. 1986.

Marie. Directed by Roger Donaldson. With Jeff Daniels. 1985.

The River. Directed by Mark Rydell. With Mel Gibson. 1984.

Missing. Directed by Costa-Gavras. With Jack Lemmon. 1982.

Coal Miner's Daughter. Directed by Michael Apted. With Tommy Lee Jones. 1980.

Welcome to L.A. Directed by Alan Rudolph. With Keith Carradine. 1977.

Three Women. Directed by Robert Altman. With Shelley Duvall and Janice Rule. 1977.

Carrie. Directed by Brian De Palma. With Amy Irving. 1976.

Badlands. Directed by Terrence Malick. With Martin Sheen. 1973.

Prime Cut. Directed by Michael Ritchie. With Lee Marvin. 1972.

19

Nicole Kidman on
The Shining

Nicole Kidman had reached a real moment in her career. Fresh from the tabloid wars surrounding the breakup of her marriage to actor Tom Cruise, she had two triumphs, one after the other, in the summer of 2001: first as a corseted, fishnet-stockinged chanteuse in Baz Luhrmann's feverish *Moulin Rouge*, and then as a haunted mother in Alejandro Amenábar's *The Others*. As we sat down to watch Stanley Kubrick's *The Shining* in a huge, ice-cold screening room in Santa Monica, the only question in most people's minds was which film would earn her an Oscar nomination (*Moulin Rouge,* it turned out). Once someone has become a boldface name in the gossip columns, it can be difficult to separate the actress and creative artist from the celebrity magazine cover girl, which made it all the more interesting that she chose a Kubrick film, unflinching about the connection this was certain to make in readers' minds with *Eyes Wide Shut,* the Kubrick film that she had made with her ex-husband.

·

The first time Nicole Kidman saw *The Shining,* she was fourteen and spent most of the movie paying more attention to her sixteen-year-old boyfriend than to what was happening on the screen. "I was meant to be going roller-skating at this rink in Sydney," she said. "But we decided to ditch that and go see a movie. I really wasn't supposed to be in there. I was too young, as I recall, but he got me in. I looked older. And I kind of watched a bit of the movie, but really, I made out through most of it."

Later, she watched it again. By this time, she was a film actress herself. She and her husband at the time, Tom Cruise, had rented a huge, ancient château in France and were staying there all alone. So they decided to rent this 1980 film, which also takes place in a big, remote, nearly empty building, and late at night they slipped it into the VCR. "We purposely watched it that way, to magnify the experience," Ms. Kidman said. "It was terrifying."

Since then, Ms. Kidman not only got to know the movie's revered director, Stanley Kubrick, but also worked for him in *Eyes Wide Shut* (1999), a movie that made almost as much news during its production as it did after its release because of the long, painstaking shooting schedule that the perfectionist Kubrick maintained. Sitting near the back of an otherwise empty screening room in Santa Monica and munching from a basket of chocolate-covered pecans that were a gift from her publicist, Ms. Kidman prepared to watch *The Shining* for the first time since she had worked with Kubrick, who died in 1999, shortly before the release of the film.

"I've seen most of Stanley's movies many times," Ms. Kidman said. "And obviously, by working with him, we talked a lot about all of his films. *The Shining* isn't necessarily my favorite Kubrick film, but I do love it. What interests me now, and why I want to see it again, is in terms of horror as a movie genre and what Stanley was able to do with it. Great directors are often able to go into a genre and really elevate it, and that's interesting to me. It was the same when David Fincher made *Seven,* really elevating that serial-killer thriller genre. I think that's really fascinating, how great directors can do that."

Although 2001 had brought the breakup of her marriage to Mr. Cruise, it was followed by a wave of sympathetic media attention and two significant critical and box office hits. First came Baz Luhrmann's

Moulin Rouge, a lush and frenetic attempt to resuscitate the movie musical by mixing contemporary songs with a belle époque setting. Ms. Kidman played Satine, the consumptive star at the Paris nightclub of the title, and sang, danced, and swung her way through the film. Later, in August, a smaller-scale horror film, *The Others,* in which she played the mother of haunted children in a creepy mansion, became one of the sleeper hits of the summer and began arguments in Hollywood about which film would eventually earn her an Oscar nomination. In December, she was declared Entertainer of the Year by *Entertainment Weekly* magazine. A month later, she won the Golden Globe for best actress in a musical, and a month after that she was nominated for an Oscar for her role in the same film, *Moulin Rouge.*

So, all in all, it's been a passable year.

Ms. Kidman, tall and slender, brushed back her russet hair and popped another pecan into her mouth, stuffing it into her cheek with her tongue to slowly savor the powdery chocolate coating. "Back when I first saw this, I really wasn't aware of moviemaking in terms of moviemaking," she said. "I would just sit and watch movies. But now, it's interesting to watch some of them again, now that I'm aware of how it's all done, technically. Ooh, look, this is scary, isn't it?"

The film (based on a novel by Stephen King, which it resembles in only a few plot elements) had begun, and its opening credits were under way—a long, slow, gliding shot from a bird's-eye view overlooked a car as it made its way along an otherwise deserted mountain road, higher and higher up the pine-flecked ridges while low, ominous music played. At one point, when the car made a precipitous turn on the cliff-hugging road, the camera did not follow it but kept flying out and over a pristine mountain lake. But it was the slowness of it and the music that made the camera seem almost predatory, stalking from above.

We have our first view of the Overlook, a huge hotel high in the mountains with a kind of frontier luxe design and a gigantic hedge maze on its front lawn.

"It's become such an iconic image, don't you think?" Ms. Kidman said. "This big, creepy hotel high in the mountains. How often since this movie came out have you seen something in a movie or a television show and thought, 'Oh, it's just like *The Shining*'?"

In the opening scenes, we meet Jack Nicholson as Jack Torrance, a former schoolteacher applying for a job as the hotel's winter custodian. Torrance and his family—his wife, Wendy (Shelley Duvall), and their son, Danny (Danny Lloyd)—would be snowed in all winter as the mountain road leading to the hotel became buried. Not a problem, Torrance tells the hotel's manager (Barry Nelson); he is beginning a new career as a writer and needs a long stretch of peace and quiet to begin work.

Two things immediately become apparent: as in many Kubrick films, the line readings are strangely flat, not to the point of unnaturalness but just enough to give them an odd feel. And the director clearly fussed about the framing of his shots, as everything appears posed and arranged.

"Stanley is the master of that, I think," Ms. Kidman said. "He was very precise about his framing, mostly because of the way he wanted to use the Steadicam in the movie."

The Steadicam was a new toy back in the late 1970s when Kubrick was making *The Shining.* He was not the first director to use it, but he was among the first. And he certainly pointed the way to how it could become not merely another tool, but also a kind of gateway into a new visual style.

Essentially, the Steadicam is what its name implies: a steady camera. Previously, directors had to use expensive and unwieldy cranes or lines of track to get smooth, bump-free camera movements. But the Steadicam attaches to an elaborately engineered harness on the camera operator's shoulders and can be moved about freely—backward, forward, sideways, up and down—without the slightest murmur or shaking.

In *The Shining,* Kubrick made these ostentatiously smooth camera movements, which were still relatively new to audiences at the time, into a motif for the film. The steadiness of the camera movements mixed with the grisly subject matter into a persistent mood of creepy unease, especially when juxtaposed with the odd, often emotionless line readings.

"Stanley would always tell us he was not interested in naturalness," Ms. Kidman said. "He was not interested in a sort of documentary style of performance. He liked it to be slightly odd, slightly off. He would never say that directly, about wanting it to be odd. He would never talk in that kind of detail about what he wanted to achieve in his films or what they were about, but it was apparent."

As Torrance talked to the hotel manager and his staff, in those fussily arranged frames, the tinge of artificiality in the line readings made it seem as if everybody was trying a little too hard to seem natural. Even in the next scenes, between Wendy and Danny, back home and talking about their move up to the Overlook, the clear affection between them is subtly tinged with the same sense of stilted portentousness.

So when the horror begins to creep into the story, it seems to flow directly out of the strange atmosphere that all these techniques have created. First, we learn that the previous caretaker at the hotel had apparently suffered a mental breakdown during the lonely winter and had gruesomely murdered his entire family. And then we discover that Danny is a lonely and friendless little boy who has taken to talking to what his mother believes to be an imaginary friend named Tony. The little boy takes on a high-pitched, raspy tone when he speaks in Tony's voice, and he curls one of his index fingers up and down in time to Tony's lines.

"I love how all of these scenes play out, so easy and very confident," Ms. Kidman said. "You know there is something odd about it, but it's done with such precision and intelligence that you know the director is in complete control. And that thing that the boy does with his finger—do you see that? Stanley said that the boy came up with that during a casting session. He just started doing it, so they wrote it into the script. It was so right and so creepy. Isn't it?"

Ms. Kidman, who was just about to head off to Sweden to begin work on a new film, *Dogsville*, for the director Lars von Trier, said she had been studying about Bertolt Brecht lately and come to believe that there was a connection between Brecht's approach to his characters and Kubrick's.

"Brecht's view of theater was that by creating naturalism you were asking the audience to become emotionally attached to the characters," she said. "What Brecht felt, and what directors like Stanley or Lars or others are saying, is that what they are doing is about ideas. It's not about becoming attached to the characters or imagining that it's really happening to you, as you often do when you watch a movie. I think it's true. That's what Stanley liked about a performance. It didn't have to be real; it just had to be slightly heightened, slightly off. Stanley was an ideas director. His overall ideas were always very profound and unusual—you know? It certainly applied to *2001* and to *Eyes Wide Shut*. But every film he made was about more than just feeling for the characters."

The peculiar line readings even begin to feel almost comical, in a dark sort of way, as the subject matter becomes more grisly. Long, expository passages as the hotel's previous murders are described to Torrance in a matter-of-fact way take on a distinct funny tinge, for instance, as does a later scene when Wendy is shown the contents of the hotel's walk-in freezer and listens to a long, seemingly pointless laundry list of its contents.

"You really get that slight black comedic thing, don't you?" Ms. Kidman said. "That is definitely no accident. From getting to know Stanley, I know that this is very much from his sense of humor. It's so unusual; that's what I love about it. And once you begin to hear the comedy in it, you pick up on more and more of it as the movie goes along. It really draws you in."

The first signs of strain in the Torrance family are felt as they drive back up to the Overlook. The forced cheerfulness of Mr. Nicholson's earlier scenes with the hotel manager are a sharp contrast to the sense of anger and tension as he drives and listens to his wife and son prattle on.

"The happy family," Ms. Kidman said, chuckling. "Look how irritated Jack looks. You can just tell that he feels trapped in that car. Let's face it, Shelley's character can be a little irritating. She doesn't do anything wrong; she can just be a little irritating." Mr. Nicholson snaps at her, dismissively. "Oh, things are going well in this relationship," Ms. Kidman said. "But this is what I love about Jack's performance in this movie. He is so bold in the way he does it. Look at how mean, how awful, he is to her. He doesn't hold back. In no sense is he winking at the audience and saying, 'Oh, I'm not really like this.' He just goes for it. Such a good combination, Stanley and Jack. Who would have guessed it?"

By this time, the audience has been let in on a secret about Danny that none of the other characters knows. Tony is more than a harmless imaginary friend. He is a real, spiritual presence—"a little boy who lives in my mouth" is the way Danny describes him—who tells

Danny a lot more than he has shared with his parents, including giving him visions of blood and carnage at the Overlook.

One particular vision is repeated three times during the film. It shows an elevator lobby at the Overlook while, in torturous slow-motion, one of the elevator doors glides open, releasing a torrent of blood that gracefully sweeps through the lobby, splashing the walls and carrying the furniture toward the camera like flotsam.

"This stuff is just so fantastic," Ms. Kidman said. "It just shows what you can do with an image."

She had just finished a film—*The Others*—in which there were several crucial scenes involving child actors, playing her young son and daughter. And she found herself repeatedly amazed by the performance Kubrick was able to draw from Danny Lloyd.

"God, he is so good," Ms. Kidman said. "And his scenes are often so long and really depend on his performance. It's so difficult to get a child to do that. This child is perfect."

One way Kubrick was able to nudge the boy in a certain direction was by concealing from him the movie's actual subject matter, which was deemed too gruesome for someone so young. Ms. Kidman said she did not know what the boy's experience on the film had been. (Ms. Duvall, who was called upon to reach and maintain a pitch of almost manic terror in several scenes later in the film, described the experience as hellish, Ms. Kidman said.) But she was not surprised that Mr. Lloyd did not pursue an acting career into adulthood and made only a couple of films more. "His parents were smart," Ms. Kidman said. "Child actors don't fare very well in Hollywood."

Ms. Kidman was particularly taken with a long scene between the young Mr. Lloyd and Scatman Crothers, playing the hotel chef, who is giving the boy some ice cream before the hotel closes down for the winter and he goes down the mountain with the rest of the staff, leaving Danny and his family alone. There is a moment in the scene when Mr. Crothers, whose character also has psychic powers, begins to communicate telepathically with the boy. The stunned Danny sits there, transfixed. "I love how he doesn't blink," Ms. Kidman said. In this scene, Danny is informed that he has a gift known as shining, and there are others like him in the world, although he is right not to tell his parents everything about it, or about Tony.

"He just lets the scene play," Ms. Kidman said, referring to

Kubrick. "He always did that. On *Eyes Wide Shut,* he'd let things play and play, even when there was nothing but silence, and I'd think, 'Ooh, no way this is getting into the movie—it's going on way too long.' And then that would be the exact take that Stanley would decide to use."

In *The Shining,* it adds to the creepiness, she said. Audiences are accustomed to scenes of a certain length; often they are awaiting the cut to the next scene with the same anticipation as someone who listens to a certain kind of music and comes to anticipate a chord change. So when the cut does not come at the anticipated point, it is felt subliminally, and focuses viewers' attention, makes them feel a little adrift, even tense.

The scene between Mr. Crothers and the boy also showed how Kubrick was intent on giving little pieces of information visually, frequently reinforcing it by showing the same things several times. "He always said that you had to make sure the audience understood key pieces of information to follow the story, and that to do that you had to repeat it several times, but without being too obvious about it," Ms. Kidman said. "Here, in this scene, look at how there is this rack of knives hanging in the background over the boy's head. It's very ominous, all of these knives poised over his head. And it's important because it not only shows that the boy is in danger, but one of those very knives is used later in the story when Wendy takes it to protect herself from her husband."

Kubrick was infamous for his perfectionism and for the number of takes he would make of seemingly ordinary scenes, in many cases more than fifty.

"There was a reason Stanley would do that," Ms. Kidman said. "He believed that what it does to you, as an actor, was that you would lose control of your sense of self, of the part of you that was internally watching your own performance. Eventually, he felt, you would stop censoring yourself. It's exhausting and difficult, so you do need to have a passion for the film that you're making and a belief in him. People would ask me, wasn't it torture to spend so much time working on that movie? And I said, no, it wasn't. It really wasn't. We were working with one of the greatest filmmakers of all time, and we were able to be in his orbit for that period of time. It was amazing. It was liberating."

By the movie's midpoint—when the creeping terror begins to seep out into actual visions of carnage, and Mr. Nicholson's performance edges toward psychosis and mania—it is clear that Kubrick had found a way to use the Steadicam to draw out his scenes. Frequently, the camera would follow characters from one room to another, out into a hallway, back into the room. Scenes would go on and on.

"Stanley would never say, 'Let's cut something'; he'd always let things play out," she said. "And he would choreograph scenes like this so carefully, down to very tiny movement, because he was so intent on the framing of the shots even as the camera was moving from place to place."

While there is music throughout the film, often foreboding classical pieces, long stretches are almost silent, or played only to the sound of ambient noise. In one scene, when Torrance is supposed to be writing, the camera focuses on his unattended typewriter. Instead, in the background, we can hear a thumping noise, almost like an ax hitting a tree, and when the camera moves it is revealed as Torrance bouncing a ball off the wall.

The most striking instance of the use of sound, though, comes in one of the film's most famous shots: that of the boy on his plastic-wheeled, low-riding tricycle, zipping around the hotel's empty corridors. The scene is shot with a Steadicam using a rig that Kubrick had specially built for the film, so the camera glides along at just a few inches off the floor, just behind the boy, chasing him through the labyrinth of the hotel. The sound in the scene is very specific: a soft rustling as the plastic wheels pass along carpeted hallways interspersed with a grating sound as they rattle over the wooden floors in between.

"It's so logical, of course," Ms. Kidman said. "That's what it would sound like. But it's so perfect; it really brings us into the scene. That's where Stanley was a master. He would just notice the small, odd details."

As Torrance begins to deteriorate mentally—and to have some frightening visions of his own, all leading him to the notion of killing his family—the sprawling hotel, buried under huge snowdrifts, begins to feel more and more claustrophobic. And Wendy, first in denial and then in growing panic, realizes that her husband is not only unhinged but also a threat.

"This is where I think Stanley is really able to elevate the horror genre," Ms. Kidman said. "He takes his big idea, that of the father figure, the protector figure, becoming a villain, turning into someone you are afraid of. I'm really noticing that this time through. The first time you watch a movie like this, you are caught up in being scared about what's coming next. But when you know what's coming next, you can pay more attention to how it's constructed and how well thought out it is."

There is one scene—in the final third of the film, when we know that Torrance is fighting the growing urge to kill his wife and son—in which Danny is sitting on his father's lap. Mr. Nicholson is rubbing the boy's back as he asks subtly threatening questions, and the boy is almost slumped over as he sits there. "Look at this," Ms. Kidman said. "Stanley doesn't cut. This is so hard to do with a child. Usually, in scenes with this kind of intensity and subtlety, you'd have to edit around. And it's such a long scene. There is only one way this scene could have happened, and that is because of the chemistry between the director, the other actor, and the child. This is what all the hard work was about."

When the boy suddenly looks over and asks his father, "You would never hurt Mommy, would you?" Ms. Kidman gasped with emotion. "Oh!" she said. "That is so powerful. And it was all one long take."

Mr. Nicholson drew barbs from critics at the time for what some felt was the over-the-top nature of his performance in the film's final half hour, when he degenerates from a taunting madman into a screaming, grunting beast with an ax. But Ms. Kidman rejects that. "I simply don't agree," she said. "I think he is being very bold. Is some of it over the top? Perhaps. But I don't think the movie would have worked half as well as it does if he'd played it down."

Just as compelling, she said, is the way Ms. Duvall's character comes apart—and then pulls herself together—in the final scenes.

"Her voice is so high-pitched that when she starts whining and crying, it seems almost comical," Ms. Kidman said. "At first, you sort of want to laugh, and then you cringe and then you scream."

There is the famous scene in which Wendy discovers that the book her husband has been laboring on all winter is actually page after page of the same childish sentence: "All work and no play makes

Jack a dull boy." She rips the pages away one after the other while, unknown to her, Torrance is sneaking up from behind.

"It drives you mad, doesn't it?" Ms. Kidman said. "A great shot, a great moment. And yet it's funny, too, in a twisted sort of way. Shelley is just wonderful here. Look at her reaction. She's not screaming or anything, just getting more and more frantic. He's coming up behind her, isn't he? Oh, I can't bear it. I really can't bear it." A short scream escaped from Ms. Kidman when Mr. Nicholson's leering face suddenly appeared on the screen.

"It's like the dam bursting on his insanity," she said. "The whole movie has been building up to this. And look at how cruel he is to her, how he mimics her. It's wonderful, how cruel he is. And Shelley is having to show so much fear, so much terror, without a break, without a cut. It's so intense. It's like a dream, you know? Where you're in a dream and you're kind of stuck, you can't move, and something is coming after you."

In the film's last few scenes—when the evil spirits of the Overlook take physical shape, so that even Wendy can see them, and the blood spills one last time from the elevator shaft—Ms. Kidman said she could not watch any of *The Shining* now without feeling the director's presence. "I can feel him in everything," she said. "I can hear his voice. I know exactly what he would have said. I can sense his particular tastes."

She set down the basket of chocolate pecans and took a few deep breaths.

"Stanley challenged me on every area of my life," she said. "He taught me so much. I can't even put it into words. What would really be interesting is to take a long stretch of time and watch each of his films, one after the other. Here is an example of a movie that just gets better every time you watch it. It's funny how that happens, when you have a really good film or a good book or even a good painting. There is always something else to see in it."

HIGHLIGHTS OF NICOLE KIDMAN'S ACTING CAREER
AS WELL AS INFORMATION ON *THE SHINING*

■

What They Watched

The Shining. Directed and produced by Stanley Kubrick; screenplay by Diane Johnson and Stanley Kubrick; original music by Wendy Carlos and Rachel Elkind; cinematography by John Alcott; edited by Ray Lovejoy. With Jack Nicholson, Shelley Duvall, Danny Lloyd, Scatman Crothers, and Barry Nelson. 1980.

Nicole Kidman's Films

The Hours. Directed by Stephen Daldry. With Meryl Streep and Julianne Moore. 2002.

Birthday Girl. Directed by Jez Butterworth. With Ben Chaplin. 2002.

The Others. Directed by Alejandro Amenábar. With Fionnula Flanagan. 2001.

Moulin Rouge. Directed by Baz Luhrmann. With Ewan McGregor. 2001.

Eyes Wide Shut. Directed by Stanley Kubrick. With Tom Cruise. 1999.

Practical Magic. Directed by Griffin Dunne. With Sandra Bullock. 1998.

The Peacemaker. Directed by Mimi Leder. With George Clooney. 1997.

The Portrait of a Lady. Directed by Jane Campion. With John Malkovich. 1996.

To Die For. Directed by Gus Van Sant. With Matt Dillon. 1995.

Batman Forever. Directed by Joel Schumacher. With Val Kilmer. 1995.

Far and Away. Directed by Ron Howard. With Tom Cruise. 1992.

Billy Bathgate. Directed by Robert Benton. With Dustin Hoffman. 1991.

Days of Thunder. Directed by Tony Scott. With Tom Cruise. 1990.

Dead Calm. Directed by Phillip Noyce. With Sam Neill. 1987.

20

Barry Sonnenfeld on
Dr. Strangelove

Ihad a certain history with Barry Sonnenfeld. He'd been one of
the subjects of a series I wrote for the *New York Times* in 1997 in
which I walked around various New York neighborhoods with
celebrities who had some connection to it. In his case, we spent
several hours traipsing around Washington Heights, where the
cinematographer-turned-director grew up. It turned out to be the
installment in that series that probably drew the biggest response, a
long rant about his awkward childhood, antagonistic relationship
with his parents, and various humiliating episodes. So I was eager to
hook up with him again, now that several years had passed, *Men in
Black* had turned him into an A-list director, and subsequent flops
had tarnished that glow a bit, to see if he was still a little nutty.

•

Being a movie director," Barry Sonnenfeld said, "is all about
answering hundreds of questions like 'Do you want the green one or
the red one?'"

He grabbed half of his sandwich, melted brie oozing from the
sides, and took a huge bite, chewing thoughtfully. "It's through the

accumulation of hundreds of these kinds of questions for your set decorators and your cinematographer and everyone else that a director eventually creates a style," he said. "And what I really love about this movie, my favorite movie of all time, is that it's all about a director setting a specific tone and style and making sure that every single aspect is completely consistent with that tone."

The first frames of Stanley Kubrick's nuclear satire, *Dr. Strangelove or: How I Learned to Stop Worrying and Love the Bomb,* were coming up on the screen of Mr. Sonnenfeld's basement screening room, a high-tech playground of projectors and digital equipment.

"The other thing that I love about this movie," he said, "and one of the reasons that it's meant so much to me, is that it's a comedy in which no one in the movie is allowed to acknowledge that they're in a comedy. To me, that's the hallmark of the best American comedies."

Mr. Kubrick's straight-faced satire may include bizarre characters with ridiculous names—General Jack D. Ripper, President Merkin Muffley, and, of course, Colonel Bat Guano—but they always deliver their lines with complete conviction, drawing comedy from the contrast between the serious line readings and the utter silliness of what's being said.

"Mostly, for me, directing is all about tone," Mr. Sonnenfeld said. "The single most important thing that a director does is to decide on a tone, whether it's sloppy or controlled or dark or absurd. And to me, this is a perfect example of a director who has picked a very specific tone and then every single thing, from the script to the performances to the way it's shot, serves that tone. And another thing: this is a movie where everyone, from the actors to the cinematographer, has been told that they are not making a comedy. If any of these actors had tried to play *Dr. Strangelove* as a comedy, it would have been a disastrous movie. There is no winking at the camera—except for one specific moment, but we'll talk about that later."

This quality—playing comedy as drama—is what Mr. Sonnenfeld strives for in his own work, whether *The Addams Family* (1991), *Get Shorty* (1995), or *Men in Black* (1997). It is definitely a quality he went after in two films that ended up being released within four months of each other in the summer of 2002.

Big Trouble, based on a comic novel by Dave Barry, was originally intended to be released in the fall of 2001. But since one of the jokes in the film involves attempts by dim-witted thugs to smuggle a nuclear bomb onto a passenger plane, Disney decided it would be better to let some time pass between September 11 and the film's release. It eventually came out in April 2002, followed on July 3 by *Men in Black II,* reuniting Mr. Sonnenfeld with Will Smith and Tommy Lee Jones.

"I don't mean to imply that the movies that I make are anything near as good as *Dr. Strangelove,* but in all of them I'm always trying to make sure that the actors don't act like they know they're in a comedy," Mr. Sonnenfeld said. "They don't act like they think they're supposed to be funny. To me, that's what makes Tommy Lee Jones so fantastically funny in the *Men in Black* movies. I just kept saying to him, while we were shooting, we're making *The French Connection* here. It just happens to be about aliens instead of drug dealers."

Mr. Sonnenfeld, forty-eight, stumbled into filmmaking, largely because of his partnership with two fellow New York University students, Joel and Ethan Coen. Mr. Sonnenfeld, whose guiding interest was photography, said he earned extra money as a cameraman on low-budget films, including some pornographic ones. When the Coen brothers were interested in making their first movie, *Blood Simple* (1984), they recruited Mr. Sonnenfeld as cinematographer. The team made two more films together: *Raising Arizona* (1987) and *Miller's Crossing* (1990), and they remain good friends. Not until *The Addams Family* did Mr. Sonnenfeld make the move into directing.

"I remember very clearly the first time I heard about *Dr. Strangelove,*" Mr. Sonnenfeld said. "My dad and my French horn teacher, who later became my business manager, were playing pinochle and talking about how brilliant this new movie was. It came out in, what, 1962?" Actually, 1964. "So I would have been nine or maybe ten years old. I just remember them raving about this movie. But I didn't actually see it until several years later, when I was something like sixteen or seventeen."

Mr. Sonnenfeld talks quickly, often in long, high-pitched bursts that flow from idea to idea, and he tends to lean his head back and stare toward the ceiling as he tries to remember something.

"There was a short period where I spent my days at the New Yorker movie theater instead of going to high school," he said of the long-gone theater at Eighty-ninth Street and Broadway. "One of the great moviegoing experiences of my life was a double feature one day of *Duck Soup* and *Hamlet*. It was pouring rain, the kind of rain where your pants are soaked from wherever your coat ends, and I was kind of depressed. I was the only person in the theater except for this old woman, who looked like a street person, and I'd brought in this tuna sandwich that really stunk the place up. All through the movie, this woman in the back of the theater kept saying over and over again in this very sad voice: 'Don't trust them, Hamlet. Don't trust them!'"

It was during one of these New Yorker excursions that he saw *Dr. Strangelove* and immediately recognized that it meshed with his own comic sensibility.

Originally, *Dr. Strangelove* was intended to be a political thriller. Based on a book by Peter George, who shares screenwriting credit with Kubrick and Terry Southern, it was a tense antiwar drama. But while the script was being developed, the dark comedy bubbled to the surface, and Kubrick found himself pulled toward satire. (It turned out to be a fortunate decision, as the movie was released within a few weeks of *Fail-Safe,* another nuclear war thriller with a plot bearing striking similarities to this film's.)

The first thing to appear on the screen is a white text crawl on a black screen, assuring the audience that the events depicted in the movie could never actually happen. The writing is so serious and so bureaucratic that it becomes comical, especially on repeated viewings, when you anticipate the absurdities to come.

"I've always wondered if this was Kubrick's idea or if the studio made him put on this crawl," Mr. Sonnenfeld said. "Because the effect is actually brilliant. Already you're smiling."

Then the opening credits: the refueling of a strategic bomber in midair that is shot as a kind of technological copulation, complete with a Muzak-like version of "Try a Little Tenderness" on the sound track.

"See how these credits are handwritten and some of the words are bigger than other ones?" Mr. Sonnenfeld said. "It's very distinctive. When I made my first movie, I tracked down Pablo Ferro, the guy who did these credits. That's why *The Addams Family* credits are almost identical to these. Hey, have you ever noticed this?"

He pointed to the screen as the writing credits appeared.

"There's a misspelled word at the bottom there, see?" he said. "It says 'base' on a book instead of 'based' on a book." He cackled happily. "That's one of the pitfalls of handwritten credits, I guess. And no one caught it."

The opening shots of Kubrick's satire are designed to look like a documentary, a series of scenes of B-52s and twirling radar antennas and the long, dark runways of an Air Force base. Only gradually are we cued to the comedy.

Peter Sellers, who plays three roles in the film, makes his first appearance in a sight gag, suddenly appearing from behind a sheet of computer printouts. As Group Captain Lionel Mandrake he looks vaguely like Terry-Thomas, with a handlebar mustache and overly proper British aplomb. His first phone conversation with General Ripper (Sterling Hayden) is played, like all their scenes, as a series of banalities that grow increasingly absurd.

"They're always repeating things to one another, but very seriously," Mr. Sonnenfeld said. "It adds to the flatness of it, the obvious banality. And it's in the contrast between that flatness and banality and the outrageous things they are discussing, like nuclear annihilation, that we get the comedy."

Ripper informs Mandrake that the United States is in "a shooting war" with the Soviet Union and that the base's planes have been ordered to attack their targets inside Russia. "Oh, hell," is Mandrake's only response.

As the orders to attack go out to the planes, we are introduced to the crew members of a B-52 whose captain is Major T. J. Kong (Slim Pickens).

"I love these shots in the B-52," Mr. Sonnenfeld said. "Notice how the guys are always eating. They're stuffing food in their mouths or chewing gum or drinking coffee, almost every time you see them. It's a way of making a joke out of how ordinary and everyday this is for them, how it's just a job and a kind of tedious one at that."

Major Kong, eyes shifting around the cockpit, pages through a copy of *Playboy* magazine. When he unfolds the month's playmate, it is a woman lying on her stomach and covered only by an open copy of *Foreign Affairs* magazine. "See that woman in the picture?" Mr. Sonnenfeld said. "She's the same woman who we see having an affair with George C. Scott a few scenes from now."

Major Kong leans back to take a nap. The camera, jittery and handheld and in the harsh glare of the bare bulbs inside the jet, works its way from one crew member to another. Suddenly the jet's radio, called the CRM-114, begins to blare. The message decodes as a "wing attack, plan R," which the crew cannot at first believe.

"Notice, the whole time this conversation is going on with Major Kong, this guy is stuffing food in his mouth and trying to talk through mouthfuls," Mr. Sonnenfeld said. "That is a very definite directorial decision because it's a motif you see throughout the movie. Even later, in the war room scenes with George C. Scott, he's always stuffing gum in his mouth. It's like, this is their job, this is where they go to work, and they're kind of bored."

The crew is ordered to program a coded, three-letter prefix into the CRM-114, a code known only to General Ripper and a code that must precede any order to abort the mission.

Once Major Kong accepts that the orders are genuine ("Well, boys, I guess this is it, nook-leer combat, toe-to-toe with the Rooskies"), he opens a safe and replaces his flight helmet with a cowboy hat. It is the first truly absurd moment in the film. And as the hat hits his head, the music starts up, a somber and serious version of "When Johnny Comes Marching Home," complete with drums and funereal chorus.

"Now, we get Kubrick's decision to allow Kong to put on his cowboy hat," Mr. Sonnenfeld said. "It is timed perfectly. He has already established the tone of the film, that it is a kind of absurdist realism, and he is ready to start pushing it a little bit, daring the audience to come along with him. At the wrong moment, a sight gag like that could have sucked all of the air out of the movie. Instead, it's exhilarating. It's brilliant. Because Kubrick has laid the groundwork for it."

The way the music is used—in a very straight-faced manner, as if this were the most serious war drama ever made—is also calculated to seduce the audience, Mr. Sonnenfeld said.

"We, in the audience, get to be smart," he said. "He doesn't underline the joke for us or stick it under our nose. He just lobs it out there and lets us discover it. That's something I always try to do as a director: to let the audience be smarter than the filmmaker, to let them discover the jokes. In this scene, it lets us make the connection that Kubrick is using serious music for a comic effect. And this, in turn, cues us how to react to the movie as a whole."

In a similar way, Mr. Sonnenfeld is taken with the way Kubrick lighted the sets.

"In the bomber, it's all very glaring and the camera is jumping around," he said. "But take a look at how he shoots General Ripper in his office."

A grid of fluorescent lights hangs over the general's desk, casting a harsh glare onto nearby Venetian blinds. The general sits behind the desk, a long cigar clenched in his teeth. As he begins his first psychotic rant—about a Communist conspiracy to impurify "natural bodily fluids"—the camera is placed very close to his face, but a few inches below.

"You can already see the stylization in the way Kubrick has shot this room," Mr. Sonnenfeld said. "The only light seems to come from this fluorescent grid above him. The rest of the room is either completely black or very dim. Yet when we look up at Ripper, there is a warmer light on his face. This is all calculated to make the image much more dramatic, and you can be sure that while Kubrick was setting up the shot he was being peppered with questions like, 'Shouldn't there be more fluorescent lights? Do you want a desk lamp?'"

Another major character, General Buck Turgidson (George C. Scott), is introduced offscreen as we watch his secretary and lover—the bikini-clad Miss Foreign Affairs, Miss Scott (Tracy Reed)—answering a phone call in the general's bedroom. As soon as the scene came on-screen, Mr. Sonnenfeld shouted out, "You have to!"

It is only seconds before the line is spoken by the general. (His secretary asks whether she should answer the phone, and the general, who is in the bathroom, yells that she has to.) Mr. Sonnenfeld is one of those movie fans who delight in yelling out their favorite lines just moments before they are spoken on the screen. And for such people, he said, *Dr. Strangelove* is a cornucopia.

"I'm always picking out lines from this movie and using them on the set of my own movies," Mr. Sonnenfeld said. "I'll suddenly shout out, 'They'll see the big board!' or 'I'm not saying we won't get our hair mussed.' And everybody else just has to figure out what I'm talking about." Other film buffs of a similar stripe tend to pick up on it, he said, and offer lines of their own in response. "Gentlemen, you can't fight in here," they'll say. "This is the War Room!"

In *Raising Arizona,* a comedy he made with the Coen brothers, they put the initials OPE on a men's room wall where a pair of escaped convicts pause to refresh themselves. Those are the code letters General Ripper uses with the CRM-114, an anagram the deranged man draws from "peace on Earth" and "purity of essence."

And Mr. Sonnenfeld said he frequently ended letters to studio executives with a final paragraph that is taken directly from a mad, rambling letter that General Ripper sends to the Pentagon. It says, "God willing, we will prevail, in peace and freedom from fear and in true health, through the purity and essence of our natural fluids."

Another bright cackle escaped from Mr. Sonnenfeld.

"It drives them crazy," he said. "They don't know what I'm talking about. Really, it's amazing, a lot of the executives, especially the television executives, have no idea where that comes from."

The scene that introduces General Turgidson—when his secretary asks whether she should answer the phone and he barks "You have to!"—is shot as one very long take.

"This is brilliant, risky filmmaking," Mr. Sonnenfeld said. "There is not a cut in this scene. Not one. And there's so much going on in it. This is the same woman who we saw earlier in the *Playboy* centerfold, and then we can tell by her body language that she's not only having an affair with George C. Scott but with the guy on the phone who's calling the general. And then look, see? George C. Scott comes into the room and takes the phone. Look at all the mirrors all over the place. Where is the camera?"

General Turgidson is informed that Ripper has sent the bombers to attack the Soviet Union, and he smacks his stomach with a loud thump. "I don't like the look of this," he tells the office on the phone, but as he does so he is staring at his lover's body.

"To do a long, complicated scene like this in one take, you really have to trust that the timing is going to work," Mr. Sonnenfeld said. "Because you have nothing to cut to. If it doesn't work, you're stuck with it. But Kubrick realized that comedy—true comedy—plays best without cuts. Cuts are the enemy of comedy. If you watch a really great comedy, like *His Girl Friday* or *Palm Beach Story,* it's always a series of actions and reactions within one shot, with very little cutting. It's just the way it is. Every cut pulls you further from the comedy."

Another example comes later in the film when Mandrake discovers that Ripper has sent the bombers to the Soviet Union on his own authority, and Mandrake tries to countermand the order. But Ripper locks the two of them in his fluorescent office and proceeds to regale an increasingly alarmed Mandrake with tales of Commie conspiracies and natural bodily fluids.

One long sequence has Sellers and Hayden side by side on a couch in the general's office. Ripper has his arm gently around Mandrake's shoulder, and the cringing Mandrake fidgets and whimpers with alarm with every psychotic rant.

"Comedy always plays best, like this, in a two-shot where you have both characters on the screen together," Mr. Sonnenfeld said. "If Kubrick had been cutting between the two of them, instead of keeping them both on the screen, the comedy would have bled out of the scene. When you have Sterling Hayden with wild eyes talking about the fluoridation of children's ice cream and then a frantic Peter Sellers right next to him, fighting panic, it's so much more funny."

In the War Room, where Turgidson and President Muffley, also played by Sellers, and the others discuss ways to recall the bombers before they strike, a ring of fluorescent lights hovers over the circular table like a halo, and the "big board," showing the attack lines of the planes, rises behind them.

"Watch how George C. Scott plays this scene," Mr. Sonnenfeld said. "He's saying the most absurd things, but he's playing it totally straight. And look at that book on the table in front of him. What does it say? *World Targets in Megadeaths*. It's absurd. It's a joke. But Kubrick just leaves it sitting there. He doesn't focus on it or cut to it. If the audience discovers the joke, fine. If they don't, that's fine, too."

A short while later—when the president invites the Soviet ambassador into the War Room to impress upon him that the attack is not official United States policy—Mr. Sonnenfeld points to the most glaring moment where, he feels, Kubrick lost his footing.

"This is that one moment I was talking about earlier," Mr. Sonnenfeld said. "It's the one time that they're winking at the camera."

As Scott fumes about the presence of the Soviet ambassador— "He'll see the big board!"—he walks backward, stumbles, rolls over, and hops back up to his feet, freezing in a position of mock exasperation.

"See that freeze?" Mr. Sonnenfeld said. "It's too much. It's over the top. It's deliberately comical. To me, tonally, it says, 'Look at me, I'm trying to be funny.'"

As he watched the film again, Mr. Sonnenfeld realized that there were two or three other similar moments—all involving Scott's performance—when he felt the actor went a little too far. At one point, when he says something particularly idiotic, he puts his fingertips over his lips and looks sheepish. Later, when he says something idiotic, he flattens a hand on his head and freezes with a comic look on his face.

"Isn't that weird?" Mr. Sonnenfeld said. "It's just a little too far again. And really, it's a wonderful performance. We're only talking about eight seconds or so throughout the whole film. But it's not right. It doesn't fit with the rest of the movie."

Mr. Sonnenfeld even has a theory of how it happened.

"Not to take anything away from George C. Scott's performance, but what sometimes happens is that the funniest stuff in the dailies turns out, in the end, not to be right for the movie," he said. "It's the weirdest thing. And then there are other scenes where the actor is just driving a car or something. It looks inert in the dailies, but then it plays like gangbusters in the movie. My guess is that this George C. Scott stuff was the funniest stuff in the dailies every day. Everyone was laughing. But then when he put it in the movie, it doesn't quite work because it's not exactly in sync with the rest of the performances."

Mr. Sonnenfeld draws a contrast to Keenan Wynn's much smaller role as an army officer who arrests Mandrake after Ripper's suicide. Mandrake has figured out the three-letter code, but he can't make the utterly serious and skeptical Wynn believe him. In the sequence, an increasingly frantic Mandrake tries to make a long-distance call from a pay phone but doesn't have enough change. Twice during the sequence, Kubrick cuts back to Wynn, whose face is completely devoid of expression.

"He's hilarious," Mr. Sonnenfeld said. "Keenan Wynn never gives an inch. He is totally, totally serious at every moment. And the truth is, in most cases, no reaction is the best reaction. But I'll bet when they were looking at the dailies and they had a shot of Keenan Wynn without any emotion in his face, no one in the room said, 'Wow, we've got gold here.' Yet in the movie, it's among the funniest moments."

When the Russians reveal that they have invented a new dooms-day machine, a series of underground bombs set to irradiate the world if the Soviet Union is attacked, the efforts to stop the American bombers become even more frantic. And when the code that Mandrake has divined is finally relayed to the bombers, and one of them—Major Kong's—refuses to turn back, the comedy slides completely into the darkest nuclear nightmare.

Dr. Strangelove, Sellers in his third role, makes his appearance, a giggling scientist with a German accent who savors words like *slaughter*. He has some strange, spastic malady that causes him to speckle his dark suit with cigarette ashes and occasionally wrestle with his own rebellious arm that periodically jerks into an involuntary Nazi salute.

"This is just so brilliant and so close to being ridiculous," Mr. Sonnenfeld said. "It's so close to being bad. But it works, and the reason it works is because of the way Kubrick has set it up over the last eighty minutes. Gradually, bit by bit, he has gotten us accustomed to accepting more and more ridiculous materials, and here, with Dr. Strangelove, he is really pushing us, almost daring us not to go along with him."

As the president and his staff plot to escape the coming nuclear holocaust by disappearing into mine shafts, Dr. Strangelove gradually lifts himself out of his wheelchair. "Mein Führer!" he shouts. "I can walk!" And the screen explodes in a series of nuclear blasts set to the tune "We'll Meet Again."

Mr. Sonnenfeld jumped up. "Mein Führer, I can walk!" he said, cackling again, and flipped on the lights in the screening room.

"I love this movie because Kubrick is always so close to being over the top, yet he keeps it so totally real," Mr. Sonnenfeld said. "And it is so difficult to walk that line. When you are trying to stylize a movie, it is so hard to figure out how far you can go at any given moment. And that's why this is such a great movie. Because Kubrick seems to have such total control. He always knows where that line is, and he's always teasing right up against it."

HIGHLIGHTS OF BARRY SONNENFELD'S CAREER AND INFORMATION ON *DR. STRANGELOVE*

■

What They Watched

Dr. Strangelove or: How I Learned to Stop Worrying and Love the Bomb. Directed and produced by Stanley Kubrick; screenplay by Kubrick, Terry Southern, and Peter George; original music by Laurie Johnson; cinematography by Gilbert Taylor; edited by Anthony Harvey. With Peter Sellers, George C. Scott, Sterling Hayden, Keenan Wynn, and Slim Pickens. 1964.

Barry Sonnenfeld's Films

AS A DIRECTOR

Big Trouble. With Tim Allen and Rene Russo. 2002.

Men in Black II. With Will Smith and Tommy Lee Jones. 2002.

Wild Wild West. With Will Smith. 1999.

Men in Black. With Will Smith and Tommy Lee Jones. 1997.

Get Shorty. With John Travolta. 1995.

Addams Family Values. With Anjelica Huston and Raul Julia. 1993.

For Love or Money. With Michael J. Fox. 1993.

The Addams Family. With Anjelica Huston and Raul Julia. 1991.

AS A CINEMATOGRAPHER

Misery. Directed by Rob Reiner. With James Caan and Kathy Bates. 1990.

Miller's Crossing. Directed by Joel Coen. With Gabriel Byrne. 1990.

When Harry Met Sally. Directed by Rob Reiner. With Billy Crystal and Meg Ryan. 1989.

Big. Directed by Penny Marshall. With Tom Hanks. 1988.

Raising Arizona. Directed by Joel Coen. With Nicolas Cage. 1987.

Throw Momma from the Train. Directed by Danny DeVito. With Billy Crystal. 1987.

Blood Simple. Directed by Joel Coen. With Frances McDormand. 1984.

21

Barry Levinson on
On the Waterfront

The installment with Barry Levinson had a long, somewhat tortured history. We'd originally made an appointment to meet in New York, which fell apart due to miscommunication, and then finally made it happen a couple of months later at the MGM offices in Santa Monica. But then when the events of September 11, 2001, naturally turned everyone's full attention to that tragedy and the nation's response, the series went on hiatus at just the moment when his installment was to run. As a result, it didn't appear for almost six months, like a lost dispatch from the Crimea. By that time, the film that he'd been hoping to promote, *Bandits,* had opened to a fairly tepid box office reception, perhaps making more poignant his comments about the painful travails of Hollywood moviemaking at the moment.

■

God knows, this is a thin age for storytelling," said the director Barry Levinson, prompted to this melancholy assessment by a midafternoon screening of Elia Kazan's *On the Waterfront.*

Watching the film, which he said had a profound effect on him as a boy in Baltimore Heights, only amplified his sense that something essential had seeped from American movies in the decades since Mr. Kazan and his star, Marlon Brando, transformed the art of film acting.

"Let's hope we're only into one of these valleys, and not think that this is where we are going to be forever," Mr. Levinson said.

Just look at *On the Waterfront,* Mr. Levinson said. "You've got Terry Malloy, this ex-fighter who is basically a bum, who works for this crooked union boss. Malloy's brother, Charley, is another crooked big shot in the organization, and they have this very complex relationship. Then you've got Karl Malden as this priest who decides to come down from the pulpit and go out into the streets to help clean things up, and Eva Marie Saint as this girl from the convent who has to deal with her brother's murder by the gangsters. Look at how many characters there are at work in this story, and they're all so rich. I may be wrong, but I just think this is much, much fuller than the way stories are told today for the most part."

Mr. Levinson is not the curmudgeon he may seem from these sentiments. Many veteran directors, including Oscar winners like Mr. Levinson, consider the current sequel-powered, corporate-driven mind-set of the Hollywood studios to be a weak broth when compared with the richness of American filmmaking in the 1970s and '80s, when they came to prominence.

"I think movies in general have gotten more and more simplistic," Mr. Levinson said. "I don't know if it's the audience or what's being delivered to them. Actually, I think this simplification came about because, these days, movies are all about television. Everything is about selling the movie, and the way movies are sold is in thirty-second television spots. And this is what we end up with."

When *On the Waterfront* was released in 1954, it seemed to fit neatly into several filmmaking trends. Its realistic setting, ripped-from-the-headlines story, and working-class milieu made it part of a continuum in postwar filmmaking that brought movies out of the studio soundstages and onto the bustling city streets. It has echoes of Italian neorealism, of the social crusading of many late '40s and early '50s movies, even of the live television dramas of the period.

None of this meant anything, of course, to the twelve-year-old Barry Levinson who went to the Ambassador Theater in Baltimore with his friends one Saturday afternoon nearly five decades ago. "We just went every Saturday afternoon and saw whatever was playing," Mr. Levinson said. "That was it. I had no sense of film history at that point. But this was the first movie where I was sitting there and I realized that it was different. You know, you see actors in movies when you're young and it doesn't really mean anything. But in this movie, the acting of Brando—it was just something that I had never seen before. It was more realistic, yet it had all of these odd moments. I was watching it and I thought, you know, I have never seen anything quite like this."

The young Mr. Levinson was so struck by the experience that he went home and wrote a letter to Mr. Kazan. "It was the first time I ever paid attention to a director," Mr. Levinson said. "I had no ambitions to be in this business, but I wrote to him and said, you know, the next time he made a movie I'd like to come out there and watch him do it. I didn't quite understand what it was about it that was so powerful to me—the subtext in the actors' performances and the humanism of the storytelling—but I knew that I just wanted to be there and see how they did it."

Mr. Kazan never wrote back, but the impact that the film had on the young man was absolutely central in shaping the screenwriter and director he was to become.

The political element in the story meant nothing to the twelve-year-old Mr. Levinson. And he said later controversies about Mr. Kazan's direction and Budd Schulberg's screenplay—including claims that the story was at least partly a celebration of those who named names before Congress in the Hollywood blacklist era—have never really colored his appreciation of the film.

"It was simply with this movie that I began to look at movies in a different way," Mr. Levinson said. "I began to analyze them, to try to figure out how they were done, rather than just going in and spending a couple of hours in the dark with my friends."

Mr. Levinson, sixty, was a comic and television writer—winning two Emmys for *The Carol Burnett Show*—before he turned to screenwriting in 1976, for Mel Brooks, and directing in 1982 with *Diner*. Since then he has made more than a dozen films, winning an Oscar for directing *Rain Man* (1988). He also helped create the popular 1990s television series *Homicide: Life on the Streets*.

In the interim, he worked with some of the biggest stars of the period: Robert Redford (*The Natural*), Robin Williams (*Good Morning, Vietnam*), Warren Beatty (*Bugsy*), Michael Douglas (*Disclosure*), Robert De Niro and Dustin Hoffman (*Wag the Dog*), and Bruce Willis (*Bandits*). But he is probably most highly regarded for the four highly personal films he set in his hometown: *Diner, Tin Men, Avalon,* and *Liberty Heights.*

Mr. Levinson sauntered into the small MGM screening room a few minutes early and quickly chose a seat in the middle of the middle row. His wavy gray hair was brushed back from his forehead, cascading over both ears and framing a pair of glasses that ringed penetrating eyes.

On the Waterfront begins with the Columbia Pictures logo and, behind it, the first brassy laments from Leonard Bernstein's distinctive score. The simple credits appear to be a sheet of typing paper, its texture blown up to screen size, alerting audiences that the story was inspired by real events.

"The music is so simple and mournful," Mr. Levinson said. "It's a great sound, very spatial and open."

Only later, while researching how the film was made, Mr. Levinson said he was told that Bernstein had written the score without seeing the specific scenes. Normally, film composers wait until a film is finished. Then the music is recorded to match specific scenes as they are played on a screen in the scoring stage, so the scream of the violins comes at the exact moment the shower curtain is pulled back and the killer revealed.

But someone told Mr. Levinson that Bernstein, supposedly unaware that this was how it was done, had simply delivered to Mr. Kazan his *On the Waterfront Suite,* a fully integrated jazz-and-classical composition with all of the musical themes in the film. Mr. Levinson said that Mr. Kazan then had to choose portions of this composition and use them behind his scenes, the music never exactly matching the action on the screen, adding to the sense of oddness.

But in fact, when a curator of the Bernstein archives in the Library of Congress went back (after this interview was published) to look at the composer's score, it was revealed that Bernstein had, indeed, composed at least some of the film in the time-honored Hollywood way, matching his score directly to specific scenes. And the

On the Waterfront Suite to which Mr. Levinson referred was actually put together by the composer after the film's release.

Still, it was telling how firmly this notion had rooted in Mr. Levinson's mind, that the film's fluctuating equilibrium was caused, at least in part, by the way the musical score had purportedly been assembled. In his own mind, it fell perfectly into place with Mr. Brando's electric performance.

"I could tell, even when I was first seeing it, that there was something different about the music, though I didn't know what it was," Mr. Levinson said. "Now, of course, it's obvious. But the end result is wonderful. Along with Brando's distinctive and unusual line readings, it adds to the sense of things being slightly off-kilter, of the movie's differentness."

A prime example is the opening shot. The camera is staring up at a huge cargo ship at dockside, the towers of Manhattan in the background, then pans down to reveal the ramshackle headquarters of the longshoremen's union on a bobbing dock just offshore. A line of men, thugs all, some in fancy suits, others in working clothes, comes out of the headquarters and walks up the gangplank to a waiting limousine. There is one cut bringing the camera closer to the men. Lee J. Cobb, playing the crooked union kingpin Johnny Friendly, pauses before getting into the car to gently pat Mr. Brando's ex-boxer, Terry Malloy, before sending him off on some errand.

What is distinctive about it, Mr. Levinson said, is the music. From the very first glimpse of the cargo ship and throughout the scene, it is a frenzy of drums—wild, rhythmic, almost insanely energetic, like something you would expect to see behind a big, climactic battle scene.

"If this movie had been scored in the conventional way, I don't think anybody would have looked at that scene and said, 'Hey, let's have a bunch of drums playing really fast and loud,'" Mr. Levinson said. "But that's what makes the opening so interesting and creates this mood that draws you into the story."

So arresting and unusual did it feel to Mr. Levinson—and so in keeping with the revolutionary methods used by Mr. Brando and others in the film—that it seemed perfectly natural to believe that the score had been written in such an unconventional way, when it apparently hadn't been.

The cacophonous opening is followed by a dark street scene. From high above, the camera sees Terry Malloy walking to the edge of a building and calling someone's name. When there is a cut and the camera comes down to Terry's level, his face is seen behind the sharp spikes rising from the top of an iron fence, menacingly, though there is nothing particularly threatening about his slightly punch-drunk line readings.

As Terry's victim is drawn out and lured up to the roof, the camera veers up and we see the silhouettes of two thugs waiting for him up there. Seconds later, with a scream, the victim is flung to his death.

"Kazan is never really thought of as a visual director, mainly because he dealt with people and emotions and behavior in a humanist kind of way," Mr. Levinson said. "So people didn't think of him as a visual stylist. But there is something very thought-out about the way these opening moments were shot. He was not a flashy director and he was never showing off, so you didn't always pay attention to this stuff, but I think he has been vastly overlooked in this respect."

Mr. Brando's first real scene comes immediately afterward. Standing in a line of four union men, including his brother, Charley (Rod Steiger), outside Johnny Friendly's bar, he is stunned by the murder in which he played a part. "I thought they were just gonna talk to him," he says, pain crinkling his eyes. "Maybe he gave them an argument," Charley responds.

"I love the fact that Kazan stuck with a four-shot through this whole sequence and didn't go in close on Brando," Mr. Levinson said. "It works so well, the contrast between Brando's response and the response of the other three. His performance feels different almost immediately. He's not doing the sorts of things you expect. He says his lines, almost softly, and then he sits there with it, an extra beat or two. He lets something happen in his eyes."

Of course, what was revolutionary and cliché-shattering about Mr. Brando's brooding, antiglamorous performances in this and in Mr. Kazan's *Streetcar Named Desire* three years earlier has now become so imitated and commonplace that it has lost a portion of its power to shock. But there is still something powerful about returning to the source and seeing it undiluted and at the moment of genesis.

"No matter how many times you see this performance, it always has the power to surprise you," Mr. Levinson said. "Look at this moment, the way he handles a phrase or whatever. I don't care how many times you look at it; there's always something new to see. To me, there is no question that Brando defined acting from the nineteen-fifties onward."

While watching the film again—for perhaps the seventh time, he thinks—Mr. Levinson found himself acutely aware of the way the director blocked out his shots. While the intention, in most cases, is to make the way the actors move around the various sets seem totally natural, in fact it is almost always choreographed to place the right actor in the right spot at the right moment. The more actors there are on the screen, the more intricate the ballet and the more complicated the blocking.

It first comes up in the scene where Karl Malden, as the parish priest, arrives to comfort Edie Doyle, the murdered man's sister, while she protects her brother's body from the eyes of a crowd of prying neighbors.

"See how Kazan shot that?" Mr. Levinson said. "It's all one master shot. The camera hangs back and watches the scene unfold, and all of the people in it are moving very deliberately. It looks natural, but it isn't. See that woman?" He is referring to one of the bystanders. "Her head pops up there, she delivers her line, then disappears for a few seconds into the background. And then here she comes back, to deliver her next line."

Such a film would never be shot that way today, he said. Audiences are much less tolerant of long master shots and accustomed to a lot of cutting within scenes. So the sophisticated geometry of blocking out a scene like that has become less important to younger filmmakers, almost a dying art.

In the next scene, when we first meet Johnny Friendly and his top goons, the blocking is even more pronounced.

"Kazan was so good about figuring out how to block these scenes," Mr. Levinson said. "Look, that one guy does his thing, and then he comes around in the background and there he is, showing up in that gap between those two people. He listens to a line, steps forward and then the camera moves into a tight three-shot. Perfect. It shows such a great understanding of the relationship of the actors to the camera, and it's all done without cutting and feels very natural."

This early scene with Cobb's union boss—presiding like Tony

Soprano over a goofball collection of his strong-arm men—is where most of the movie's plot points are painstakingly laid out. The union is worried about a crime commission investigating waterfront rackets. The worst thing a person can be is a "canary" or a "cheese-eater," testifying against the mob. Terry is treated like a dim-witted pet; a former boxer whose career went sour, he is pampered because Friendly likes him and because his smarter brother is one of Friendly's top lieutenants. At the end of the scene, Terry is sent away with table scraps before the mob actually divides its crooked take.

"Essentially, it's a pure exposition scene," Mr. Levinson said. "Kazan has to tell the audience what's going on, lay out the basics of the plot. But he always finds a way to make it entertaining. There is so much going on in the scene, so much humor. Like, look at how, when two of the men are squabbling, Lee J. Cobb gives them this little smile, like he finds them so endearing. But then he pulls himself together and gets tough again because he has to be the boss. It really humanizes his character and shows how he's the boss not just because he's tough but because he's smarter than they are. And it's all done with a smile."

When Brando's performance in *On the Waterfront* is dissected, critics and historians tend to focus on two scenes, both illustrating idiosyncratic choices the actor made. In one, as Mr. Brando's inarticulate character tries to make friends with Edie, he picks up her dropped glove and unconsciously puts it on his own hand as he struggles to make conversation.

"It makes him seem so vulnerable," Mr. Levinson said. "But there is also something symbolic about it, about this ex-boxer putting on the glove of a convent girl, as though signaling this change that he is going through."

The other scene is the one in the back of a taxi between Terry and Charley, one of the most frequently studied scenes in American film.

"So much about that scene is interesting," Mr. Levinson said. "The way it's shot, for instance, is so simple and strange. They're riding in this car and for some reason it has venetian blinds on the back window. So all we see are the two of them with these blinds behind them. I don't know if Kazan did that to make it look distinctive, or they didn't have enough money for rear projection or whatever. But it works beautifully."

Charley has been sent by Johnny Friendly to find Terry. Friendly is worried, with good reason, that Terry intends to testify to the crime commission. Charley must persuade Terry not to testify or kill him.

When Charley cannot persuade Terry ("There's a lot more to this than I thought," Terry tells him), he pulls a gun. Terry reacts with disappointment. "Charley, Charley," he says, sadly. "Oh, Charley. Wow." Terry blames his brother and his gambler friends for wrecking his boxing career by forcing him to throw fights. "You don't understand, Charley, I could've been a contender," Terry says. "I could've been somebody. Instead of a bum." Shamed, Charley lets him go, only to find out that the cabdriver is in cahoots with Friendly and drives Charley to his own death.

"You hear these stories, and I don't know if they're true or not," Mr. Levinson said. "Take this scene, for instance. The story I heard is that they were just getting ready to shoot it and Brando walks up to Kazan and says, 'You know, this scene doesn't make any sense.' Kazan says, 'What do you mean?' And Brando says, 'I'm in the car with my brother, and he pulls a gun on me and I'm supposed to be afraid? I'm supposed to think he's really going to kill me? It doesn't make any sense to me.' Okay, Kazan says, play it that way. So they shoot the scene and instead of Brando going, 'Charley, Charley!' like he's terrified, he says it like he's so disappointed in his brother. It's what makes the scene great.

"Now, that's a very interesting acting lesson," Mr. Levinson said, "because whether it's true or not—and I've never been able to find out for sure—it shows how you can take this one line and, depending on how you deal with it, shape and elevate a whole scene. It's all about how you treat a scene, rather than just saying, okay, here's my line, where do I stand?"

As Mr. Levinson watched the blocking of the shots and Mr. Kazan's camera placements and found fresh ways to appreciate Mr. Brando's performance, he also found himself reassessing the entire movie. As a young man, he had been drawn to it partly because it seemed so street-savvy and realistic. But now, watching it again, he found himself picking out all the ways it was anything but realistic.

One sequence, about midway through the film, in which Terry takes Edie to a saloon for a beer, Mr. Levinson found particularly evocative.

"Look at how Kazan and Schulberg are letting us into the characters' behavior in ways that are not just straight ahead," Mr. Levinson said. "And how Kazan keeps this long sequence compelling by varying the rhythm and the way different shots are made. Really, when you look at it logically, it doesn't make much sense."

The scene begins in what seems like a half-deserted barroom. Terry and Edie are seated at a table. All we hear is some piano music, and then even that stops. They have a drink. Edie asks Terry to help her find out who killed her brother. He says he can't, but we can tell his conscience is tormenting him. During this conversation, Mr. Kazan cuts from one to the other as they talk. As the scene progresses, the camera gets closer and closer to their faces.

Then, all of a sudden, an angry Edie stands up and rushes into the next room. Although there is really no partition between the two rooms, as soon as she goes into the next room there is an explosion of raucous music. A wedding is under way. Large crowds swerve through a gaudily decorated room, pushing Edie this way and that until Terry rescues her. They retreat to a corner, where they continue to spar. But this time, Mr. Kazan's camera watches their conversation in a two-shot, with both on-screen throughout rather than cutting from face to face.

They reconcile, dance, and then spin into an incongruous cluster of plants at one end of the room. The light dims and, once again, Mr. Kazan cuts from face to face as they talk. Then, when they emerge back into the room and argue once more, Mr. Kazan goes back to a two-shot, but this time it is more choreographed as they spin around each other as they talk.

"Notice how Kazan keeps shifting things, whether it's the sound or the lighting or even the way he cuts between them," Mr. Levinson said. "He realizes that with a scene this long and complicated, you can't stay in one place too long or shoot it all the same way. That would be boring. This way, you almost don't realize that all of this stuff is happening, supposedly, in the same bar. On the one hand, it's very realistic, but on the other hand, it's highly stylized. I mean, how could they not have heard that loud wedding going on in the next room?"

Mr. Levinson has also been praised for his realistic approach, particularly in the Baltimore films. But what audiences don't realize—

nor should they—is that realism is just another form of stylization, he said.

"That's always the interesting trick," he said. "You're creating what appears to be a very real thing, but you can do it in a highly stylized way and it still feels real. In this movie, we can see how Kazan takes this sense of reality and tweaks it and comes up with this highly stylized approach to it."

This is borne out in a scene a few minutes later, when Terry confesses to Edie that he played a role in her brother's death. They are standing on a muddy stretch of riverfront, industrial towers in the background. But as soon as Terry begins to speak, a shrill boat whistle fills the sound track. We can't hear a word he's saying.

"Notice, this is the first time in the movie, I think, that Kazan went to a really extreme close-up," Mr. Levinson said. "But this just shows you how stylistic this movie really is. All we see is her with her hands up to her ears and the look on her face. Why did he shoot it this way? I would assume it's because Kazan realized that we already knew what he was going to tell her, so we didn't need to hear it. All we're really interested in is her reaction to it. So shooting it in this stylized kind of way really magnifies her reaction."

As the film moved to its bloody, bombastic climax, Mr. Levinson found himself wondering what it would have been like if it had been made today.

"In contemporary movies, we don't deal with issues and we rarely deal with working people," Mr. Levinson said. "We have moved away from this kind of sophisticated storytelling to a place where everything is stories about someone who has a gun and is coming to kill you. If we did this movie today, if we could even get it done, we would feel compelled to kick it up, to really exploit the violent aspects in the story."

Mr. Levinson gathered up his jacket and papers as the lights came back up.

"That's the problem," he said. "Movies are not set in the real world today. We're much more into a comic-book sensibility. We've gotten more and more divorced from films about people."

HIGHLIGHTS OF BARRY LEVINSON'S DIRECTING CAREER
AND INFORMATION ABOUT *ON THE WATERFRONT*

■

What They Watched

On the Waterfront. Directed by Elia Kazan; produced by Sam Spiegel; screenplay by Budd Schulberg; original music by Leonard Bernstein; cinematography by Boris Kaufman; edited by Gene Milford. With Marlon Brando, Eva Marie Saint, Karl Malden, Lee J. Cobb, and Rod Steiger. 1954.

Barry Levinson's Films

Bandits. With Bruce Willis, Billy Bob Thornton, and Cate Blanchett. 2001.

An Everlasting Piece. With Barry McEvoy. 2000.

Liberty Heights. With Adrien Brody. 1999.

Sphere. With Dustin Hoffman. 1998.

Wag the Dog. With Robert De Niro and Dustin Hoffman. 1997.

Sleepers. With Jason Patric. 1996.

Disclosure. With Michael Douglas. 1994.

Bugsy. With Warren Beatty. 1991.

Avalon. With Aidan Quinn. 1990.

Rain Man. With Dustin Hoffman and Tom Cruise. 1988.

Good Morning, Vietnam. With Robin Williams. 1987.

Tin Men. With Richard Dreyfuss. 1987.

Young Sherlock Holmes. With Nicholas Rowe. 1985.

The Natural. With Robert Redford. 1984.

Diner. With Steve Guttenberg. 1982.

ACKNOWLEDGMENTS

First of all, I have to thank John Darnton, the former culture editor at the *New York Times*, who hired me as a general assignment correspondent, transformed me into a Broadway columnist, encouraged me to become the paper's Houston bureau chief, and then lured me back to the culture desk to take over the movie beat in Los Angeles. Marty Gottlieb, his indefatigable deputy, has become not just a wise editor but a trusted friend.

All of these pieces first appeared in the paper's Weekend section, where they were treated with gentle intelligence by its editor, Myra Forsberg. One of her assistants, Diane Nottle, was the primary editor on most of the pieces and I could not have asked for a better one. Raphael Paganelli, the section's photo editor, put up with an almost endless series of postponements and cancellations to schedule the photos, most of which were shot by the estimable Misha Erwitt. Anne Mancuso was indispensable in helping assemble the filmogra phies.

I also need to thank Michael Kimmelman. He knows why.

My book editors—Mike Levitas and Susan Chira at the *New York Times*, David Sobel and Heather Rodino at Henry Holt—were unceasingly supportive and encouraging. I'd like to watch a movie with each of them someday. Although she didn't get a dime out of it, the legendary Amanda Urban was always willing to offer advice and reassurance.

And although he once expressed to me nothing but icy disdain for newspaper writing about movies, I want to thank one of my English professors at Indiana University, James Naremore, whose amazing lectures on Hitchcock, Welles, and others first nudged me in this direction many years ago.

For my wife, Barbara Whitaker, and for our daughters, Katie and Laura, no amount of thanks would be sufficient to express what I owe them.

INDEX

A.I., 12, 18
A-list, 3, 4, 177, 225
Abbott and Costello Meet Frankenstein, xvi
Academy Awards, 60, 110
   A Man for All Seasons, 131
   D. Washington, 156
   see also Oscars
Academy of Motion Picture Arts and
    Sciences
   film library, 79–80
Addams Family, The, 226, 227, 228, 236
Addams Family Values, 236
Affleck, Ben, 94, 104, 137
Affliction, 203, 211
Air Force One, 89
Alexander, Jane, 59
Alford, Philip, 202
Alice, 150
All the President's Men, xii, xvi, 155
   information on, 65
   S. Soderbergh on, 55–65
Allen, DeDe, 11
Allen, Woody, 137, 180, 201
   highlights of career, 150–51
   on *Shane*, xv, 139–49
Alonzo, John A., 13
Altman, Robert, 13, 197, 203

Amarcord, 93–94
Amenábar, Alejandro, 213
"America," 106, 110
American Beauty, 16, 41, 158
American Graffiti, 21, 25, 31
American in Paris, 110
American New Wave, 60
Amistad, 18
Anatomy of a Murder, 94
Anderson, Texas, 189
Anderson, Wes
   highlights of career, 199
   on *Small Change*, 189–99
Andy Griffith Show, The, 21, 23
Angels with Dirty Faces, 168
Annie Hall, 151
Antonioni, Michelangelo, 73
Antwone Fisher, 153, 163
Apollo 13, 24, 31, 188
Argent de Poche, L'
   see *Small Change (L'Argent de Poche)*
Armageddon, 104, 112, 113
Arthur, Jean, 144
As the World Turns, 118
Astaire, Fred, 172
Austin Powers, 184–85
Avalon, 240, 248

B-list, 4
Bacharach, Burt, 184–85
Backdraft, 31
Bad Boys, 104, 112, 113
Badlands, 203, 212
Badham, Mary, 202, 204
Baldwin, Alec, 197
Bananas, 151
Bancroft, Anne, 22
Bandits, 237, 240, 248
Barry, Dave, 226
Basie, Count, 184
Basinger, Jeanine, 103, 105, 106
Bass, Saul, 94
Batman Forever, 224
Battle of Algiers, 57, 178
Battlefield Earth, 175
Bay, Michael
  highlights of career, 113
  on *West Side Story*, xv, 103–13
Beatty, Warren, 159, 240
Beau Geste, 81
Beautiful Mind, A, 21–22, 24, 30, 179, 187
Bedroom Window, The, 42
Begin, Menachem, 98
Ben Gurion, David, 98
Bergman, Ingmar, 73, 139
Berkeley, Busby, 168
Bernstein, Carl, 57, 63
Bernstein, Elmer, 202, 210
Bernstein, Leonard, 106, 240–41
Beymer, Richard, 110, 111–12
Bicycle Thief, The, 73, 140
Big, 236
Big Brother (reality series), 128
Big Chill, The, 49
Big Lebowski, The, 126
Big Trouble, 226–27, 236
Billy Bathgate, 224
Birthday Girl, 224
Blackmer, Sidney, 118
Blast from the Past, 211
Blazing Saddles
  B. Glazer on, 177–87
  information on, 187
Bleu, Ella, 166
Blier, Bertrand, 167
Blood Simple, 227, 236

Bodyguard, The, 53
Boetticher, Budd, 3
Bogart, Humphrey, 34–35, 36, 37, 40, 41, 89
Bogdanovich, Peter, 6
Boleyn, Anne, 134
Bolt, Robert, 128, 129, 130, 133
Bonanza, 4
Bone Collector, The, 163
Bonnie and Clyde, 11, 15, 23, 44, 60
Bonnie Parker Story, The, 6
Boogie Nights, 41, 118, 126
Boot, Das (The Boat), 84, 90
Born Yesterday, 141
Bottle Rocket, 190, 199
Bound for Glory, 60
Bowfinger, 188
Bradley, Ben, 62
Brando, Marlon, 167, 238, 239, 241, 242–43, 244, 245
Braveheart, 159
Brecht, Bertolt, 217
Bridges, Lloyd, 82, 85, 86
Broadway Danny Rose, 151
Broken Arrow, 175
Brooks, Mel, 178–79, 180, 182, 183, 184, 185, 186, 187, 239
Broyles, William, 99
Bruckheimer, Jerry, 103, 104, 177, 180
Bugsy, 240, 248
Bull Durham, 43, 53
Bullets Over Broadway, 150
Buñuel, Luis, 191
Burning, The, 102

Cabin in the Cotton, The, 171
Caesar, Sid, 179
Cage, Nicolas, 104
Cagney, James, 89, 165, 167, 168–69, 172–73, 174–75
Cagney, Jeanne, 171
Cameron, James, 113
Candidate, The, 155
Cannon, J. D., 45
Captain Blood, 171
Carbon Copy, 164
Carey, Macdonald, 6
Carol Burnett Show, The, 239

Carrey, Jim, 179, 186
Carrie, 176, 203, 212
Casablanca, 171
Cassavetes, John, 36, 117, 120–21, 123
Catch Me If You Can, 12, 18
Cat's Cradle, 94
CBS Studio Center lot, 127, 128
Celebrity, 150
Chabon, Michael, 40
Chakiris, George, 109, 110
Chaney, Lon, Jr., 82
Chaplin, Charlie, 140
Chaplin, Ben, 12
Chasing Amy, 138
Chicago, 102
China, 68–69, 70, 73
Chinese films, 71–73, 74, 75
Chinese opera, 69, 70–71, 72, 74–75, 76
Chocolat, 93, 102
Christie, Julie, 125
Cider House Rules, The, 102
Citizen Kane, xv–xvi, 140
Civil Action, A, 174, 175
Clerks, 129, 138
Coal Miner's Daughter, 203, 211
Cobb, Lee J., 98, 241, 243, 244
Cocoon, 31
Coen, Ethan, 227, 232
Coen, Joel, 227, 232
Cohan, George M., 165, 167, 169, 170, 171, 172, 173, 174
Columbia Pictures, 34
  logo, 240
  lot, 154
Communism, 12, 14, 17
Connelly, Jennifer, 22
Connery, Sean, 104
Cook, Elisha, Jr., 117, 144
Cool Hand Luke, 23
  K. Costner on, 43–52
  information on, 52
Cooper, Gary, 43, 143
  in High Noon, 81, 82, 83–84, 86, 87–88
Costner, Kevin, 159, 165
  on Cool Hand Luke, 43–52
  highlights of career, 52–54
Courage Under Fire, 163

Courtship of Eddie's Father, The, 23, 31
Crimes and Misdemeanors, 150
Crimes of the Heart, 211
Crimson Tide, 164
Cromwell, Oliver, 130, 132, 133
Crosby, Floyd, 83
Crothers, Scatman, 219, 220
Crouching Tiger, Hidden Dragon, 55, 70, 75, 77, 78
Crowe, Cameron, 17
Crowe, Russell, 21, 33–34, 35, 179
Crucible, The, 136
Crudup, Billy, 118
Cruise, Tom, 167, 213, 214
Cry Freedom, 164
Crystal, Billy, xiii
Cuban missile crisis, 43, 48
Curse of the Jade Scorpion, The, 150
Curtz, Michael, 167, 171

Damon, Matt, 137
Dances With Wolves, 43, 46, 47, 53, 159
Darktown Strutters, 5
Davenport, Nigel, 132
Davis, Bette, 171
Day, Doris, 26
Days of Thunder, 224
Daytime Emmy Award
  J. Moore, 118
DeLuise, Dom, 186
De Niro, Robert, 240
De Palma, Brian, 50, 203
De Sica, Vittorio, xvi, 73
De Toth, Andre, 3
Dead Calm, 224
Dean, James, 39
Deconstructing Harry, 150
Deep End, 102
Deep Throat, 63, 64
Delerue, Georges, 192
Deluca brothers, 193
Destry Rides Again, 185
Devil in a Blue Dress, 164
Di, Le, 70–71, 73, 76
Diary of a Chambermaid, 191
Dick Tracy, 4
Dietrich, Marlene, 185
Diner, 239, 240, 248

Dirty Dozen, The, 100
Disclosure, 240, 248
Discreet Charm of the Bourgeoisie, The, 191
Disney, 91, 103, 105, 192, 227
"Do Not Forsake Me, Oh My Dar-
  lin'," 83
Do the Right Thing, 131
*Dr. Seuss's How the Grinch Stole Christ-
  mas*, 21, 24, 30, 187
*Dr. Strangelove or: How I Learned to Stop
  Worrying and Love the Bomb*, xvi,
  226
  information on, 236
  B. Sonnenfeld on, 225–35
Dogma, 137, 138
Dogsville, 217
Domestic Disturbance, 175
Domingo, Placido, 15
Double Indemnity, xvii, 142
Douglas, Michael, 34, 40, 240
Dragonfly, 48, 53
DreamWorks, 115, 116, 139
Duck Soup and Hamlet, 228
Duvall, Shelley, 216, 218, 219, 222–23

Eastwood, Clint, 86, 159
Easy Rider, 13, 16
Eat Drink Man Woman, 78
Eclipse, 73
EdTV, 24, 31
8 Mile, 34, 42, 187
*Eine, Der, Der Andere (The One, The
  Other)*, 90
Einer Von Uns Beiden (One or the Other),
  90
Election, 41
Ellroy, James, 33
Eminem, 34
Emma, 102
Emmys
  B. Levinson, 239
End of the Affair, The, 118, 126
Enemy Mine, 90
English Patient, The, 102
Entertainer of the Year
  N. Kidman, 215
Entertainment Weekly, 215
Erin Brockovich, 56, 57, 66

Evans, Dale, 2, 3, 6
Everlasting Piece, An, 248
Everyone Says I Love You, 150
Evolution, 115, 116, 118, 125
Exodus
  information on, 101
  H. Weinstein on, xv, 91–101
Eyes Wide Shut, 156, 213, 214, 218,
  220, 224

Face/Off, 175
Fail-Safe, 228
Fandango, 54
Fapp, Daniel L., 110
Far and Away, 31, 224
Far from Heaven, 125
Farrelly brothers, 179
Farrow, Mia, 117, 118, 120, 121, 123
Fell, Norman, 26
Fellini, Federico, 73, 93, 94, 141
Ferro, Pablo, 228
Field of Dreams, 43, 53
Fields, W. C., 141
Fincher, David, 214
Fisher, Antwone, 157
Five Graves to Cairo, xvi
Flynn, Errol, 171
Foote, Horton, 203
Footlight Parade, 168
For Love or Money, 188, 236
Ford, John, 3, 36, 180, 181
Foreman, Carl, 85
Forman, Milos, 162
Forsberg, Myra, xiii
"45 Minutes From Broadway," 172
Foster, Jodie, 201
Four Cohans, 171
Four Daughters, 171
400 Blows, The, 140, 191, 192, 194, 195
French Connection, The, 57, 227
French New Wave, 93, 191
Freundlich, Bart, 118
From Dusk Till Dawn, 9
From Here to Eternity, 182
Full Frontal, 66

Gangs of New York, 102
Garfield, John, 171

"Gee, Officer Krupke," 106
General's Daughter, The, 175
George, Peter, 228
Germany, 79, 82–83, 88, 89
Get Shorty, 175, 226, 236
Gibson, Mel, 159
Gigi, 141
"Give My Regards to Broadway," 172
Gladiator, 55, 93
Glass, Ned, 109
Glory, 157, 164
Glover, Danny, 190
Godard, Jean-Luc, 69
Godfather, The, xv
Going Places, 167
Gold, Ernest, 96, 101
Golden Globe
  N. Kidman, 215
  S. Spacek, 203
Golden Stallion, The
  information on, 9
  Q. Tarantino on, 1–8
Goldman, William, 61
Gonzalez, Elián, 15
Good Machine, 68
Good Morning, Vietnam, 240, 248
Good Will Hunting, 102
Goodfellas, 162
Gordon, Ruth, 118, 120, 123–24
Graduate, The, 44, 60, 178
  R. Howard on, 21–30
  information on, 30
Grahame, Gloria, 34, 37
Grand Illusion, 140
Grass Harp, The, 211
Gray's Anatomy, 66
Grazer, Brian, 21, 24
  on *Blazing Saddles*, 177–87
  highlights of career, 187–88
Grease, 176
Great Escape, The, 93, 100
Guest, Judith, 155
Gypsy, 170–71

Hackman, Gene, 190
Hamlisch, Marvin, 160
Hand That Rocks the Cradle, The, 42, 126
Hanks, Tom, 167, 172, 179

Hannah and Her Sisters, 150
Hannibal, 118, 125
Hanson, Curtis, xiv
  highlights of career, 41–42
  on *In a Lonely Place*, 33–41
Hanxiang, Li, 68
Happy Days, 21, 24
"Harrigan," 172
Hawks, Howard, 3, 7, 81, 87, 181
Haworth, Jill, 96, 97
Hayden, Sterling, 229, 233
He Got Game, 163
Heflin, Van, 144
Henry VIII, 128, 130, 131–32, 133, 135–36
Hidden Dragon, 55
High Noon, xvi, 11, 142, 143
  information on, 89
  W. Peterson on, 79–89
Hill, The, 142
Hiller, Wendy, 133, 141
Hirsch, Judd, 153, 155
His Girl Friday, xvii, 232
Hitchcock, Alfred, xvi, 36, 94
Hoffman, Dustin, 22, 26, 27, 167, 240
  in *All the President's Men*, 56, 59, 61
Holbrook, Hal, 64
Hollywood, xiii, 79, 83
  response to television, 95
  studios, 41, 238
Hollywood Ending, 150
Homicide: Life on the Streets, 239
Hope, Bob, 95
Hopper, Dennis, 13, 45, 49
Hours, The, 118, 125, 224
Housesitter, 188
Houston, xiii, 189, 190
How to Make an American Quilt, 19
Howard, Leslie, 141
Howard, Rance, 23, 24–25
Howard, Ron, xiv, 178, 179
  on *The Graduate*, 21–30
  highlights of career, 30–31
Hudson, Rock, 26
Hughes, Dorothy B., 39
Hurricane, The, 157, 163
Hurt, John, 132
Husbands and Wives, 150

Huston, Anjelica, 190
Huston, John, 143
Huston, Walter, 170, 173
Hutton, Timothy, 155, 156, 160

"I Feel Pretty," 106
Ice Storm, The, 77, 78
Ich Werde Dich Töten, Wolf (*I Will Kill You, Wolf*), 90
Ideal Husband, The, 126
Ikiro, xvi
Imagine Entertainment, 21, 24, 178
In a Door, Into a Fight, Out a Door, Into a Chase (Witney), 4
In a Lonely Place
  C. Hanson on, 33–41
  information on, 41
In the Bedroom, 203, 211
In the Heat of the Night, 23
In the Line of Fire, 86, 90
Informer, The, 142
Interiors, 137, 151
Irving Thalberg Building, 154

Jackie Brown, 1, 5, 9
Jackson, Janet, 110
James Bond films, xvi
James Bridges Theater, 34
Jarmusch, Jim, 92
Jaubert, Maurice, 192–93
Jaws, 60, 131, 133
Jay and Silent Bob Strike Back, 128, 138
Jeremiah Johnson, 155
Jerry Bruckheimer Films, 104
Jerry Maguire, 17, 19
Jewison, Norman, 157
Jews, 93, 95–96, 97, 98–100, 101
JFK, 53, 131, 203, 211
John Q., 156, 163
Johnny Guitar, 35
Johnson, Ben, 144
Jones, Tommy Lee, 227
Jordan, Michael, 149
Jules and Jim, 197
Jungle Girl, 4

Kafka, 66
Kahn, Madeline, 185

Kaminski, Janusz, 79
  highlights of career, 18–19
  on *Vanishing Point*, 11–18
Kazan, Elia, 237, 238, 239, 240, 242, 243, 244, 245, 246, 247
Keaton, Buster, 140
Keaton, Michael, 179
Kelly, Grace, 82, 87, 88
Kennedy, George, 45
Kidman, Nicole, 118
  highlights of career, 224
  on *The Shining*, 213–23
Kill Bill, 1
Kimmelman, Michael, xiii
Kindergarten Cop, 188
King, Stephen, 215
King of Kings, 35
King of the Hill, 66
King Pulp: The Wild World of Quentin Tarantino (Woods), 9
Klute, 58
Knife in the Water, 118
Konsequenz, Die (*The Consequence*), 90
Korman, Harvey, 183
Kramer, Stanley, 95
Kubrick, Stanley, 55, 190, 213, 216–18, 219, 220, 221, 222, 223
  Dr. Strangelove, xvi, 226, 228, 229, 230, 232, 233, 235
  Shining, The, xvi, 213
Kurosawa, Akira, xvi, 162

L.A. Confidential, 33–34, 40, 42
Ladd, Alan, 143, 145, 149
Lamar, Hedy, 183
Lamour, Dorothy, 190
Last Picture Show, The, 15
Last Temptation of Christ, 131
Laura, 95
Lawford, Peter, 96
Lawrence, Martin, 104
Lawrence of Arabia, xvi
Lean, David, 95
Leavitt, Sam, 96
Lee, Ang, 55
  highlights of career, 78
  on *Love Eternal*, 67–78
Lee, Harper, 202

Lee, Spike, 131
Lehman, Ernest, 106
Lelouch, Claude, 167
Leno, Jay, 166
Leslie, Joan, 173
Levin, Ira, 118
Levinson, Barry
  highlights of career, 248
  on *On the Waterfront*, 237–47
Liang Shan Bo Yu Zhu Ying Tai
  see *Love Eternal*
Liar Liar, 186, 188
Liberty Heights, 240, 248
Limey, The, 66
Little, Cleavon, 15, 181, 182, 186
Lloyd, Danny, 216, 218–19
Look Down on the Hudson, 25
Look Who's Talking, 176
Look Who's Talking Now, 176
Look Who's Talking Too, 176
Losin' It, 42
Lost Souls, 11, 12, 13, 18
Lost World, The: Jurassic Park, 18, 126
Love and Death, 151
*Love Eternal (Liang Shan Bo Yu Zhu
    Ying Tai)*
  information on, 78
  A. Lee on, 67–78
Lucas, George, 21, 25, 60
Lucasfilm, 106
Lucky Numbers, 175
Lhurmann, Baz, 213, 214–15
Lumet, Sidney, 142
Lusitania, 170
Lynch, David, 203
Lynn, Loretta, 203

Macbeth, 124
McCabe and Mrs. Miller, 125
McFarland and Company, 5
McGovern, Elizabeth, 161
McQueen, Steve, 45
Mad City, 175
Mae Day: The Crumbling of a Documentary, 138
Magnificent Seven, The, 93
Magnolia, 125
Malcolm X, 164

Malden, Karl, 238, 243
Malèna, 102
Malick, Terrence, 203
Mallrats, 138
Man and a Woman, A, 167
Man for All Seasons, A, xvi
  information on, 138
  K. Smith on, 127–37
Man with the Golden Arm, The, 95
Manhattan, 141, 151
Manhattan Murder Mystery, 150
Mann, Anthony, 3
Marie, 211
Martin, Strother, 49, 51
Marvin, Lee, 203
Marx Brothers, 141
"Mary," 172, 173
Meet Me in St. Louis, 141
Men in Black, 225, 226, 236
Men in Black II, 227, 236
Mercury Rising, 188
Message in a Bottle, 53
Mewes, Jason, 129, 132
Michael, 175
Midnight Express, 178
Mighty Aphrodite, 150
Mighty Quinn, The, 164
Mila 18 (Uris), 93
Miller, Arthur, 136
Miller's Crossing, 227, 236
"Million-Dollar Movie," 167
Mineo, Sal, 39, 95, 96, 97, 99
Minnelli, Vincente, 109, 110
Minnie and Moskowitz, 123
Minority Report, 12, 18
Miramax Films, 91, 92, 93,
    94–95
Misery, 236
Missing, 211
Mississippi Masala, 164
Mitchell, Thomas, 82, 85
Mo' Better Blues, 164
Moore, Julianne
  highlights of career, 125–26
  on *Rosemary's Baby*, 115–25
Moore, Mary Tyler, 155, 156, 160, 163
More, Sir Thomas, 128, 129, 130,
    131–32, 134, 135–36, 137

More American Graffiti, 31
Moreau, Jeanne, 191
Moreno, Rita, 110
Moulin Rouge, 213, 215, 224
Much Ado About Nothing, 164
Mulligan, Robert, 203, 205
Murphy, Eddie, 24, 186
Murray, Bill, 198
Music Man, The, 23, 31
My Fair Lady, 110, 141
My Girl, 188

National Board of Review, 40
Natural, The, 240, 248
Natural Born Killers, 9
Nelson, Barry, 216
Network, 60
Never Cry Wolf, 42
Never-Ending Story, The, 90
New Line Cinema, 13
New York City
  celebrity walks, xiii, 225
New York Times, xii, xiii, 67, 140, 189,
  225
  Weekend section, xiii
Newman, Barry, 12
Newman, Paul, xvi
  in *Cool Hand Luke*, 44–46, 49, 50,
  51–52
  in *Exodus*, 93, 94, 95, 96, 97–98,
  99, 100, 101
Nichols, Mike, 22, 24, 27, 28, 178
Nicholson, Jack, 216, 218, 221, 222,
  223
'Night Mother, 211
Night of the Hunter, 204
Night Shift, 31, 179, 188
Nine Months, 126
1960s, xvi, 27
  social upheavals of, 26
  youth culture, 14
Nixon, Richard M., 57, 61
No Way Out, 53
Nutty Professor, The, 24, 186, 188

Oakland, Simon, 109
Ocean's 11, xii, 66
Olvidados, Los, 140

On the Waterfront
  information on, 248
  B. Levinson on, 237–47
On the Waterfront Suite, 240–41
One Day in the Life of Ivan Denisovich, 123
Opatoshu, David, 98
Ordinary People, xvi
  information on, 163
  D. Washington on, 153–63
Oscar, 33, 40, 118, 159, 213, 215
  American Beauty, 158
  Beautiful Mind, A, 179
  J. Cagney, 167
  J. Connelly, 22
  K. Costner, 43, 46
  Dances With Wolves, 47
  Exodus, 96
  R. Howard, 21, 24
  independent films, 91, 92, 93
  J. Kaminski, 12
  B. Levinson, 238, 239
  Miramax, 92, 93, 95
  Ordinary People, 153, 155
  G. Peck, 202
  S. Soderbergh, 55, 57
  S. Spacek, 203
  Training Day, xv
  D. Washington, 157
  West Side Story, 110
O'Steen, Sam, 22
Others, The, 213, 215, 219, 224
Out of Sight, 66
Outbreak, 90
"Over There," 166, 170, 174
Ox-Bow Incident, The, 142
Ozu, Yasujiro, 73

Pachelbel Canon, 156, 161
Pakula, Alan J., 56, 58, 59, 61
Palance, Jack, 146–48
Palm Beach Story, 232
Paltrow, Gwyneth, 94, 191
Panic in Needle Park, 13
Paper, The, 31, 188
Paramount Pictures, 33, 40, 154
  logo, 143
  lot, 190
Paratroop Command, 6

Parenthood, 31, 188
Peacemaker, The, 224
Pearce, Guy, 33–34, 35
Pearl Harbor, 103, 104–5, 109–10 112–13
Peck, Gregory, 202, 205, 207, 210
Peck's Bad Boy, 170
Pelican Brief, The, 164
Perfect Storm, The, 80, 89
Perfect World, A, 53
Petersen, Wolfgang
    on High Noon, 11, 79–89
    highlights of career, 89–90
Phenomenon, 175
Philadelphia, 164
Pickens, Slim, 182, 183, 229
Po, Ling, 71, 75, 76
Poitier, Sidney, xv, 93
Poland, 14, 17, 79
Polanski, Roman, 116, 117, 118, 119,
    120, 121, 123
Portrait of a Lady, The, 224
Postman, The, 43, 47, 52
Practical Magic, 224
Preacher's Wife, The, 163
Preminger, Otto, 92, 95, 96, 98, 101
Preston, Ella, 167
Preston, Kelly, 166
Prêt-à-Porter (Ready-to-Wear), 102
Pride of the Yankees, The, 81
Primary Colors, 174, 175
Prime Cut, 203, 212
Provine, Dorothy, 6
Psycho, xvi
Public Enemy, 168
Pulp Fiction, 2, 9, 102, 167, 174, 175
Purple Rose of Cairo, 151
Pushing Hands, 78
Pygmalion, 141

Quentin Tarantino: Shooting from the Hip
    (Clarkson), 9
Quentin Tarantino: The Cinema of Cool
    (Dawson), 9
Quentin Tarantino: The Man and His
    Movies (Bernard), 9

Radio Days, 150
Ragtime, 162

Raiders of the Lost Ark, 130
Rain Man, 239, 248
Raising Arizona, 227, 232, 236
Ramsey, JonBenet, 15
Randall, Tony, xiii
Ransom, 24, 31
Rashomon, 140
Ray, Nicholas, 34, 35, 37, 38, 39, 40
Rebel Without a Cause, 35, 39, 40
Redford, Robert, xvi, 153, 154, 155,
    157, 159, 160, 161, 240
    in All the President's Men, xvi, 61, 62,
    64
Redgrave, Vanessa, 134
Reds, 159
Reed, Tracy, 231
Reincarnation of Peter Proud, The, 117
Remember the Titans, 163
Republic Pictures, 4
Repulsion, 118
Reservoir Dogs, 2, 9
Restoration, 102
Richardson, Ralph, 92, 96
Richie, Lionel, 104
Ride the High Country, xvi
Ride with the Devil, 78
Ridgely, Robert, 183
Rio Bravo, xvi, 81
Ritter, Tex, 83, 180
River, The, 211
River Wild, The, 42
Robards, Jason, 62
Robbins, Jerome, 105
Roberts, Julia, xiv
Robin Hood: Prince of Thieves, 53
Robinson, Edward G., 171
Rock, The, 104, 112, 113
Rocky, 57, 60
Rogers, Roy, xi, 2–3, 4, 5, 6, 7, 192
Rogers, Wayne, 45
Roma, 73
Romeo and Juliet (Shakespeare), 106
Rosemary's Baby
    information on, 125
    J. Moore on, 115–25
Roosevelt, Franklin D., 169
Roper, Will, 128
Rosenberg, Stuart, 44

Ross, Katharine, 29
Roth, Eric, 99
Rowlands, Gena, 36
Royal Tenenbaums, The, 190, 197–98, 199
Rudin, Scott, 177, 180
Rushmore, 190, 192, 199
Ryder, Winona, 12

Safe, 126
Saint, Eva Marie, 92, 96, 238
Sarafian, Richard C., 12
Sargent, Alvin, 155
Saturday Night Fever, 167, 173, 176
Saturday Night Live, 69, 179
Saving Private Ryan, 12, 17, 18
Schatzberg, Jerry, 13
Schindler's List, xvi, 12, 19
Schizopolis, 66
Schrader, Paul, 203
Schulberg, Budd, 239, 246
Schwalbach, Jennifer, 132
Schwarzenegger, Arnold, 179
Scofield, Paul, 128, 131, 133, 134, 135
Scorsese, Martin, xiii, 131, 162
Scott, George C., 229, 230, 231, 232, 233, 234
Scott, Ridley, 55
Sea Wolf, The, 171
Searchers, The, 36, 47
Sellers, Peter, 229, 233, 235
Sense and Sensibility, 77, 78
September 11th, 154, 157, 166, 170, 227, 237
Sergeant York, 81
Seven, 214
Seventh Seal, 140
sex, lies and videotape, 66
Shakespeare, William, 106, 110
Shakespeare in Love, 102
Shane, 192
    W. Allen on, xv, 139–49
    information on, 150
Shattered, 90
Shaw, Robert, 133, 134–35
Shaw Brothers, 68, 73
She's So Lovely, 175

Shining, The, xvi
    information on, 224
    N. Kidman on, 213–23
Shipping News, The, 118, 125
Shire, David, 63
Shootist, The, 31
Shop Around the Corner, The, 141
Short Cuts, 126
Siege, The, 157, 163
Silent Partner, The, 42
Silverado, 54
Simon and Garfunkel, 22
Simpson, O. J., 15
Sinatra, Frank, 26
Singer, Isaac Bashevis, 73
Singin' in the Rain, 141
Sleeper, 151
Sleepers, 248
Small Change (L'Argent de Poche)
    W. Anderson on, 189–99
    information on, 199
Small Time Crooks, 150
Smith, Charlie Martin, 25
Smith, Kevin
    highlights of career, 138
    on *A Man for All Seasons,* 127–37
Smith, Will, 104, 227
Soderbergh, Steven, xi–xii
    on *All the President's Men,* 55–65
    highlights of career, 65–67
Solaris, 66
Soldier's Story, A, 164
Solidarity, 14
"Somewhere," 106
Sondheim, Stephen, 106
Sonnenfeld, Barry
    on *Dr. Strangelove,* 225–35
    highlights of career, 236
Sophie's Choice, 58
Sorkin, Aaron, 131
Sound of Music, The, 110
"Sounds of Silence, The," 22, 24, 29
Southern, Terry, 228
Spacek, Sissy
    highlights of career, 211–12
    on *To Kill a Mockingbird,* xv, 201–10
Spacey, Kevin, 118

Spartacus, 93, 94
Sphere, 248
Spielberg, Steven, 12, 15, 17, 21, 60, 130–31
Spies Like Us, 188
Splash, 31, 188
Spy Smasher, 4
Stalag 17, 95
Stanton, Harry Dean, 45
Star Wars, 60, 106, 129
Stardust Memories, 151
Steadicam, 216, 221
Stevens, George, 140, 142–43, 144, 14, 146, 147
Stewart, James, 36
Stiller, Ben, 190
Sting, The, 155
Stone, Oliver, 131, 203
Story of Adele H., The, 196, 197
Straight Story, The, 203, 211
Stranger at My Door, 6
Streep, Meryl, 118, 201
Streetcar Named Desire, A, 14, 242
Stroheim, Erich von, 95
Sugarland Express, 15
Summer of Love, 23
Sunshine Sisters, 171
Surviving Picasso, 126
Sutherland, Donald, 156, 158, 161
Sweet and Lowdown, 150
Swordfish, 175

Taiwan, 69, 70
Take the Money and Run, 151
Tamblyn, Russ, 109
Tarantino, Quentin, xi, xiv, 94, 189
   on *The Golden Stallion*, 1–8
   highlights of career, 9
Tarantino A to Zed (Barnes and Hearn), 9
Taxi Driver, 60
Thalberg, Irving, 91
That Obscure Object of Desire, 191
Thelma and Louise, 16
Theresa, Sister, 129–30
Terry-Thomas, 229
They Got Me Covered, 95
Thirteen Days, 43, 48, 53

Thompson, Emma, 77
Three Kings, 41
3,000 Miles to Graceland, 48, 53
Three Women, 13, 203, 212
Throne of Blood, 140
Throw Momma from the Train, 236
Thunder Road, 14
Thurman, Uma, 2, 5
Tin Cup, 43, 53
Tin Men, 240, 248
Tiomkin, Dimitri, 84
Titanic, 113
To Die For, 224
To Kill a Mockingbird
   information on, 211
   S. Spacek on, 201–10
Tokyo Story, 73
"Tonight," 106
Traffic, 55, 56, 57, 58, 62, 63, 66
Training Day, xv, 156, 163
Travolta, Jett, 167
Travolta, John, xi
   highlights of career, 175–76
   on *Yankee Doodle Dandy*, 165–75
Travolta family, 170–71
Treasure of the Sierra Madre, 142
Trier, Lars von, 217
Trigger (horse), 2–3, 5, 7–8
Trouble in Paradise, 141
True Romance, 9
Truffaut, François, 190, 191, 199
   influence on Wes Anderson, 191–93, 194–96, 197, 198
Trumbo, Dalton, 92, 93, 94, 95, 96, 99, 100
"Try a Little Tenderness," 228
Tuck Everlasting, 211
Turner, Tina, 104
Two English Girls, 197
2001: A Space Odyssey, 55, 218

Umberto D, xvi
Underneath, The, 66
Unforgiven, 159
United States
   in films, 14, 15, 17
Universal Pictures, 21, 24

Universal Studios lot, 56
University of California Film and
 Television Archives, 34
University of Texas library, 194
Untouchables, The, 47, 50, 54
Urban Cowboy, 169, 176
Uris, Leon, 92, 93, 99

Van Fleet, Jo, 50
Vanishing Point
 information on, 18
 J. Kaminski on, 11–18
Vanya on 42nd Street, 126
Vertigo, 36, 94
Vietnam War, 14
Virgin Spring, 73
Vonnegut, Kurt, 94

Wag the Dog, 240, 248
Waite, Ralph, 45, 51
Ward, Bumble, xiv
Warner Bros., 165, 171
 logo, 168, 180
 lot, xi, 79, 80, 83, 89, 186
Washington, Denzel, xv
 highlights of career, 163–64
 on *Ordinary People*, 153–63
Washington Post, 57, 60, 62
Watergate, 57, 58, 63, 64
Waterworld, 43, 53
Wayne, John, 36, 81, 93
Wedding Banquet, The, 78
Weinstein, Bob, 91, 92
Weinstein, Harvey
 on *Exodus*, xv, 91–101
 highlights of career, 101–2
Welcome Back, Kotter, 167
Welcome to L.A., 211
"We'll Meet Again," 235
Welles, Orson, xvi, 133, 143
West Side Story
 M. Bay on, xv, 103–13
 information on, 113
West Wing, 131
What's Up, Tiger Lily?, 151
When Harry Met Sally, 236
"When Johnny Comes Marching
 Home," 230

White Dog, 42
White Heat, 142
White Sheik, The, 141
Wild Strawberries, 140
Wild Wild West, 236
Wilde, Brandon de, 144
Wilder, Billy, xvi, xvii, 95
Wilder, Gene, 186
Williams, Robin, 240
Willis, Bruce, 104, 240
Willis, Gordon, 58, 63
Wilson, Luke, 190
Wilson, Owen, 190, 198
Winkler, Henry, 179
Winslet, Kate, 77
Wise, Robert, 105, 106, 108,
 111
Witney, William, 3, 4–5, 6, 7–8
Wizard of Oz, The, xvi
Woman Under the Influence, A, 36
Wonder Boys, 33, 34, 40, 42
Wood, Natalie, 39, 110
Woodward, Bob, 57, 61, 63–64
World Traveler, 118
World War I, 170, 174
World War II, 5, 6, 8, 95
Wroclaw (Poland), 12, 14
Wyatt Earp, 53
Wyler, William, 143
Wynn, Keenan, 234

"Yankee Doodle Dandy," 172
Yankee Doodle Dandy
 information on, 175
 J. Travolta on, 165–75
Yentl, 73
Yojimbo, xvi
York, Susannah, 132
Young, Victor, 143
Young Sherlock Holmes, 248
Your Show of Shows, 179, 182
"You're a Grand Old Flag," 166

Z, 57
Zaillian, Steve, 99
Zelig, 151
Zinnemann, Fred, xvi, 79, 80, 84, 87,
 88, 89, 129, 131, 134–36

ABOUT THE AUTHOR

RICK LYMAN, who reports on the film industry for *The New York Times,* began writing the "Watching Movies With" column in 2000. He lives in Los Angeles with his wife and two daughters.